IT'S NEVER *just* ADHD

SANDRA CORAL

IT'S NEVER *just* ADHD

FINDING THE CHILD BEHIND THE LABEL

1 Oliver's Yard
55 City Road
London EC1Y 1SP

CORWIN
A Sage company
2455 Teller Road
Thousand Oaks, California 91320
(800)233-9936
www.corwin.com

Unit No 323-333, Third Floor, F-Block
International Trade Tower, Nehru Place
New Delhi 110 019

8 Marina View Suite 43-053
Asia Square Tower 1
Singapore 018960

Editor: Delayna Spencer
Production editor: Imogen Roome
Copyeditor: Neil Dowden
Proofreader: Leigh Smithson
Marketing manager: Dilhara Attygalle
Cover design: Wendy Scott
Typeset by KnowledgeWorks Global Ltd
Printed in the UK

Library of Congress Control Number 2023944872

British Library Cataloguing in Publication data

A catalogue record for this book is available from the
British Library

ISBN 978-1-5297-9221-8
ISBN 978-1-5297-9220-1 (pbk)

In memory of Cem and Serra.
Being your teacher changed everything.

Contents

Acknowledgements

In 2019, I started an Instagram page and podcast called *The ADHD Good Life*. As my following grew in 2020, my page morphed into *Neurodivergent Narratives* and with it more writings that centred on the complexities of managing neurodivergence in society for marginalised communities. Since then, many more people have followed along with my learning and unlearning about neurodivergence. I hope this book proves to be a continuation of this journey and you get as much out of reading it as I did writing it. As always, thank you for being here.

In true ADHD fashion, this book was meant to be published (many) months earlier. At the time, I didn't realise I had other unrecognised neurodivergence which inevitably made writing this book that much more challenging for me. However, I'm incredibly grateful for the unending patience, open-mindedness and kindness of my editor, Delayna Spencer, and the support of everyone I worked with at Sage Publications. Thank you for trusting me with this task and providing me the opportunity to write the book I've always wanted to write.

There are far too many students for me to thank individually for the honour of being their teacher. But I can honestly say I learned far more from them than I ever taught. Teaching has truly been one of the greatest jobs I've ever had and that's because of all of you.

I've been humbled by the opportunity to work with some of the most talented educators during my 18 years in classrooms. There are way too many to mention here, but I know that I couldn't have written this book without the influence of dear friends and peers I've worked with over the years: Zeyneb, Oylum, Deniz, Ros, Will, Natasha, Nurcan, Taslim, Dagmar, Leyla, Paraminder, Maryanne, Briton, Vicky and Catherine. I'm a much better teacher due to the privilege of learning from all of you. Thank you.

Speaking of teachers, I can't forget to give a very special thank you to Mr Desjardins, who taught me in 7th and 8th grade. You were the only teacher who would ask, years after you taught me, if I still was writing. Now almost 30 years later I can finally say, I am. Thank you for always trying to see the many facets of this person behind that student label. I would never have believed I could write a book without hearing it from you first.

I owe an immense debt of gratitude to my dear friends and fellow autistic advocates, Tiffany Hammond (@Fidgets.And.Fries), Tiffany 'TJ' Joseph (@Nigh. Functioning.Autism) and Dr Mari L. Cerda (@Autie.Analyst). Through your guidance and care I continue to learn about what it truly means to be in community. You've all taught me how to be a better person and I could never thank you enough for that gift.

I might never have uncovered my own neurodivergence if it wasn't for knowing about the advocacy my adoptive parents did for my biological brother when he was a child. Thank you Mom and Dad for always doing what you could. I know it's not always been an easy journey, but I'm truly grateful for all of it. And for both of you.

Over ten years ago I met my husband, Dean, and it was then that he first told me I'd write a book. Even though I laughed at the idea Babe, you've not once wavered in your belief in me, or that book. I love that I can share this moment with you now. Thank you for being right.

And always, to Otis. You show me what it means to truly embody self-compassion while embracing the fullness of life, every day. I have so much more to learn from you.

About the author

Sandra Coral is a queer, Black femme and transracial adoptee who grew up in the countryside of Southern Ontario, Canada. She has a masters in Educational Psychology (University of Connecticut) and has taught for over 18 years in schools all over the world. Sandra is the person behind *Neurodivergent Narratives*, a podcast and Substack newsletter that centres the unique challenges and experiences of neurodivergence for historically excluded groups. Currently, Sandra works with a content creator, coach and education consultant. They utilise their training in education, narrative therapy and somatic attachment therapy to support people, schools and workplaces in better understanding neurodivergence and creating neurodiversity-affirming environments.

Sandra lives just outside London, England with her partner and son.

About the book

I wrote this book with teachers, school administrators, paraeducators, additional learning needs teachers, speech learning therapists, occupational therapists and other specialists in mind, but anyone who has an Attention Deficit Hyperactivity Disorder (ADHD) child in their life could gain lots from it. It's also not just a book about ADHD *symptoms*, strategies and accommodations either. It's so much more than that, much like the ADHD children that you know, care about and work with every day.

This book aims to offer a wider lens for understanding our ADHD students. It asks us to consider what culture, beliefs and life experiences we all bring into our learning environment every day. It asks us how these influences might impact the ways we've learned to see these students, interpret their *behaviour* and decide on how to support their learning needs. The book explores the experiences of different ADHD learners told through my lens as their teacher. It asks us to consider the ways ADHD manifests in our learning environments depending on the combination of different lived experiences, co-occurring neurodivergence, physical conditions, or even students' relationship with the teacher.

As educators, we've got a lot on our plate and students who show ADHD presentations can add a lot more to it. We're all doing the best we can, every day. The ideas I have for support are not based on any new system or a programme that you have to implement, but like many changes we wish to see in our lives, they tend to begin with us. Therefore, you'll notice that I've added reflection questions throughout each chapter. What's important when you answer and discuss these questions is to take a moment to connect with your body. It might help you to be in a space where you feel more grounded and have capacity to engage with the questions before you begin.

When you read the questions, notice any discomfort that comes up.

Were there any words or phrases that stood out for you? Was there a sense of tightness or constriction somewhere in your body? Can you describe this space as you experience them? The colour, shape, size, texture, intensity or temperature?

Can you stay with those sensations as they shift and change or do you need to take some deep breaths or find another place in the body or room around you that evokes a sense of more ease and capacity in you?

Then take a moment and write (or record) what you noticed, whether it be thoughts, memories, questions or anything else that comes to mind. Sharing your insights with trusted others is also important. We grow through this discomfort when we share with others and learn to take steps to do better. All these explorations and reflection questions should be engaged in with the utmost compassion. Get curious about your responses. There's no room for growth in judgement and self-criticism.

There are a few key ideas I share that create the basis of any learning environment. Amongst them are being trauma-informed and equity-centred (see Ameera's story to start with ideas on that), culturally responsive (see Ji Yeon, Diego and Darnell's stories) and of course neurodiversity-affirming (which is essentially the overarching theme of this whole book). When it comes to classroom support, what I've written are simple suggestions, strategies, or tools for your learners. Many suggestions I make aren't just for ADHD students but are beneficial for all our students.

It's important to recognise that there's a lot more information that I could add in each chapter of this book, but then it would go on forever. The topics touched on could be individual books in their own right. This book is merely an introduction to bigger societal issues like **white supremacy culture**, patriarchy and capitalism and how they can influence the ways we've been taught to interpret and define ADHD. You'll notice how each chapter explores a story of an individual student (all fictional stories, but each created from my 18 years of teaching experiences). You'll get an idea of the *perceived behaviour* of each child based on the title of each chapter. The names of each student are chosen deliberately to hint at their ethnicity. I did this in the hope that it'll help you recognise some conscious and **internalised biases** you might hold that impact your interpretations of their behaviours. Within each chapter there are different ADHD presentations explored in depth, offering practical classroom support, strategies, ideas and tips to easily incorporate into your teaching, classrooms or lesson planning.

I've also written the book in a way in which you don't have to read from start to finish to get some of the answers you're looking for. It's enough to choose specific chapters as you narrow in on what you need, whether that be on certain ADHD presentations, co-occurring neurodivergence, or how various social identity markers might be impacting the ways that you're interpreting the behaviours you're noticing. I do think it might be helpful that you read the Introduction to get an overview of ADHD before you start though.

Remember, just like how all people are unique, our ADHD learners are too. The children in each chapter don't present the same way and not all ADHD presentations that we notice stem from the same causes. Some strategies and tips I suggest may not work in your classroom for a variety of reasons (lack of physical space, equipment, teaching knowledge or experience, number of students, etc.) and some strategies may work initially and need to be changed. Even still, some might work well for you with some tweaks or modifications for your specific situation. That's OK too. I trust you know your students best and what you are capable of implementing as their teacher with the current support that you have at your disposal.

Don't be surprised if as you read a chapter you feel like you might have tried something different for a learner or you would have changed some things quicker than I did. That's natural too. I'm an imperfect educator, just like everyone else. We bring different experiences, skills and observations into our classrooms because of our cultural backgrounds, training and lived experiences. We're not monoliths and we don't have to be to find this book helpful.

Another thing this book highlights is that ADHD doesn't travel alone (meaning it often co-occurs with other neurodivergence, impacting a person physically, socially, emotionally, or mentally). Sometimes ADHD presentations can indicate other learning or emotional challenges too. I'm not suggesting that ADHD is always present with the different neurodivergence briefly mentioned in the book or that it's never ADHD. What I am suggesting is nothing's ever that simple. Whatever I share about any co-occurring neurodivergence, it's my hope that it encourages you to learn more and see how some simple changes initially made for ADHD learners might benefit more students than you initially realise. The truth is that it isn't always easy to pinpoint ADHD and maybe the whole point is doing what we can to reduce the barriers to learning whether what we're noticing is actually ADHD or not.

Finally, I don't think I could write a book about supporting ADHD learners without discussing the significant challenges they experience with emotional regulation. Since ADHD brains tend to protect bodies that carry more sensitive nervous systems, looking at ways to increase a felt sense of safety in the learning environment seemed a necessary component to include in the book. So each chapter includes a common emotional struggle for ADHDers, showing how it might manifest, while offering some initial suggestions for support. This is also where developing a better understanding of trauma-informed, equity-centred and culturally responsive teaching comes in handy too. The ways we set up our learning environments make all the difference.

The use of language and labels in this book

I've thought carefully about the language used in this book because of the way that labels impact us all. Their meanings can carry a lot of influence on how we see ourselves and each other. I wanted to write with the belief that there were many reasons for the ADHD presentations noticed in the students I taught, but also there were many reasons for the responses I gave as a teacher too. We bring our whole selves into the classroom almost as much as our students do and there's a vulnerability in being a student or an educator. Remembering our common humanity was the thought that guided all the language choices I made. That meant finding language that kept me from pathologising, shaming or blaming the people whose stories are shared. It meant writing from a place that focused on the complexities of being human while offering myself, other teachers and students compassion. Our experiences as educators and learners are linked, intertwining and impacting each other.

Keeping these thoughts in mind, when you read this book you might notice I often use the term *ADHD presentations* over ADHD behaviour or symptoms where I can. This is to keep away from pathologising what I believe are natural responses in the child's body based on what they're experiencing in that moment. When I choose to use "presentations" over behaviours, there's a subtle shift for me in how I'm thinking about what I notice too. Behaviours tend to be about something a person is doing, often intentionally and towards others. It focuses on the problem being something only the person acting out can solve and is usually only solvable by somehow changing themselves. It limits others' ability in finding ways to support the person too, especially since the expectation is that the behaviour can only be changed if the person chooses to. When I describe *presentations*, I'm noticing the child's actions while sticking close to the facts. I'm keeping my emotions out of it and sticking only to what I observe. This helps me stay out of my own interpretations of what *I think* a behaviour means about them (or me), thus influencing the way I might decide to respond to them rather than react.

I refrain from using terms like "ADHD symptoms" and limit my use of terms like "condition". I'm not writing about curing an illness. Although I know that ADHD medication works wonders for many people, medication still doesn't solve all the challenges ADHDers go through in school. But even more so, the nature of ADHD is that it rarely, if ever, travels alone. That makes it more difficult to see if what we're noticing on any given day is actually just ADHD, another neurodivergence or a combination of physical, social, mental, emotional and/or biological influences. When I use ADHD presentations, I'm also admitting that I'm not 100 per cent sure what label I could place on the "behaviours" I'm noticing either. Instead, I tried to do what I could to support the student based on what I noticed as potential barriers to their learning, whether they were diagnosed with ADHD or not.

Other language considerations of note

I've tried to keep from unnecessarily gendering people and things (see Alex and Emma and Henry's stories on gender too). The only people that have a specific gender in this book are the students who are the focus of each chapter. Everyone else, including myself where I am referenced as the teacher, is referred to as they/them, by name or by a degendered "title". For example, the learners in the book either refer to me by first name or simply as "teacher". I interchange the terms ADHD students, ADHD learners, ADHDers along with children, students, learners with ADHD. I also do the same for educators and teachers, and parents and carers. There are many words we might use to describe ourselves, each other and the children we teach. Each term might have subtle differences for you too. I think it's important to reflect on how they influence the way you see yourself, the children you work with and the adults that care for them.

Language changes quickly, so some terms in this book may not be used a year from now. I wanted to choose terms that were as affirming and current as possible, with careful consideration of terms used around race, gender, culture and other social identities, as well as any disability and social justice principles. I've tried to be as specific as possible when referencing different cultures, communities or areas people might be from. I also decided not to use the term BIPOC (Black (including Black Indigenous), Indigenous, People of Colour), which doesn't centre other races, but rather continues to subtly suggest that **whiteness** is what to compare all others against. Instead, I try to refer to race or groups specifically or use the term melanated people where necessary.

There are also **bolded words** throughout the book that correspond to a Glossary if you need any assistance understanding key terminology.

A final thought on labels

My hope is that this book will encourage you to think a lot more about labels. I hope it will make you stop and think about the labels that have been used to define you, who had the power to create and place them and how they've impacted you. How do you think the various labels attached to you might be interpreted by your students and influence how they relate to you? I hope this book encourages you to reflect on the labels that you've worked to unlearn or redefine about yourself and maybe start to reflect on some you've learned to use on others too, and how they might need to be redefined or removed altogether.

Finally, I hope that this book will help you reconsider the ways that you've learned to label the children you work with – but especially the labels you've learned to place on ADHD learners and how they've changed depending on what the child looks like, their age, their gender, their financial status, their academic ability and more. All these social identity markers, whether we acknowledge them or not, play a role in the ways that we decide to support our students with ADHD. Unpacking and changing these beliefs is a huge step we can all take in creating the conditions for children with ADHD to thrive in, allowing them the chance to define all they could be for themselves.

Preface

The limitations of labels

We automatically group and classify ourselves and others with lots of different labels: labels about our character, our appearance, our talents, our jobs and our lives. When we can group things and create a story about what they mean, then we know what to expect of ourselves, each other and what should happen in our lives. Labels help the brain derive some sense of certainty (and therefore safety) about what we believe we should expect from the world around us.

As teachers, we all have various definitions of this label and what to expect from ourselves because of it. The same goes for the label of student too. It feels necessary to label our students with specific learning disabilities or behaviours. Labels are often needed for legal reasons, like getting an Education, Health and Care Plan (EHCP) or other learning accommodations. When we can anticipate the kind of behaviour they might display in the classroom, we believe we'll know what to expect from the children we teach. The right label can help us find definitive ways to support our learners. But our students have interpretations of what it means for us to be teachers and for themselves to be students too.

Labels often encourage us to interpret and define our students' behaviours through the narrow lens of the **dominant culture**; a culture that encourages conformity and places blame on the individual when they can't or won't comply with its expectations. In this way, the label can become the focus that threatens to erase the wholeness of their identity. We don't consider the cultures and the experiences our students bring into our classrooms or how this knowledge could be used to support them (and us) too. Without actively interrogating the labels placed on ourselves and others we'll struggle to see how they might limit our belief in the capacity for growth and change, not only for our students but also for ourselves. We're whole people with an array of experiences and beliefs under these labels of teacher, student or ADHD learner.

We all deserve the dignity to define who we are for ourselves.

Introduction

They placed the paper down before me without even a glance in my direction. I stared motionless at first, as the shame rose in my body.

I'd been given this coloured paper before, but they'd forgotten again. It was the same paper all the kids fought over when doing self-portraits, the precious *flesh-coloured* paper. *Flesh colour* which looked like the *flesh* of my teacher and every single other student in my class. *Flesh colour* that looked like every single student and teacher at my school. Everyone but mine. It was as if I didn't have a *flesh colour*. The coloured paper that was for me was just called *brown*.

No one wanted that colour.

I quickly tapped my teacher on the arm which made them turn abruptly to me and shake their head disapprovingly. I started to stammer. I was nervous and speaking a little louder and quicker than I probably needed to. I finally told them, "I don't look like this. Where's my paper? I need brown paper …" I trailed off, looking over briefly to see the students around me pointing and snickering. My teacher glanced at me as if to brush me off. Everyone was used to me getting upset about something. I was already called all sorts of names and labelled for how others interpreted my behaviour, so the shame I felt in even mentioning this problem appeared instantly.

"Yes, yes, Sandra! I know. I know", they snapped at me. "There's no need to panic or get upset about it. Your paper is coming …"

They finished handing out the *flesh-coloured* paper to everyone else in the class and went searching for a brown scrap of paper for me. It wasn't quite the shade of my skin colour, but my teacher tossed it down, saying, "See? There! No big deal!". They walked off, leaving me deep in my pit of shame that was now coupled with humiliation, as some of my classmates whispered and giggled about the incident amongst themselves. Strangely, I was the only one who heard anything, my teacher never addressed it at all. That left me wondering if maybe it wasn't a big deal. Maybe I shouldn't have spoken up. Maybe I should have just taken the *flesh-coloured* paper and been like everyone else.

At least until someone would inevitably point out someday when our work was displayed that I wasn't *that* colour. And laugh.

They always laughed.

Tears welled up in my eyes, but thankfully, this time I managed to wipe them away before anyone noticed. Regulating my emotions had never been easy for me anyway, but no place more so than school. For as long as I could remember I would easily become dysregulated, and this could end up being very explosive. It would get to a point where I couldn't take it anymore. I'd end up screaming and shouting, throwing and hitting things (and sometimes people), running out of the classroom and hiding from my peers until someone found me and I had to go back to class, or until I had no choice but to slink my way back into my seat in front of all my peers. Or I could get so upset that I would be silent for hours, unable to engage with my classmates or most of my teachers.

I also had no idea that what I was dealing with was unmanaged ADHD.

But why am I starting a book about supporting ADHD in schools with a story about racism? Because I can't separate the two. As a student, I wasn't just a girl who couldn't manage her emotions well, who wasn't great at organising her things or who couldn't listen before she spoke; I was also Black. Whether it's admitted or not, that's what the people around me saw first. That influenced the way my behaviour was interpreted by others. I didn't fit what was expected of a girl, but being a Black one meant that the dysregulation I was displaying regularly (especially while being an academically successful student) meant something different. That tended to revolve around somehow being my fault.

Yes, undiagnosed ADHD was a part of the problems I was dealing with, but it wasn't the only thing. Everyone saw the Black skin while never acknowledging the added difficulties it created for me at the same time. Colour Blindness was one thing that made the learning environment unsafe for me. How I *felt* in my learning environments and the messages I got about how others felt about me fuelled a lot of how my ADHD presentations manifested in school. The best strategies and accommodations could have been implemented for my ADHD, but without feeling like I belonged exactly as I was would have impacted my ability to implement them effectively. Improving how I felt in my learning environments would have included everyone involved with overseeing my learning and care regularly unpacking the ways their own cultural lenses, lived experiences and **internalised biases** were influencing how they interpreted and labelled my behaviour and what it indicated about my needs.

Without these things happening, any support would have been forcing me to fundamentally change who I was in order to fit who they expected me to be, rather than creating support that worked for me. The labels I was given weren't in service to me but limited me to a disconnected, shrunken version of myself. There was so much more to me than the expectations those labels forced on me, but the weight of them kept me from fully understanding who I was and what best supported my needs.

ADHD and Black children

I'm a **transracial adoptee** and was placed with my adoptive family when I was 3 years old. It was a closed adoption that happened during the early 1980s, so I don't remember much about it. My parents had biological children quite a lot older and had previously adopted a Black child many years earlier too. When they adopted my biological baby brother and I, things hadn't changed that much with the **transracial adoption** process. They were instructed to go to what they were told was "racial sensitivity training" in order to "help them learn how to raise a Black child". It was a presentation that took maybe half a day and when completed, left my adoptive parents questioning its ultimate usefulness. There were many things that they would not have truly foreseen or understood about how growing up isolated in white spaces might impact me, but they always did their best with the knowledge and resources that were available to them at the time.

Intersectional insight: Adoptees and fostered children

ADHD is more prevalent amongst adoptive children than it is in the general population. "Simmel, Brooks, Barth and Hinshaw (2001) conducted a study examining 808 adopted children aged between 4 and 18 years old. 21% of the children had ADHD compared to 3–5% in the general population" (Lanc UK, accessed April 2023). With foster children those numbers range between 18 and 21 per cent (Peñarrubia, Navarro-Soria, Palacios, and Fenollar-Cortés, 2021).

The United States Commission on Civil Rights' publication "Beyond Suspensions" (Lhamon et al., 2019) looked at the impact of discipline policies, the connection to the **school-to-prison pipeline** and how it disproportionately impacted Black, Indigenous and Brown, disabled students. When considering the impact on Black girls it noted that

> behaviors, particularly of Black girls, are misinterpreted as defiant and violent and disruptive and sometimes those are just expressions of their critical thinking. But based upon some of the ways in which we have portrayed Black femininity in our society, the way those words come out or the very act of dissent is perceived as an act of defiance … Educators believe that Black girls are more independent, need less comfort and need less support than their white peers. (p. 193)

Black children are found to be either overrepresented or underrepresented when it comes to diagnosis and receiving support services too. Both are the result of misidentification because of systemic racism. When overrepresented (particularly for emotional disturbances and conduct disorders – see Darnell's story in Chapter 1 for more), there are more students when compared to the overall school enrolment for that group of children. Underrepresentation recognises fewer children when compared to the amount of children in that group that are enrolled. Either way, for Black students the impact on them is the same. Whether in general classrooms or segregated into "special education" classes, they were more often met with lower academic expectations and harsher disciplinary actions, and endured more school suspensions and expulsions than their peers (Lhamon et al., 2019).

It wasn't until I was well into adulthood that I truly learned and understood these differences in treatment for Black children and how they appeared in my education experiences too. I remembered plenty of times when teachers would treat me differently than the white girls in my class for doing much of the same behaviours. I was the one who got reprimanded in front of others, was kicked out of classes or received "in-school suspensions". My emotional dysregulation was seen as the key problem. My reactions in situations were more often considered defiant and I remember constantly feeling either misunderstood or simply unseen. I never saw myself in the stories told by my teachers or through representation that didn't go beyond incarcerated people, enslaved people or the occasional athlete. It sent the message that I wasn't as valuable as everyone else. I was easily disposable and not seen as human too.

The majority of my primary and secondary school life was spent being the only Black girl learning amongst a sea of white children. To compensate for being so visibly different from my classmates, I tried to be extremely studious and hardworking. I never wanted to be the reason anyone was upset with me. In fact, I tried to be perfect in hopes that getting the best grades, being the captain of all the sports teams and volunteering for all the jobs would help me to fit in. Only, my inconsistent work efforts, emotional dysregulation, significantly lower test scores compared to my class work, and disorganised, messy school desk often meant that I was far from that aspiration, which only added to the shame I increasingly felt. With no reason for why this was happening, I began to see these failings as character flaws that I needed to hide. That left me no choice but to just *try harder* and change more of myself so I could hopefully be considered to be like everyone else.

I became incredibly anxious and was often depressed. Even though school was a place that offered me the predictability of a routine and the security of clear expectations that I craved, it also became a secret source of torment for me. I lacked social understanding compared to others in my classes, which only made me more hyperfocused on what made me different from everyone else. I lived with the fear that at any given moment anyone could use my differences to ridicule, bully and humiliate me. My self-esteem plummeted as an immense fear of making mistakes and an unending search for perfection took its place. My need to feel a sense of control got stronger as I got older, leading me to obsess about and criticise my hair and body. I developed a dysregulated relationship with food, which if I had been white and in a bigger (or smaller) body, might have been recognised as a sign of an eating disorder.

Unfortunately, challenges surrounding food and eating are not uncommon with neurodivergence. In fact, I often wonder if when dysregulated eating patterns are noticed, perhaps neurodivergence is not the exception but the rule. Disordered or dysregulated eating behaviours can show up in a multitude of ways for children and adults with ADHD, which include

- using food as a way to manage uncomfortable emotions like boredom, stress;
- forgetting or ignoring hunger cues due to hyperfocus on a task or activity;
- reduced appetite because of ADHD medication;
- difficulties noticing hunger or satiation cues;
- eating past the point of comfort due to impulsivity;
- executive functioning skills delays that impact planning, shopping or cooking meals in the time needed, leading to overeating what's available or skipping meals completely.

Studies also show that ADHD often co-occurs with eating disorders, most commonly with those where binge eating rather than food restriction is present. Both ADHD and eating disorders can co-occur with mood disorders like depression or anxiety (both of which are also considered neurodivergence). With so much overlap, maybe it's not so surprising that ADHD presentations have been reported in 5–17 per cent of people being treated for eating disorders (Reinblatt, 2015).

Much of the anxiety I felt in school came from the messages I received about being a Black girl which drove me to hyperfocus on more extreme ways to try to fix myself. Using food became a way to exert some control over my life. If the label of "the *good* Black girl" or "the *cool* Black friend" could easily be stripped from me at the whim of every white person around me, I always needed to prove I was *better than that*. Better than what I'd gleaned it meant to be the *unacceptable Black girl*, which was any reactions I had that could potentially make the white people around me uncomfortable. I eventually learned that being myself would never be enough and these labels would be the ones others would define me by.

I now understand that it was my proximity to my adoptive parents' **whiteness** that allowed me to access therapy in high school. In fact, if they hadn't had their own children, they wouldn't have realised that the Black children they adopted were displaying different needs. I have no doubt being white made a difference in approaching professionals in the 1980s demanding support for their Black sons for what they believed was ADHD. Even with their privilege, I know that it wasn't easy for them to accomplish, but for many Black people during that same time period (or even still today), an ADHD diagnosis wouldn't have been a consideration, let alone a possibility.

If I hadn't remembered my brother's childhood ADHD diagnosis, I don't think I'd still be diagnosed today. My circumstances for recognising my ADHD in many ways were an exception. But because I'm Black, the time and effort it took to secure a diagnosis was still the rule.

What is ADHD?

Attention Deficit Hyperactivity Disorder (ADHD) is the current term for a specific developmental delay of executive functioning seen in children and adults. It's often talked about as three different types: ADHD hyperactive, ADHD inattentive or ADHD combined (meaning a mix of the first two types mentioned). ADHD is a specific neurodivergence (clinically referred to as a neurodevelopmental condition) that is often genetic and hereditary but can occur if someone experiences a brain injury or trauma. It's important to note that not all ADHDers have every single possible presentation at one time. They also may display more of some presentations and none of the others. Due to the way that ADHD can look like other neurodivergence or mental health needs, it can sometimes be difficult to decipher whether it is ADHD or not, especially if you're unfamiliar with all its manifestations.

Many other neurodivergence like Autism, trauma and Obsessive-Compulsive Disorder (OCD) have presentations that significantly overlap with ADHD too. Not to mention, many neurodivergence co-occur with ADHD which can make it difficult to determine root causes of dysregulation in order to ensure the appropriate supports are in place. "The 2007 National Survey of Children's Health (NCSH) found that 33% of the children with ADHD had one coexisting condition, 16% had two, and 18% had three or more" (Larson, Russ, Kahn, and Halfon, 2011, accessed through CHADD.org 13 June 2023). But ADHD doesn't just co-occur with neurodivergence that are considered mental health, mood disorders or specific learning disabilities. It can also co-occur with physical developmental delays like dyspraxia and has high co-occurrence rates with epilepsy, eating disorders, sleep disturbances and even

Table 0.1 ADHD hyperactive and ADHD inattentive

ADHD Hyperactive	ADHD Inattentive
Fidgets with objects or hands, or taps feet while sitting	Daydreams and becomes easily distracted, doesn't appear to be listening when talked to
Finds it difficult to be still when necessary	
Engages in excessive physical movement – always doing something or moving without considering if it's the right time to be doing so	Has a hard time staying focused on tasks that require sustained focus, difficulty sustaining attention during play or tasks, such as conversations, lectures or lengthy reading
Talks a lot or non-stop	
Talks over others or blurts out answers without questions being completed	Misses details and makes seemingly careless mistakes in schoolwork or during other activities
Acts before thinking of consequences or possible dangers	Has trouble following instructions and often shifts from task to task without finishing anything, gets sidetracked easily
Runs or climbs where not appropriate and with no apparent goal but to keep moving (older children and teens may feel more restless energy)	Has trouble getting organised (time, materials and/or tasks), loses track of things (losing homework assignments or space can be cluttered)
Interrupts games and conversations	
Struggles to wait for turns or in line-ups	Is forgetful in day-to-day activities (misses deadlines, forgets homework)
Loses or forgets things repeatedly and often	
Inability to stay on task; often shifts activities, bringing very little, if any, to completion	Is easily distracted by unrelated thoughts or stimuli

asthma too. When left untreated, ADHD results in a higher prevalence of addictions, alcohol and drug misuse, and reckless behaviour. If anything, binary charts of symptoms about ADHD like Table 0.1 above make it appear that it's all so simple or straightforward, but unfortunately that's never the case. These kinds of charts provide us with a starting point, but each child with ADHD shows their own unique combination of ADHD presentations.

There are many different theories about the causes of ADHD, but what I think is important is how the range of difficulties ADHD students experience appears on a spectrum. This means that on any given day or moment, what impacts an ADHD learner could change depending on many different factors, including how they can meet their personal physical and emotional needs (sleep, hunger, feeling confident or capable), co-occurring conditions (any neurodivergence or physical conditions listed in the paragraphs above), environment conditions (how comfortable they feel with others or in the space) or their interest in the task at hand. No two ADHD students are the same but can have many similar needs at different times.

Executive functioning skills development

Executive functioning skills are what we develop to help us decide what we need to pay attention to and direct our focus towards (Dawson and Guare, 2008). We access these skills in the thinking brain which is within the frontal lobe of the prefrontal cortex. These skills assist us in linking our prior knowledge to our new learning and present lives so we can reflect on our actions, organise our thoughts and ideas, and make decisions that we can continue to tweak as we get more information. The most commonly talked about executive functioning skills are self-awareness, inhibition, working memory (both verbal and non-verbal), emotional regulation, self-motivation, and planning and problem-solving. In this book, I've described them in slightly different ways so that they are easier to centre and practise in a classroom:

- perseverance;
- time management;
- sustaining attention;
- cognitive flexibility;
- working memory;
- meta-cognition (reflection);
- impulse control;
- planning and prioritising;
- organising.

From infancy to young adulthood, the development of cognitive functioning is reflected in behaviour that is less reflexive and stimulus-bound, but rather more goal-directed, self-organised and flexible (Stuss, 1992, in Matthews, Nigg, and Fair, 2014). This is why our executive function skills development is considered so important. As we grow, these skills develop so our independence increases. This means the younger the child, the more unreasonable it is to expect them to effectively self-regulate – they just don't have the skills yet. It's why teachers, parents and carers or other adults will scaffold the use of these skills through their own executive functioning, gradually reducing the child's dependence on them as they age.

But since ADHD is a developmental delay, it often takes more time for these skills to develop, even with direct teaching, introducing new tools and practising new strategies regularly. It's also important to remember that "developmental delay" in this sense means that each ADHDer's brain structures and skills continue to develop throughout their lives at different rates. This is why we see changes in ADHD presentations as a child grows, but at the same time why ADHD is something people never grow out of.

The executive functioning behind emotional regulation

In my experience, many ADHDers share about feeling emotions intensely and often talk about being more sensitive to rejection in particular. These feelings can often lead to becoming emotionally flooded, which triggers the (over)reactions that we might witness in our students' responses. Emotional regulation also happens in the prefrontal cortex. This skill allows us to manage our behaviour and social interactions in ways that ensure we meet our needs without causing too many disruptions for ourselves or those around us. ADHD students are often known for emotional outbursts that can include aggression or excitability or can appear moody or demotivated at times. Part of what makes emotional regulating in ADHD challenging is noticing the sensations we experience in our bodies, and learning to choose strategies and tools to help us better navigate any potentially dysregulating experiences. Although there are programmes and tools that teach about emotional regulation in schools, it might be helpful to consider how different strategies might look for students who must implement them while navigating an ADHD brain too.

For instance, ADHD learners tend to expect the work they're asked to do not to be rewarding, which leaves them more apt to avoid or withdraw from tasks, taking longer to complete them, if at all. It's often difficult for an ADHDer to consider doing a task that someone else has deemed "important" enough to create an emotional connection that feels strong enough to do the task. In fact, ADHD brains err more on the side of negative bias and will avoid tasks more than approach them (Barkley, 2018). They feel more willing to take action when something is a novelty, interesting or in some way *feels* rewarding enough to them. This can fluctuate from day to day and moment to moment impacted by environmental factors that can leave ADHD students *feeling* less capable, ready or willing to engage. Their efforts to work towards a goal can often be thwarted by the ways their ADHD manifests at the same time. This can be due to any number of challenges experienced, including with impulsivity, working memory and sustaining attention.

ADHD students may *feel* that something is important to them, but when another task or situation creates a stronger sensation in their bodies that must be met in order to regulate it, their attention immediately goes towards that. This often leads to them forgetting about the other task entirely. Delays in executive function skills affecting impulse inhibition and metacognition make it challenging to reflect on whether their actions are in support of the initial goals they set for themselves or not. Working memory only compounds difficulties when they struggle to remember what action they took the last time the same situation arose, what actions weren't effective, or even what the initial goal they were working towards was before they were distracted in the first place.

Not to mention that some tasks take so much additional effort to complete for various reasons beyond managing ADHD presentations (for example, co-occurring neurodivergence or physical needs that require attention) that the reward of completing the task doesn't feel worth it. At the same time, there's no guarantee that the ADHD learner will feel rewarded by doing the same task at another time or *feel* whether it would be rewarding again even if they *know* it was previously and genuinely *want* to do it. The negative bias that the same task will not achieve the same sense of satisfaction becomes harder to engage with when you consider they're often thwarted by working memory delays too.

Considering the nervous system with ADHD

Our thinking mind holds a lot of knowledge about the world around us. It's the part of us that understands the expectations and assumptions that society places on us. It creates the labels we put on people and things so we can make meaning of the world. But it's not the only place we keep knowledge. Our bodies hold a lot more of what we know, only they speak to us in a way that isn't cognitive. Instead, they speak in sensations that we feel. These sensations are like wordless narratives about what feels dangerous or safe (Menakem, 2017). When our bodies constrict or expand, feel tight or at ease, activate or are numb, feel pain or comfort, they're sending us messages about what we need. Our bodies only consider whether something (either felt internally within our bodies or externally from our environment) is a threat or not. A threat can be anything that is real or perceived and not just what is happening to us at that moment either. Our memories, thoughts, actions or beliefs can bring up sensations in the body too.

The vagus nerve is a complex system of nerves that connects the brainstem, heart, lungs, pharynx, stomach, gut and spine. It's directly connected to a part of our brain that doesn't use cognition or reasoning as a primary tool for navigating the world, called the amygdala, which is the centre for emotions in our brain. The amygdala is only focused on survival, and for ADHDers who are thought to have smaller amygdala volumes that means when faced with any sensation that makes them *feel* uncomfortable (frustration, excitement, apprehension or rejection that could be real or perceived, for example) it will be interpreted as a threat much quicker (Tajima-Pozo, 2015). This results in reactions that keep ADHD students protecting themselves in a variety of different ways, including avoidance and procrastination or acting out because of emotional flooding.

An "amygdala takeover" is when the amygdala senses a threat and automatically sends its signals of fight or flight through the body, resulting in uncontrollable aggression and anger (Saline, 2023). This reaction keeps ADHD students from accessing the thinking part of their brain, therefore they react without logic or reason, and can't access the skills and strategies necessary to make a different decision so they can regulate the rising emotions in their bodies. When ADHD students are trying to manage emotional flooding, "research has shown that it takes the body 15–20 minutes to fully recover from an amygdala takeover" (Saline, 2023). I think many of the ADHD presentations that we see in our classrooms have a lot to do with this difficulty in emotional regulation. It's important to remember that a dysregulated nervous system is one that is not feeling safe. When we're dysregulated, we're reacting to what our body interprets as a threat (even if it's just perceived). We can't access our frontal lobe to engage in reasoning and decide what response is appropriate. If we can't access our frontal lobe, then we're not learning effectively. When ADHD learners become dysregulated, they need additional time to self-regulate so they can come back to thinking again.

The environment we learn to set up for our ADHD students will help develop a stronger felt sense of safety. Feeling safer in a space leaves room to eventually try out new suggestions to strengthen self-regulation. Our strategies and tools in helping our ADHDers must support them in developing a stronger connection to their bodies too. They need to understand the messages behind their physical sensations and how to meet these needs in alignment with the best versions they envision for themselves. While our ADHD learners are calm and socially engaged, we frequently practise developing their self-regulation skills.

Putting the themes in this book together

We all have brains that are conditioned by the world around us. The **dominant culture** has told us who we should be in order to be considered "good teachers", and what our students should be and do in order to be considered "good students" too. All of how we feel about these beliefs and assumptions are stored in our bodies and this knowledge goes far beyond what we consciously think. We create learning spaces built on these beliefs and assumptions, and how we feel about these things impacts how we teach and act. But our students also come into our classrooms with their own beliefs and assumptions that impact how they interpret our behaviours and behave in school too. Since we know all this, how can we create a space where they feel safe enough to learn, especially for ADHD learners?

For our ADHD students, whose amygdala quickly filters any uncomfortable sensory input it receives as a threat to the body, finding safety in any environment becomes even more challenging. Not only do they have a nervous system that is highly sensitive to stimuli, but their brains are also wired to react quickly in order to protect it (remember: quickly doesn't always mean their ideal choice for the environment they're in). This keeps their bodies hypervigilant for threats in the environment (hence partly responsible for the attention and focus problems), and struggling with impulse control that keeps them from easily pausing and connecting with their thinking brain before taking action first. This makes it harder for ADHD learners to discern whether the stimuli they sense are actually a threat or not so they can choose how they want to act accordingly.

This is a big reason why educators need to regularly unpack and move through the sensations connected to **internalised biases** about our students, their ADHD presentations and what we've made their behaviour mean about the learner – and ourselves. Our bodies remember what our brains try to tell us we've let go of. Our bodies have a much different idea of what it considers safe than what we think it does, especially if we're not regularly doing the work to better understand what we notice in them. We will keep reacting from that **unconscious bias** rather than learning to become more regulated ourselves so we can question these reactions and decide if there's a way to respond that better aligns with the teachers we want to be. It's also why regularly practising self-regulation skills with our ADHD students while everyone is calm and collected works to support them in eventually feeling safe enough to use them when they need to. But all of this takes lots of time, patience and effort; after all, it's not just the body that we're working with, but the developmental delays of the ADHD brain too. It's necessary to remember that consistency in utilising any new strategies and tools comes when the body feels safe enough to automatically engage in them regularly. For the ADHD student, that can take longer than for many of their peers.

I know with all that teachers have going on in classrooms today, especially with how underfunded we are, how dangerous and overwhelming our jobs can be and the pressures of standardised testing. With the many hats we often feel forced to wear to do other jobs that we were neither trained for nor ever wanted to do in the first place, it becomes that much more difficult to meet the specific needs of all our students – especially those who frequently become dysregulated. We're told we're superhumans for all we accomplish in a school year, but the problem with this is it keeps us on pedestals, disconnected from our humanity and meeting the needs that come with being human. We learn that we must keep taking on jobs that aren't ours and be the ones to meet all our students' needs over our own. We fear what might happen when we fall from these heights, damaging our wellbeing or losing our jobs, but then also blamed for not working hard enough to achieve what was expected of our students.

I think the most challenging suggestions in this book for educators don't necessarily come from implementing the strategies and tools for our ADHD learners. Instead, they come from the ability to accept and embrace the needs that come with the messiness of teachers being humans too, especially in a society that doesn't always want to see us as such. When we can start to see and connect with the human behind the teacher label, we begin to get curious about the human behind the ADHD label and what they bring to the learning environment too. From here, more possibilities emerge for offering our ADHD students support and guidance in ways that work best for all of us, exactly as we are.

Resources to explore

Neurodiversity and education

Neurodivergent Narratives Podcast and Substack by Sandra Coral
The Cult of Pedagogy Podcast by Jennifer Gonzalez
The Neurodiverse Classroom, A Teacher's Guide to Individual Learning Needs and How to Meet Them by Victoria Honeybourne

ADHD

Black Girl, Lost Keys blog by Rene Brooks: https://blackgirllostkeys.com/
What Your ADHD Child Wishes You Knew by Dr Sharon Saline
The ADHD Dude: https://adhddude.com/
ADHD Foundation: www.adhdfoundation.org.uk/
ADHD Experts Podcast by ADDitude

Neurodivergence

Divergent Minds by Jenna Nerenberg
Neurodivergent Insights blog by Dr Megan Neff: https://neurodivergentinsights.com/

1

"He's so defiant!":

Darnell's story

This chapter asks us to reflect on:

- the ways **internalised bias** creates harmful interpretations of ADHD when discussing Black students;
- the diagnosis of oppositional defiant disorder and what this means for Black, Brown and Indigenous students;
- when dyslexia co-occurs with ADHD and why we might not recognise it;
- how prioritising reading and writing for expressing understanding impacts ADHD learners;
- how standardised testing impacts ADHD students while also centring **whiteness** in school.

I came back from the break time only to find Darnell at the principal's office, again. There was always something he'd been accused of doing: teasing other students, refusing to do classwork, arguing with teachers, or just general class disruptions like walking around or talking during class instruction. Today it was about a playground scuffle he'd had with some younger students. Darnell was also never one to take responsibility for his own behaviour and often accused others of causing the issues he found himself in. Many of his subject teachers were becoming concerned about his "lying and aggressive behaviour". Words like "defiant" were being tossed around to describe him, and frustrations about his lack of engagement in lessons were also rising.

It wasn't long before I noticed that Darnell was the only student with ADHD who was considered defiant. I could easily name a few (white) students who behaved much the same way, but unlike Darnell, ADHD was frequently mentioned and misbehaviour was usually excused. Now, I couldn't deny that Darnell would frequently argue, refuse to do work or lie about his actions, but I also couldn't unsee how quickly he was accused of being in the wrong either. He was in a difficult position, already considered guilty before he opened his mouth. No wonder he'd lie or lash out. When Darnell is seen as defiant, it only fuels the belief that his behaviour is done purposely in order to harm others and it's up to him to decide to change it. If he can't do that, then the result is usually being punished for it. But it was becoming quite evident that this approach wasn't working at all.

Meet Darnell:

- 8 years old
- Black, Caribbean ethnicity
- identifies as a boy
- fluent in the language of instruction
- outgoing, funny, creative
- loves: maths, music, science
- detests: writing, reading, drawing
- interests include: space, computer games
- future aspirations: astrophysicist
- best known for losing his temper, resisting reading and writing tasks, disrupting classes
- learning challenges: ADHD (possibly ODD), dysgraphia, suspected dyslexia
- additional information: new student to the school, newly divorced parents

---

Darnell had been diagnosed with ADHD when he was much younger and took medication for it, but many teachers wondered if, instead, he had oppositional defiant disorder (ODD; see Dhruv's story for PDA comparison). He had arrived at the school only a semester before me and we were two of only a few Black people in a predominately white school environment. That can be hard enough on anyone who isn't white, but often more so when you're Black. To make matters worse, Darnell wasn't an easy-going student either, which only amplified his difficulties. I also noticed that he had significant learning challenges in reading and writing that never seemed to be discussed as often as his *defiant behaviour*. From what I knew of Darnell, he didn't seem to be a particularly angry or vindictive child. He could get discouraged easily, but when considering his learning challenges, it was easy to see why. Under all the "defiance", he seemed more disheartened, untrusting and anxious than anything else.

Intersectional insight: What's in a name?

Okonofua and Eberhardt (2015) conducted two different studies, where teachers were given school records describing two incidents of misbehaviour by "male" students with names that were either more typically Black-sounding or white-sounding. The teachers were then asked if they believed the behaviour was a pattern, how badly they were upset by the misbehaviour, how severe the punishment should be and if they felt the student was a troublemaker. They found that the Black-sounding names led teachers to see the child's behaviour the second time around as being more troubling than compared with white-sounding named students. After the second offence, the teachers considered the behaviour a pattern for the Black-sounding named students that needed more severe consequences and envisioned suspension in future. They were also more apt to call Black students troublemakers, believing that after the second infraction their behaviour could not be changed. It makes you wonder how a label like defiant might further influence the interpretation of behaviour and treatment of Black students too.

The racism of oppositional defiant disorder

Oppositional Defiant Disorder (ODD) is diagnosed when a child has a pattern of acting out in hostile, aggressive, vindictive and argumentative behaviour (generally towards authority figures), which happens over a period of time of at least six months. Their behaviour must be interpreted as so disruptive that it impacts their relationships and aspects of their daily life. While it's suggested that possible causes of ODD could be a combination of biological, psychological and social factors, additional possible causes can include a lack of structure, inconsistent discipline practices, parenting practices, abuse and exposure to community violence too. A disproportionate number of Black, Brown and Indigenous students are diagnosed, leading many to question whether ODD is an actual neurodivergence or whether it's a diagnosis as the result of systemic and institutionalised racism instead.

School, for example, is a very different experience for Black students than for their white peers. They are more apt to be severely punished for subjective reasons like "disrespect" when they express themselves in their own vernacular. Their behaviour is more closely monitored with less room to make mistakes, harsher punishments when they do and even less support to make things right. Black students are seen as older than they are, making it easier to rationalise treating them more strictly than their same-aged peers. This keeps Black learners from accessing the skills development and resources required to support their social-emotional needs. It's as if ODD was created for a group of students that were already considered to be defiant whether they had an ADHD diagnosis or not.

Diagnostic tools for ADHD were initially normed for white male-presenting children and therefore further excluded historically marginalised groups, often resulting in Black, Brown and Indigenous Peoples being diagnosed with what are seen as more "severe" social or emotional conditions. ADHD was considered something that only white children had, even within Black communities. Centring white children for ADHD diagnosis also meant that similar behaviour in Black children was seen as more aggressive or violent.

Children who are considered to be "more aggressive" than their peers are said to have more trouble identifying and interpreting social cues from peers. These children tend to see hostile intent in "neutral situations" and think they should be rewarded for their aggressive response too (American Academy of Child and Adolescent Psychiatry, 2019). But living in a culture that designed the **systemic inequalities** which created many of the conditions for ODD would make many "neutral situations" hostile. For historically excluded students, these "neutral situations" are often infused with **microaggressions** and other forms of discrimination which they're expected to accept as "neutral" in order to avoid the repercussions that come from being seen as more threatening and aggressive than they already are. They must endure many situations throughout a school day that may be defined as "neutral" to those with more privilege, but in actuality are incredibly harmful and violent to those who are most marginalised.

Describing a student as defiant may seem neutral, but depending on the context in which someone is describing and the student being described, labels like this can indeed be interpreted as hostile. Studies have shown how having a diagnosis for disruptive behaviours (like a conduct disorder or ODD) negatively impacts a teacher's ability to objectively evaluate other behaviours such as inattention or hyperactivity. Without even considering **internalised bias**, a label like defiant or any kind of conduct disorder would have a negative impact, particularly on Black, Brown or Indigenous students who are already perceived as a threat simply by existing. But when these diagnoses are decided in place of ADHD (or ADHD is not included as a co-occurring diagnosis), this limits the child's access to medications, therapy and other supportive services that an ADHD diagnosis would otherwise provide.

Without access to these treatment options, ADHD students aren't just at risk for poor grades or relationship problems. Unmanaged ADHD can also lead to riskier sexual choices, car accidents, addictions, smoking and eating disorders, and takes an average of up to ten years off a person's life. Some research suggests that anywhere between 25–45 per cent of people[1] in prison also have unmanaged ADHD (Fields, 2021). Labels help us categorise our students' possible needs, but only when we learn to interpret them in ways that consider the identity and experiences of the whole child, through a lens that's as free from **internalised bias** as possible.

---

1   Black and Indigenous students are more likely to be incarcerated and the pathway to incarceration begins in the education system. Studies repeatedly show that the more a student is suspended or expelled, the more likely they will not complete high school and end up in the **school-to-prison pipeline**.

By the time Darnell came back into the classroom, we had already started on a writing assignment we began a few days earlier. Darnell moaned loudly as he entered the room.

"I'm not doing this!" he declared, before announcing he had finished already. He went over to his seat, tossing aside his paper that awaited him there. While learners were scattered around the room writing drafts, revising drafts with partners or doing writing workshops with myself or my teaching assistant (TA), Darnell proceeded to then pick up his pencil and doodle on his eraser instead.

Here we go ... again, I thought to myself as I walked over to him.

"Darnell ..." I said as gently as possible, "You're not quite finished yet. You had to write at least half the page. Remember?"

"No. I'm done ... I just write small." He continued doodling on the eraser.

"Really?! This is done, is it?"

I looked at the paper again. He had written a few words that were more like bullet points. His writing was varied in size, with a few upper-case letters incorrectly mixed with lower-case ones. The one sentence he'd written started with a capital letter and had a full stop (neither of which happened often). He did have some interesting initial thoughts (which to his credit actually *did* happen often). But I always hoped he'd continue by clarifying them with more details.

"Darnell ... I've made notes on the paper with some questions for you to answer to help you expand on your thoughts."

He wouldn't budge. I pushed the paper towards him, pointing at it insistently with my pen as if it might be the "on switch" that would urge Darnell to finally get started. Only he leapt up and pushed the paper across his desk.

"No!" he shouted, "You're always getting me in trouble and no one else!"

I paused and backed away. When Darnell reacted like this, I knew that debating with him wasn't going to get us anywhere. All I'd successfully done in this interaction was continue to try the same ways to get him to express his understanding, hoping that this time it would be different. I'd have to talk with him another time.

Reading and writing are often fraught with a lot of insecurity in students if they can't perform to grade-level expectations. Darnell would have angry outbursts over what he believed he couldn't do in literacy lessons. I knew it was an area that I would have to address delicately. The longer the school year went on the less reading and written tasks he would attempt to do. It was impacting his confidence as a learner and his overall self-esteem. But when you consider the messages we get in school about the importance of being "good readers and writers" it's not surprising it was affecting Darnell so deeply.

The prioritising of the written word

The messages we receive about English-language usage and the written word in **white supremacy culture** are everywhere. As educators, we bring our beliefs and experiences about how we see ourselves as readers and writers into the classroom, influencing the ways we teach literacy too. Written communication is used as a way to preserve the power of **whiteness**. It not only tells us what writings are deemed most important (the ones that centre **whiteness**, of course) but also insists that the ideas and beliefs of white people are best too. Societal norms for student behaviour when it comes to reading and writing create **internalised biases** about which students are more often criticised, and assumed to be less intelligent, careless or lazy for their efforts and who are deemed worthy of more support.

It's seen when it's assumed that Black students who speak African American Vernacular English (AAVE; which is its own unique language, not a form of slang) are less intelligent than those who *speak white*. They must **code-switch** in order to be perceived as intelligent (but not *too* intelligent, as that can be interpreted as a threat too). Or how Brown, Indigenous, Asian, Arab, Pacific Islanders and other melanated peoples who speak English with an accent (even while communicating fluently) are considered less intelligent than white people who do the same. Or how non-speaking people are frequently assumed to be incompetent and unable to understand the world around them. It's also why many non-white immigrant families impress upon their children to learn the language of their new school and country, not prioritising learning their **home language**. The message is clear in the education system: if you can use (English) written (and spoken) language well, you're perceived better than if you can't.

The belief that the written word and all the knowledge produced by it is inherently more valuable than anything else (while also deciding that it's been best used and shared by white people) simultaneously erases, **whitewashes** and **appropriates** the knowledge, skills and histories of Black, Brown, Indigenous, Asian, and other melanated peoples. **White supremacy culture** conditions us to ignore and disregard the many other ways that wisdom has been passed down through historically excluded groups over centuries and the ways that different people learn and work together. We learn we must prioritise centring **whiteness**, limiting students in what they learn (either from each other or their communities) and expressing what they know. But attempting to decentre written work, especially within a system that has used testing for almost a century, is not an easy feat. We've all internalised a lot of messages about our proficiency as writers and readers both as educators and learners.

Since ADHD learners can struggle with emotional regulation, Darnell's reactions in writing class make sense. His writing challenges would impact how he saw himself as a learner and what he felt capable of. Like every other student, Darnell would receive the messages of what makes a good reader or writer and from those messages determine whether he fits the description or not. Couple these messages with the ones that inform him about how he is perceived as a Black child in this society, it's no wonder his nervous system would become much more hypervigilant to threats in his environment, even if he didn't have the words for it. All of this could further impact his ADHD presentations too, perhaps by being more easily dysregulated. His body was already aware of the threats in his environment that reminded him that no matter what he did, his efforts or any of his accomplishments, would never be good enough.

Reflect now

Where have you been quick to judge repeated similar behaviours as worse in one student over another? What beliefs did you have about that student that kept you from seeing them as perhaps not having the skills or knowledge to deal with a problem rather than simply being one?

Darnell huffed himself around his peers and went over to the corner of the class which had the carpet, a bunch of pillows, a teacher's chair and a small tent. It was where we had our class library. He sat with his arms crossed, purposely looking away at me next. I stood back for a minute and decided to give him some space. Darnell had set himself up quite comfortably in the space and conveniently next to another learner who was working at a mini-table. This led to him trying to push his peer's pencil as they wrote, which of course frustrated them. Darnell laughed. Clearly, there wasn't going to be any more writing today.

It had only been a few weeks into the school year but writing had already become a source of contention for us. It seemed strange that he would struggle with something so intensely, especially when there were signs of how talented he was in other subject areas. Darnell was a creative kid who showed this most often through hands-on, problem-solving tasks. I was impressed with his wide vocabulary and many insightful contributions he'd add to class discussion. This initially surprised me because it was never previously mentioned when talking about him, but since Black students are not often recognised for their academic strengths, I shouldn't have been surprised at all. What was certain to me was that reading was not the best way for Darnell to acquire new knowledge and writing was certainly not his best way of expressing it. I had to make some changes.

Standardised testing, whiteness and ADHD

Decades of research show that Black, Brown, Indigenous students, and some Asian groups, when compared to white students, experience bias from standardised tests. These assessments, given from childhood to higher education, are designed to measure intelligence and knowledge. But since they are often normed to the **dominant culture**, they are an inherently biased tool, showing inaccurate scores of a student's knowledge and ability (Rosales and Walker, 2021). Standardised testing doesn't consider how differences in race, gender, **culture**, language, socioeconomic background and more can impact student learning outcomes. Instead, it keeps **whiteness** (and with it the written word) as the primary benchmark to measure students' academic success. It's no wonder we consider learners (and even more so if they aren't white) who make frequent mechanical errors or use "simplistic" vocabulary as being less intelligent. Students that can't conform to these expectations learn that they won't be seen as successful unless they reach these standards. They don't realise that these tests were designed to exclude them from the beginning.

Our focus on the written word as a measure of success and expression of understanding can have a detrimental impact on the academic outcomes of ADHD learners. Challenges with written expression are seen through "less organized written work, writing fewer words, and making more mechanical errors (e.g., misspelt words and poor handwriting) in comparison to their peers and are still apparent even when they have the basic rules of writing" (Molitor, Langberg, and Evans, 2016). In fact, "writing composition difficulties are twice as common (65%) as learning challenges in reading, mathematics and orthography individually" (Mayes and Calhoun, 2006). This is thought to be because of the cognitive load of working memory and sustained attention that writing entails over other academic subjects. ADHD children "score 5–6 points lower on average on standardized tests of intelligence" (Frazier, Demaree, and Youngstrom, 2004), and depending on the severity of ADHD and how it presents has also been shown to affect students' academic performance (Barry, Lyman, and Klinger, 2002; Riccio, Homack, Jarratt, and Wolfe, 2006). When the written word is considered the most valued way of communication and accessing information alongside our unchecked implicit biases, it keeps the lens of what we believe our learners are capable of and how we support them extremely limited.

And it's students like Darnell who continue to endure the consequences.

Reflect now

What have you learned about the importance of being a good writer or reader and how has that influenced how you see yourself? How has a student's ability to speak or write influenced the ways that you saw them or their abilities? What might need to change in your beliefs when race, gender, socio-economic status or other social identity markers are considered while assessing a student's reading, speaking or writing ability?

When ADHD co-occurs with dyslexia

Dyslexia appears in up to 15 per cent of the population, but only 4.5 per cent of students are diagnosed and that number is even less for Black children. With such a significant emphasis on literacy in schools, struggling in reading, writing, grammar or spelling can create immense stress and a loss of self-esteem for children. Without proper support, these students end up having increased anxiety and depression (both of which can co-occur with ADHD too), which can also manifest in increasingly disruptive and/or challenging behaviour. This might make us want to look at how we can eliminate the behaviour rather than get to the root cause of it. For Black, Brown and Indigenous children, whose behaviour is closely monitored for mistakes and harshly policed in schools, the needs under the behaviour often go unnoticed and remain unmet.

Intersectional insights: Mental health in marginalised students

It's important to remember that many of our most marginalised students also come to our spaces with anxiety or depression just because of the challenges they must deal with in this **white supremacy**, patriarchal culture. Multiracial/biracial youth report experiencing anxiety and depressive symptoms at higher rates than their monoracial peers (Fisher et al., 2014, in Campbell, 2020). Additionally, multiracial/biracial youth with non-white mothers have far lower emotional well-being than their monoracial minority and white peers (Schlabach, 2013, in Campbell, 2020). Black and Latine trans students experience significantly more intense mental health challenges when compared to white trans students. Indigenous Peoples have reported the highest rates of depression, more than any racial group. Even though "depression and anxiety are reported at lower rates in the Asian and Pacific Islander communities, they are also least likely to seek treatment options. Southeast Asian refugees are more likely to be diagnosed with post-traumatic stress disorder (PTSD) because of difficulty adjusting to a new culture or escaping conflict in their home countries" (Hsu, Davies, and Hansen, 2004; Office of the Surgeon General (US), 2001). Even though anxiety and depression commonly co-occur with ADHD, they also can be further triggered by systemic and structural racism and victimisation due to gender and sexuality too. We can't always know if it's anxiety or depression that's driving dysregulation, but there are plenty of daily realities for marginalised students that explain why they could be present.

About 50–60 per cent of ADHDers have co-occurring learning challenges (Olivardia, 2022) and dyslexia is the most common with estimates of 25–40 per cent having both (McGrath and Stoodley, 2019). Dyslexia is a language-based neurodivergence that impacts phonemic awareness, which is difficulty recognising and breaking down the sounds of letters. Dyslexia is not always easy to spot right away, especially when initially learning to read or when alongside co-occurring conditions like ADHD, which have a significant overlap in presentations. We often think of dyslexia as writing letters backwards or not being able to read, but it's a lot more than that. Although they can overlap in terms of information-processing speed challenges, working memory deficits, and naming speed and motor skills deficits, the ways these presentations manifest in both are slightly different. With ADHDers, you see these challenges appear at any time and usually not connected to specific skills or subjects. For dyslexics, you see these issues predominately around reading and writing tasks. However, each condition often exasperates the other.

With dyslexia, it's helpful to notice the "unexpected learning challenges" with a student as early as possible. For example, dyslexic learners have a spiky profile. This means they have incredible strengths in some learning areas while struggling significantly in others. They might have a wide vocabulary and strong oral skills, yet struggle with identifying the letters of their name, finding the right word to say or making rhymes. They might have significant maths ability but can't recite the days of the week, recall information from rote memory or name all the letters of the alphabet. Having dyslexia (or even ADHD for that matter) doesn't equate to being unintelligent, but it's often treated as if it does.

If we believe that the learner should be able to do the task but can't, especially in light of having significant strengths in other areas, we need to be asking ourselves why that is. What is it that we need to address in order to reduce barriers to their learning? However, problems arise when teachers have unchecked biases that consider a student's learning challenges as evidence of what they are capable of. Conroy (2021) writes:

> For an educator to suspect dyslexia, the educator must first expect that a child can be taught to read. Given the research on implicit bias and lower teacher expectations, the reliance on *unexpected difficulties* negatively affects Black children with dyslexia.
>
> When educators are unaware of their bias, there is no internal check to self-monitor, which increases the likelihood of perpetuating bias when applying the definition of dyslexia as *unexpected*.

Black children are often given lower learning expectations; their strengths go unnoticed and therefore their learning challenges don't raise any alarms with their teachers. It leaves Black dyslexic children undiagnosed and unsupported. They aren't seen as intelligent enough to have unexpected learning difficulties in the first place.

Reflect now

Consider the importance society places on the written word and what you've learned as a person and teacher about what it means if you're not proficient in it. What might it mean to Black boys like Darnell who are routinely seen for what they can't do and it is assumed their behaviour or attitude is why they're not working as expected? How might this story be different when considering different social identity markers including white children? When or with whom might you be quick to assume a student is less competent or have lower expectations for them?

I knew that I needed to make an intentional effort to create extra time to connect with Darnell. He was visibly hyperactive and often emotionally dysregulated, becoming easily frustrated and lacking cognitive flexibility. But it wasn't a surprise either. Darnell had experienced a lot of changes lately, both in his home and with starting a new school setting – both of which would take time to adapt to, but with complaints against him rising, Darnell's adjustment period was already quickly coming to an end, so I needed to move faster.

When I first brought my lunch over to the dining hall and took a seat next to Darnell, he rolled his eyes and looked suspiciously at me. I knew he wouldn't be pleased to see me there but it worked in my favour because he had to eat and there was nowhere else to go. It wasn't going to be easy. He didn't want to talk about writing, reading or any kind of problems we had in the class. Luckily, that didn't matter. I was there to talk about whatever he wanted to share – which wasn't all that much at first. Eventually, he answered a few questions that involved the others at the table initially too. I didn't want my presence at the table to become overwhelming for him. What I soon realised was that I barely knew him beyond school work and what he couldn't do. At that point, I decided I'd have to spend a couple of minutes with him each day to further develop our relationship. I wanted him to know that I genuinely liked him and maybe that could help him learn to trust me as a teacher too.

Lunch was almost over when I realised that I hadn't addressed the issues around his literacy lessons. As the bell went for playtime, I walked alongside Darnell on his way to break:

"I'm really glad I got the chance to talk to you today, Darnell", I said.

He didn't say anything, so I just continued.

"I know the writing is a lot in class. We're going to find better ways to get your ideas out."

He paused before telling me, "I don't wanna write anything!"

I nodded. "I get that. And teachers always want you to write so much … but we'll figure something out for you."

He didn't respond, only racing outside to the playground. I wasn't surprised by that either. I certainly hadn't earned his trust yet, but working together to reduce these learning barriers would be a good start. I wasn't sure whether his reactions stemmed from the uncertainty in his life or not, but for whatever reason, he didn't have the skills or capacity to manage them, yet. If I continued to interpret his outbursts to mean something personally about me, then I'd still be expecting him to make changes to his behaviour on his own and experience was telling us both that this approach wasn't working. For Darnell to believe that he could depend on me, he'd have to know that I saw that he was capable of learning. It would be an integral part of creating a space he felt safe enough to take the risk to learn in.

ADHD Support: increasing perseverance and managing anger and aggression

Darnell needed additional support to address the gaps in his executive function skills, but because of the way he experienced dyslexia, alternative ways to access the curriculum and express his understanding were needed too. Although ADHD and dyslexia can overlap in strategies for support, helping students with dyslexia often means providing additional, specialised, daily support for building phonemic awareness too. We knew that Darnell became easily dysregulated, so that meant tracking his reactions to see whether we could note some triggers. We also realised that his ADHD presentations weren't going to miraculously improve because we made a few curriculum changes. Anything we implemented was going to take time for him to incorporate it into his self-management strategies. There would be a lot of scaffolding we'd have to do in the meantime.

Forcing learning on students who feel like Darnell isn't going to make it happen any faster. Helping these students might mean prioritising their mental and emotional well-being first. For Darnell, that meant looking at how he could better manage his emotional regulation for his anger and frustration. We also realised that helping him build more perseverance with learning meant creating more opportunities for success. But he'd also have to be engaging in appropriately challenging learning experiences in order to do this (no one feels particularly successful doing things that don't have a purpose or are noticeably simple). Accepting that the learning outcomes expected for Darnell's age might not ever become achievable or visible to us this year helped shift the focus to monitoring his well being and self-regulation instead. It didn't mean that we didn't care about his academic achievement, but that we recognised that his frequent dysregulation was a sign of his lack of readiness for learning in the current environment. The priority for Darnell became building the skills necessary to engage in his learning more effectively.

Table 1.1   ADHD support: increasing perseverance and regulating anger and aggression

Perseverance (goal-driven persistence) Being able to complete a goal or task even when challenges arise, it gets difficult or feels boring. It's staying the course even when another goal or project feels more interesting

Possible ADHD presentations	Possible accommodations
Doesn't feel capable of doing a task (and gives up quickly)	• Offer solutions when the learner feels calm. Under the resistance are emotions (not being seen or heard, shame, embarrassment, uncertainty, anxiety) that can be addressed by scaffolding the task through breaking it down into smaller parts, offering encouragement, working alongside them, having the focus remain on the process rather than the outcome (which might be the part that feels unsurmountable)
Struggles to complete a task at the same level of quality and attention as when they started	• Offer examples of what mastery might look like in a task so that the outcomes are clear, with an open invitation to meet and adjust where necessary
	• Reducing the number of questions needed or writing expected and slowing down to engage more deeply in the topic or task rather than adding more content
Teases or fights other students; argues with teachers about assigned tasks rather than attempt given tasks	• Developing collaborative learning skills that are easily integrated into the class like Kagan structures

- Adjusting your language to show empathy to students' frustrations and undesired behaviour without engaging in it, rather than ignoring it, which is another way of abandoning the student
- Consistently checking in during independent tasks at a set time (with a timer) to praise specific examples of on-task behaviour

Emotional regulation: Managing anger and aggression

What's under the aggression presentations and frequent flight or fight outbursts is high levels of anxiety. This anxiety could stem from various roots besides ADHD. When a student acts out like this but also has ADHD, there is the complication of developmental delays with executive functioning skills that make interpreting the cues in the environment around them more challenging. Including trauma alongside possible ADHD makes the student even more hypervigilant, interpreting interactions with others as possible threats, resulting in the need to attack.

Possible ADHD presentations	Possible accommodations
Lies and won't often take responsibility for actions	• Lies happen automatically without thought, or when dysregulated (feeling anxious or another discomfort they can't necessarily name) or when they can't find the words they need right away in the topic or task • When tempers are high, it's best to give all parties space to think about what happened, before they speak. This is about finding out the facts of what happened, different perspectives and how to make things right, not punishment and blame, which would only bring up more anxiety and not get to the root of the problem
Anger and frustration seem to happen quickly	• When calm, give direct teaching for strategies to self-monitor for clues that anger is arising. Introspection difficulties or sensory challenges can make it even more difficult for some students to recognise changes in their bodies that indicate volatile emotions are emerging • Teach strategies to practise pausing before reacting when the learner is calm. (Pausing allows for time to reconnect to the thinking brain.) Practise **perspective-taking** skills so students can learn how their decisions and reactions impact others and what choices they might make in future with this different insight
Seems like the student is purposely trying to manipulate or upset others	• Keep the focus off ODD labels and on what works to create an environment of safety for the student • Look for patterns in their reactions to identify possible triggers and what helps de-escalate situations quickly

(Continued)

Table 1.1 (*Continued*)

Decides work is complete when it could be improved and will not engage with the reflection process	• Be clear on the expectations of projects. Give examples to avoid confusion. Be flexible depending on difficulties shown in the process of engaging in the learning (other skills beyond the outcome could be difficult for the learner to further engage in) • Choose intentionally about what outcomes are worth insisting on. Where else has this competency been met or are there other ways they could meet it? • Rethink completing lots of questions as a way to show understanding or competency
Becomes easily emotionally flooded	• Have a calming space in your classroom that also has short activities that help refocus a student's attention from the incident so they can calm down and come back to the thinking part of their brain • Separate students to give some space and time to calm down first before discussing the incident. The body is in flight or fight, so any kind of discussion to "reason with them" will likely further upset the student and escalate the situation. Stand by as a way to offer co-regulatory support as they calm down, but refrain from pressuring them to "explain themselves" • Don't engage with the anger, language or complaints. After they've calmed down and had some space from the incident, it's easier to explain what happened and discuss with them/give them a chance to make things right (this isn't necessarily an apology either, but what they could do that actually helps them fix things for the other person and makes them feel better about doing this) • Share stories, role play and guide class discussions for students to hear various ways to solve problems and how to manage anger and other big emotions, during times of calm. Include exercises that connect these emotions to what they might feel in the body. Practise these skills often when students are regulated • Develop their ability to visualise how their actions impact others and reflect on what they think are other people's perspectives on problems and solutions through stories, simple small-group discussions using social and emotional learning (SEL) problem-solving cards and role play

	• Model your own strategies to address big emotions in class (this helps address some SEL needs where there is no curriculum)
Becomes easily argumentative and defensive (may physically or verbally attack someone quickly)	• Tone of voice and how you present requests and demands are important to students who experience anxiety. Phrases that give simple choices or are an invitation like, "I wonder whether…", "Let's see if…", and talking about the object or task rather than directly asking the student themselves and telling them what they must do helps create a sense of autonomy and a felt sense of safety. Using **declarative language** is important
Struggles with confidence	• Daily two-minute chat for ten days (or more!) on topics of choice to develop a relationship with the student
	• Finding ways to encourage the student to share any talents with younger students or to be willing to help others
	• Make a point to catch them on task and doing as expected. We often notice when some of our more difficult students are doing things wrong, but rarely check in with them when they are working well independently or with a friend

Supporting Darnell

Darnell was getting frustrated. I could see it. It had started slowly at first but I knew that if I didn't get over to him then it could become something bigger. He was staring at the paper, his face scrunched up as he angrily scratched out the last thing he wrote. Darnell's aversion to writing wasn't changing overnight but the additional support was helping him make progress. I approached him just in time to avoid the paper ending up in a ball on the floor.

"Hey. It's OK." I leaned over and whispered, "Let's take a break."

Darnell looked down at his work for a moment, before getting up and shuffling over to the classroom's newly improved quiet corner. There he found a small handheld fidget toy from the **sensory bin**.

I looked closer at his paper. Anything he'd managed to do was significant. I needed to tell him that when we met after his break. If I had checked in sooner, I might have helped him see that his efforts weren't unnoticed and they mattered too. Although I'd managed to connect more with Darnell, he still became easily dysregulated when I wasn't careful with the learning activities I planned. I was learning to recognise when he was becoming dysregulated sooner and found I could de-escalate them a little quicker when I did.

I went over to him now engaged in a simple Sudoku activity he found in a box filled with short paper activities alongside the sensory bin. Since Darnell would naturally walk away when he'd had enough, incorporating his go-to strategy along-side a short activity helped him to take his mind off the problem, calm down and come back ready to discuss solutions. This way, he could do what he already did to self-regulate, but the added activity gave him a way to cool off so he could engage better with me later on. I waited for a few minutes before I went over.

"Great choice of activity." I tried to consistently praise Darnell when he worked effectively independently. I wanted him to know that I noticed him working well when he worked alone too. He was so used to being talked to when he did things wrong that it was important for me to keep noticing the little things that he did well or made progress with, even when they were expected behaviours for his age. I set the visual timer for the corner to three additional minutes.

"Darnell … The timer is set for three more minutes. Do you see that?"

He briefly looked up and nodded.

"Great. Three more minutes, then we can decide what to do next."

"OK", he spoke quietly.

Timers don't always make for smooth transitions as they can be easily ignored, so Darnell still needed support with this. When the timer went off, my TA was quick to use a reminder that shared why they needed Darnell's help.

"Let's see about turning off that timer, Darnell." They wandered over and I watched Darnell's attention go towards turning it off. I could see his body droop as he looked back at his desk and where a moan of displeasure would have been interjected, he heard my voice instead.

"Darnell …" I called over. He looked up to see me waving the chromebook in my hand with a smile, motioning him over. I could see the relief wash over his body. He would have input on how learning could look for him too. I could see his body's increasing ease as he walked over to me. I breathed deeply as he approached, so I could continue with responding calmly. If we were going to work together, it was imperative that no matter how Darnell might react, I wouldn't react because I'd decided to take it personally. He needed to trust that I could consistently handle my own discomfort however he behaved.

Key takeaways:

- **Internalised bias** keeps many Black, Brown and Indigenous children from being diagnosed with ADHD and dyslexia, while oppositional defiant disorder (ODD) and other conduct disorders are disproportionately diagnosed in historically excluded groups over white children exhibiting the same presentations.
- ADHD has many overlapping presentations with dyslexia. One way to distinguish between the two is if the similar presentations are only seen during reading or writing or noticeable in different subjects and environments too.
- Prioritising writing and reading in schools not only serves as a way to centre **whiteness**, but also keeps us from considering other ways students could engage with the curriculum and share their understandings.

- ADHD students are 65 per cent more likely to also have challenges with written expression, which is also seen to create lower academic outcomes for these students in standardised testing.
- Standardised testing was created to ensure that Black, Brown, Indigenous and melanated immigrant students were excluded from accessing higher education opportunities.
- Supporting students with significant social and emotional needs often means prioritising their well-being over learning expectations.

Resources to explore

Dyslexia

Black, Brilliant and Dyslexic by Marcia Brissett-Bailey
Dyslexia and Me: How to Survive and Thrive If You're Neurodivergent by Onyinye Udokporo
British Dyslexia Association: www.bdadyslexia.org.uk/
Dyslexia Action: https://dyslexiaaction.org.uk/

Irlen syndrome

Irlen Institute: https://irlen.com/

Restorative justice

Hacking School Discipline: 9 Ways to Create a Culture of Empathy & Responsibility using Restorative Justice by Nathan Maynard & Brad Weinstein
This Restorative Justice Life Podcast with David Ryan Castro-Harris

2

"They're just shy":

Emma and Henry's stories

This chapter asks us to reflect on:

- the difficulty in recognising inattentive ADHD presentations in the classroom;
- how the **gender binary** perpetuates the conditions that leave many ADHD children undiagnosed or unsupported;
- how we support ADHD students who also have high academic achievement, (the twice exceptional (2E) student);
- the ways ADHD students might learn to cope and hide their ADHD presentations.

"She spends hours doing homework in the evenings. She wants to make sure that everything is done perfectly."

Emma's parents beamed, and how could they not? She was an easily likeable student, doing well academically and had a couple of good friends too. Her parents continued, "As soon as Emma gets home, we give her a snack and immediately have her do homework before she plays". I nodded enthusiastically. That sounded like something Emma would do.

"We always make sure that she reads before she goes to bed. But now Emma does this herself."

They smiled. Clearly, Emma had a system in place that was helping her achieve in all the right areas. She was having a great start to the year.

Our parent–teacher evening was just before the first half term, but there was much to say about Emma. She was a kid who would be going places, especially if she kept up this kind of dedication and commitment to her studies. I really couldn't think of a single thing … except … maybe … she was a bit quiet in class. She seemed incredibly shy about speaking up and could be a bit anxious about feedback that wasn't absolutely positive. I wondered if they had any ideas as to why Emma reacted like this. Her work was always meticulously done, so she really had nothing to worry about with her academic achievement. Any feedback was minor and, besides, no one was perfect, after all. But Emma could often look deflated, taking any corrections to heart.

"Well …" Emma's carers looked at each other for a second. "She can be a bit quiet, that's true … But at home, she's so chatty! She's very creative and loves to write. We have noticed that she doesn't like being corrected …"

They took a pause before continuing. "She can be sensitive at times, but we're not worried. Girls are like that sometimes."

I nodded and shrugged it off. These weren't problems by any means, just little things I'd noticed so far in my short time with her. Perhaps Emma needed some time to get used to the pace of the class or just get used to me being her teacher. After all, I was one of the few Black teachers working on staff. Teachers aren't the only ones that come to school with beliefs and expectations that influence the ways they act and interpret the actions of others; students do too. It wouldn't be strange to assume that Emma needed a bit more time to feel comfortable with me. I might have been the first Black teacher she had.

Meet Emma:

- 9 years old
- European ancestry, white, blonde hair
- identifies as a girl
- fluent in the language of instruction
- shy, kind, sensitive
- loves: writing stories, reading, social studies, music
- detests: speaking in front of the class
- future aspirations: author
- best known for: high academic achievement, impeccable classroom behaviour
- learning challenges: none currently known
- additional information: meticulous in completing tasks

I would never have considered Emma to be anything like the next kid on my parent–teacher meeting list.

Henry wasn't the type to cause problems in class. He was a very likeable student who usually got his work done on time too. But when he'd finally get around to starting, he'd manage to complete the bare minimum required and rarely anything more. Henry participated in class discussions when he had an interest in our topic. There was no way he'd volunteer an answer or a thought without being sure of its correctness though. You would see Henry speak more often in smaller groups and share his work with a partner, speaking if he had to. Occasionally he'd take a little longer to express his understanding than expected. Sometimes he couldn't quite organise his ideas on what he wanted to say, which would make for some very confusing shares at times, but I wasn't clear on whether he recognised this in himself.

Henry's parents grimaced as they voiced their concerns.

"Henry has so much potential", they exclaimed, "if only he'd just stop getting lost in the details and get the thing done!". I smiled and nodded knowingly. That sounded a lot like the Henry I'd met only a couple of months earlier. He would just lose track of the bigger picture and get stuck in one area of the work that appealed to him rather than just getting things done.

"We know he's capable of doing great things", they continued. "He's so creative and such a brilliant problem solver. He just needs to show this side of himself more often!"

The conversation went on as they shared their concerns about Henry having times when he'd be lost in thought. I knew what they were talking about. I'd frequently catch him drifting off into space in the middle of class instruction. He'd always answer me when I called him and he rarely interrupted others, but many times you got the sense that he lucked out in finding the appropriate response.

Henry's parents lamented that he needed frequent reminders to get his homework started for fear he'd just stare at the wall and lose track of time. He was often resistant about completing homework, but without reminders, it was debatable if it would get done at all. He just wasn't motivated enough. They shared that they understood that boys weren't concerned with neatness in their work as much as girls were and they could accept that. But the problem came with what they saw as his inconsistent efforts towards doing his best work. They believed that Henry just needed to "buckle down a little more and try harder". After all, "he could do so much more if he just put his mind to it". Initially, I was inclined to agree. Henry definitely had the intelligence and skills to be a more successful student. Sometimes there just seemed to be a disconnect between what he *appeared* capable of and what he *actually* produced.

Meet Henry:

- 9 years old,
- white, European ancestry, brown hair
- identifies as a boy
- fluent in the language of instruction
- quiet, insightful, creative
- loves: reading, maths, art
- detests: writing stories
- future aspirations: architect or engineer
- best known for: good academic achievement and classroom behaviour
- learning challenges: none currently known
- additional information: can appear "unmotivated"

Henry showed more of a sporadic effort with his studies, which resulted in inconsistent good outcomes with the occasionally amazing ones. Emma routinely went above and beyond to do her best, but Henry acted as if his efforts were determined by whether he felt like doing the work or not. In reality, it was the furthest thing from the truth. Both Emma and Henry were dealing with many of the same learning challenges, but they manifested slightly differently. Their genders played a significant factor in how their behaviours were interpreted, determining what was expected of them and the kind of support, if any, that was suggested. Labels influenced by behaviour expectations of the **gender binary** can quickly turn ADHD presentations into descriptors of a child's personality. This creates the ongoing diagnosis problems where many children with ADHD aren't recognised because they're assumed to be *acting out of* or *acting in* character with their gender assigned at birth and are therefore blamed and/or shamed for their difficulties in school because of it.

The case for degendering ADHD traits

The perception of ADHD is heavily influenced by how children are expected to behave according to their assigned gender at birth. This plays a significant role in who's recognised, diagnosed and supported, and who's not. ADHD is often described through the lens of gender where we read about how *boys and girls present differently*. The idea here is that girls remain undiagnosed until they are much older than boys because they learn *to mask* (or hide) their ADHD presentations so as to appear like everyone else. It's suggested that since hyperactivity is not *socially acceptable* behaviour for girls, they learn to internalise those presentations instead. This is why girls are most often diagnosed with inattentive ADHD and why they have been historically either frequently misdiagnosed (often with mood disorders, feminine-presenting people are considered more emotional) or underdiagnosed. Boys, on the other hand, it's argued, are permitted to have more visible presentations of hyperactivity because that is an expected behaviour for them and therefore is considered more *socially acceptable* until it's interpreted that their behaviour is unmanageable. Since boys can be seen acting differently, that makes it easier for them to receive diagnoses. These differences in behaviour are influenced by how boys and girls are "socialised to behave" according to the gender they're assigned at birth.

The socialisation premise assumes that most girls and boys, regardless of their environment, social identity and lived experiences, would have ADHD that presents more or less the same. While it's true that we get many messages about how we're expected to behave in the **dominant culture**, it doesn't quite explain the many children who *don't* neatly fall within the expected behaviours of their assigned gender and receive a diagnosis or those who *do* but still remain undiagnosed. It assumes that all genders have the same binary experience and expectations from being socialised according to their assigned gender at birth, as if Black girls, Asian girls and white girls are diagnosed (or misdiagnosed) at the same rates. Socialisation doesn't account for the children whose **gender identity** doesn't fall into the boy or girl labels of the **gender binary** either. We're not socialised with the same expectations or interpretations of masculinity and femininity either because of the influence of our privileges and oppressions.

Transgender, non-binary and other **gender-expansive** children's experiences are often erased in schools due to cultures that promote **cisnormativity**. But when compared to their **cisgender** peers, they have three to seven times higher rates of diagnosis (Kaiser Permanente, 2018). The socialisation theory doesn't quite seem to explain or account for the high ADHD diagnoses percentages for this part or the student population either. In *Whipping Girl: A Transsexual Woman on Sexism and the Scapegoating of Femininity*, Serano (2016, p. 74) suggests that rather than explaining gender differences through how we're socialised we consider how "socialisation acts as a way to exaggerate biological gender differences that already exist. It coaxes those of us who are already exceptional (for example, boys who are seen as 'more sensitive' or 'quiet' and girls who are seen as 'more aggressive' or 'outspoken') to hide or curb those tendencies rather than simply falling where they may on the spectrum of gender diversity". In other words, viewing gender differences from the lens of how we're socialised creates the impression that the natural differences between men and women exist as "mutually exclusive *opposite* sexes" (p. 74) and how we've been *conditioned to interpret* these differences has no bearing on how we see them. When gender differences are given meaning and interpreted through completely artificial and performative beliefs about what is feminine and masculine, we not only ignore the biology that plays a role in creating these differences (like hormones), but we also fail to recognise how these biological differences are interpreted in society. Biological differences in people are real, but the meanings, assumptions and values we place on what is considered masculine or feminine are not. Social constructs of gender do not adequately define the varied lived experiences of anyone, let alone those with ADHD.

Identifying ADHD presentations through a child's "socialised" gender also hides the societal oppressions that influence access to ADHD diagnosis. It doesn't acknowledge how the ADHD diagnostic criteria have historically been based on the behaviour of white, cis-gendered, affluent, heterosexual boys in schools who weren't acting like the successful, perfect, future leaders of society they were expected to be. Prioritising ADHD diagnosis for *these* white boys allowed them to continue accessing their privilege because the message has always been clear that they were naturally superior to everyone else. ADHD helped explain why the white boys from *socially acceptable* backgrounds didn't fit the expectations, but *they*, unlike anyone else (including those white boys from much lower socio-economical backgrounds), could be fixed (see Alex's story for more on gender). Hyperactive white boys with ADHD could be the problem while never having to address the ways that patriarchal, **white supremacy culture** are inherently toxic and harmful for them too.

The many articles emphasising ADHD as a diagnosis initially for *white boys* are rarely written with **intersectionality** in mind. When no marginalised identity details are mentioned, the default has always been *white girls* (and *white women*). They weren't afforded the same access (read: privilege) as *white boys* (and *white men*) to support in upholding their expected gender role. Their reasons for being under- and misdiagnosed weren't quite the same as those from more marginalised communities. Suggesting that socialisation was the main reason for *women* being underdiagnosed continues to hide all the systems of oppressions that have kept marginalised identities from accessing diagnosis and appropriate provisions for support – including *white women*. Labelling ADHD presentations through expectations about gender excludes all those children we don't see because they aren't considered within the **dominant culture's** interpretations of masculine and feminine behaviour that centres **whiteness**. Until we start expanding our beliefs about gender beyond the **gender binary**, we will continue to exclude students. When we don't see the real problems and how they impact our thinking, we'll continue to struggle finding other possibilities for solutions too.

Reflect now

What messages did you learn about what's expected for behaviour when it comes to gender? How do those beliefs change when you incorporate race, socio-economic status and other intersecting social identities? How do you see these ideas reflected in your teaching and the expectations of your students' academic achievement, social skills and learning behaviour?

Since Emma and Henry's behaviour didn't seem too out of the ordinary with what I'd been conditioned to believe about gender, I assumed there weren't any real problems for their learning. Emma was a hardworking and diligent student. She took her time being neat and organised with her work. I never thought that maybe she didn't want to take extra work home or spend as long on every task. Maybe she never knew how other students who had similar academic achievement to her could prioritise and organise their thoughts in ways that she couldn't. It allowed them to work a lot more efficiently in ways that she couldn't.

I also believed that it wasn't out of the ordinary for Henry to struggle with writing and not enjoy it. That seemed pretty common for lots of boys his age. I never considered that maybe he felt limited by what was blocking his written expression, or that the inconsistency in his achievement outcomes and focus were barriers for him too. My perceptions of their effort and outcomes were limited by how I interpreted their behaviour for their assigned gender at birth. I often wonder what I might have done differently for them if their behaviours had been reversed.

Like many ADHD learners, Emma and Henry learned to cope with and meet these expectations in school by hiding behaviours that they learned were unacceptable for them. Some ADHD students can become so effective, you might not think they're struggling at all. What makes this even more challenging to spot is how they're praised for some of strategies they use too. A strategy like checking and rechecking your work could be interpreted as working carefully and being reflective. But the same strategy could become maladaptive too, like if checking and rechecking leads to late or uncompleted tasks. As their teacher, I struggled to see the subtleness in the overlap of learning challenges alongside high academic. What if the skills or strategies that I interpreted as their *strengths* were also being used to mask or compensate for challenges they were having instead?

When does a learning strategy become a barrier to a student's learning?

Hiding inattentive ADHD

The consistently inconsistent manner of all types of ADHD presentations makes it hard to decipher whether a student has ADHD inattentiveness, dealing with trauma, illness, tiredness or just having a challenging day. Pair this with a student who's generally doing well academically and socially, and it doesn't seem like there are any problems to be solved. When a student meets our school's academic and social expectations, it feels like you're looking for problems where there aren't any. How do we know whether, given the right support, our ADHD inattentive learners could see more of what they could do? Are we simply expecting more of them than they're capable of? Is there a way to know for sure that what we'd see is the right thing to do?

Inattentive ADHD impacts learning in ways that we don't often expect because we don't realise that a student's coping strategy has already taken over. So much of what ADHD inattentive learners struggle with remains internalised and therefore invisible to us watching for any unusual learning behaviours. Whatever keeps these children from being diagnosed with ADHD is often buried deep beneath what teachers might see as *acceptable* learning behaviours. By the time commonly recognised ADHD presentations become visible for a diagnosis, it's usually a sign that whatever strategies they were using could no longer match the demands of what is expected of them in school. By then, many students are older, feel shame and have lowered self-esteem because they've been living with the subtle realisation that they've never quite reached the potential they once believed possible for themselves.

There are things we can do that support inattentive ADHD students when we support all students. But creating learning environments where students can feel safe enough to explore what helps them learn and what feels difficult for today – even when it's not an everyday occurrence – is a good start. We can support them in the inconsistencies of energy that impact their outcomes which are a natural part of human experiences. We can help them remember that just because we did something really well once, doesn't mean we can't make mistakes or need guidance in making improvements next time around, and that's natural too. Creating a learning culture that normalises the fact that we all have "off days", we're all continually learning and some days we might need some extra guidance or even a little more grace. It sends the message that it's enough to come to school as our imperfect human selves.

Reflect now

How does your behaviour change depending on who you're around? Which people do you feel like you can be most like yourself with? What kind of things do they do to help you feel like it's safe enough to be who you are? What ideas and beliefs could you bring from your own experience of safer people and spaces to your classroom?

Table 2.1 Possible ADHD presentation that might suggest the need for support

Possible ADHD presentation that might indicate additional support	How students might cope and therefore hide the ADHD's impact	What teachers might notice (or what behaviour they could question)	How teachers might support their suspected needs
Daydreams and becomes easily distracted, doesn't appear to be listening when talked to	– taking notes on everything said in classes – asking friends what needs to be done (or working with the friend that knows what to do)	– notice who consistently jolts back to attention when they hear things like "this is important" – how often and when does a student seem lost in thought (do other students often comment on them not doing the work either?)	– having other students repeat the instructions in their own words – framing what is important to listen to at the moment: "This part is important …" – make time for regular movement breaks and keep teacher talking time short – give students skills to break apart instructions and order specific steps to complete
Has a hard time staying focused on tasks that require sustained focus, difficulty sustaining attention during play or tasks, such as conversations, lectures, or lengthy reading	– might doodle or fidget as the teacher speaks – might move feet while seated or other inconspicuous movements – might ask for clarification on tasks often	– work might be rushed to be completed by the end (if completed at all) – the quality of work might deteriorate as they progress – might be stuck in tasks that aren't as important as the main project but spending excessive time on them	– put instructions in the same place on forms and in the classroom – break down projects into small tasks (and share how to break down tasks and why) – give plenty of brain breaks or allow movement throughout the work session
Misses details and makes seemingly careless mistakes in schoolwork or during other activities	– might work with someone who is particular about getting things done – might spend longer time to do work so that there are (hopefully) less mistakes	– mistakes happen often where you normally wouldn't think they would – parents/carers share that the child takes a long time to do homework, eat or other tasks	– check in even when they're on task to see how they're planning out their work – model reflecting and checking on work and the kind of careless mistakes they might find

Has trouble following instructions and often shifts from task to task without finishing anything, gets sidetracked easily	– might check or recheck their work with the teacher or another trusted adult often – might give excuses for why things aren't important to complete anymore or why ideas changed – might deflect attention from uncompleted tasks to a newer, "more improved" idea	– misses part of the questions in a task or a chunk of an assignment – might struggle to relay what they are expected to do more often – might be unsure of how they'll prioritise what needs to be done	– give one task to do at a time (or a limited choice) – give regular time to go back to previous tasks and check for mistakes or what is incomplete (often we find missing things when we have space from working on them) – remind students to check their work with a very short checklist
Has trouble getting organised (time, materials and/or tasks), loses track of things (losing homework assignments or space can be cluttered)	– could be overly particular about the way they organise their things – inconsistent in their organisation of materials (at school very organised, but at home, they're not) – might ask to take work home to finish it, often	– difficulty planning what to be done in the amount of time they have so might leave things unfinished or rush through the final part – might give them time to work independently but they've not completed what they could or have planned – become stuck in the small details of a task that keep them from doing the work they need to complete	– bag checks to review what materials are needed for home and school – provide an effective filing system for paper and materials or give time for students to put their materials and excess papers in the right spots (this helps students get a feel of what organisation strategies might work for them to use in future) – go over estimated times to complete tasks with students as they plan (then reflect on the effectiveness of their time during and after)

(Continued)

Table 2.1 (*Continued*)

Is forgetful in day-to-day activities (misses deadlines, forgets homework)	– may resist taking home books or materials – overly concerned about forgetting anything or being late (may seem anxious about that happening)	– needs reminders often – has friends collect things for them (or friends are often asked to give them things they forgot) – might remember one thing that is important to them and forget everything else	– keep homework days on the same days as much as possible – model using a planner and make time for doing this daily – give students an option to make things right when they forget, but also deal with natural consequences for forgetting (rather than shaming, blaming or guilting)
Is easily distracted by unrelated thoughts or stimuli	– might not share in class or share things that are entertaining to the class rather than risk making mistakes or shares when they've had adequate time to think of and hear responses	– talks a lot or tells stories and they are unrelated or trouble getting to their point	– model ways to share thinking out loud and how to prioritise what is important to share – repeat their words back to them for support with clarifying their ideas – allow time for processing new information in regular short intervals (5–10 minutes to draw, write or share thinking)

Weeks following our parent–teacher meetings we had literacy class as usual. I had stopped the class for a quick check-in, which included a couple of examples and modelling my thinking aloud for some reflection strategies. Afterwards, I gave the students some time to continue their writing. It wasn't long before I saw Henry's hand raised. I looked over at him.

"I'm finished", he proclaimed as he handed me his work. I looked over Henry's list of very short-sentence answers. I noticed that the pencil lead seemed dark on the paper and a small hole had permeated through it where he'd erased right through. That's usually a sign for me that the a student isn't aware of the amount of pressure they need for writing or are erasing over and over again, becoming overwhelmed or frustrated. Henry had attempted the start of a short paragraph, following most of the criteria I set for him. I began to review the questions with him again, breaking them down for him so he could share in more detail about each one. I scribed the rest of his answers as he spoke.

It was clear that Henry was enthusiastic about the topic. His understanding went far beyond what he'd shown in the task I'd set for him. I quickly began to realise that Henry was clearly a lot more talented than he was able to show us. Writing wasn't his strongest way of expressing information but, on the days when he could do the writing, it went somewhat well. Today wasn't as bad as it could have been, but I was never sure when the better days would be.

As I had these thoughts my mind went to Emma, who I glanced over at and saw her gazing out the classroom window, rather than getting started on her task. Generally Emma rarely looked as if she wasn't paying attention. In fact, she had a way of looking at you that made it seem as though she hung on your every word, but today she looked lost in thought.

"Emma … are you ready to get started?" She jolted at the sound of her name. I didn't mean to startle her.

She looked over at me and smiled, getting back to the task at hand. When asked to get started on something, she normally knew what was expected. Sometimes a simple chat with Emma to see what her plan was for her tasks could help her get on track if she was taking too long with less important details. When I was clear on what I was looking for in an assigned project, it seemed to help her confidently continue what to do. Emma worked diligently, but slowly (or perhaps, cautiously is more accurate). Once she got started, she would normally get things done on time. There wasn't a single detail out of place, often going beyond what was expected. I often wondered what Emma would be capable of if she just had a little more confidence in getting started without believing she had to include every little thing she could think of in order to complete the learning activity.

ADHD Support: time management and reducing overwhelm

On the surface, Emma and Henry didn't seem all that similar and ADHD inattentiveness wasn't very clear in either of them. Like all students, they'd received messages about what they were expected to do or be in class in order to be successful. When they struggled to feel they could meet those expectations their ADHD brains could get stuck. For ADHD learners, the pressure of what they *feel* they *should* be able to do within a certain time but can't, quickly becomes a source of overwhelm. This affects task initiation and/or completion, impacting their time management which leads to increased overwhelm, and less action. Until they can become unstuck, they can't effectively access their thinking brain. This in one thing that keeps ADHD learners utilising strategies for time management.

Table 2.2   ADHD support: time management and reducing overwhelm

Time management The ability to have a sense of the passing of time, estimating the amount of time needed to complete a task and meeting deadlines while making sure that everything else you need to complete gets done too

Task initiation Getting projects done in good time without having to procrastinate or avoid them

Possible ADHD presentations	Possible accommodations
Becoming stuck on a small detail that they believe needs to be done in a specific way	• Include check-ins that are based on self-assessing progress and discuss what parts of the plans could be changed when necessary and when and why those decisions should be made
Unable to estimate the time it takes to complete a task (taking tasks home to complete them, or rushing through the final parts of a project)	• Ensure tasks are broken down into smaller steps alongside a time frame so that the student can visualise what needs to be done
Unable to estimate accurately the length of different tasks within a project in order to complete the project on time	• Make time visible with timers. Have students colour on the timer how long they have for the task • Reflect on what helped them stay on task and what was completed. Remind students of these strategies in later tasks across the curriculum too
Assignments completed late (or not at all)	• Consider what outcomes have already been met in another subject area so that tasks can be reduced • Give projects in even smaller steps or stages in order to avoid overwhelm and check in on progress often

Hyperfocuses on a single idea or task that keeps them from finishing work on time (or not completing key parts of the project)	• Hyperfocus can go one of two ways – in "flow", where the challenge, interest and ability come together to ensure the student is effortlessly completing the task, or it becomes a strategy to anxiously complete the task that's been avoided for a variety of reasons (unsure of how to do the task a certain way, insecure of their ability, not interested or can't see the need for the task …) • Regular check-ins for planning and reflection (not necessarily with the teacher all the time) to learn to accurately estimate time and learn realistic time frames to complete certain tasks • Avoiding or hyperfocusing on unimportant tasks are often signs of overwhelm so consider additional support in breaking work into smaller tasks and/or rethinking expectations or outcomes of the project • When doing something enjoyable, including oneself in the task can help the student separate themselves from it. "Let me do this one while you finish that one and we can come back to it later" • Adding more simple mindfulness activities in the time cracks of the day and specific descriptions of how the body feels before, during and after
Struggles to start a task when it's different from what was expected	• Offer possible alternatives for processes, materials and workspaces depending on the challenge they're having. (Remember, learning is a messy process, fraught with confusion and discomfort. Gentleness and compassion best support students in regulating their underlying fears about a task)

Emotional regulation: Reducing overwhelm

Overwhelm is frequently seen in ADHD students because their attention is spread everywhere and filtering the information received is not easily accessible or as reliable. This is not just information about the environment around them, but also cognitive and emotional information. ADHD learners then struggle to decide what is important to focus on, making the amount of input too much to handle and resulting them in becoming dysregulated. This means teaching them to slow down so they can notice the signs of overwhelm in their bodies and begin to pinpoint what exactly has become too much is important. Once they take a break from the stimuli they can utilise different tools and strategies to help make their executive functioning skills more visible (rather than trying to think through things in their heads) and work through their next steps

(Continued)

Table 2.2 *(Continued)*

Possible ADHD presentations	Possible accommodations
Appears *stuck* on a way forward in the task (so does nothing and may even appear "zoned out")	• Discuss the planning of the activity to support the executive functioning skills to be outside their head. (I like to see what they do know and offer guiding prompts so they can see the knowledge they have but don't realise. Often overwhelm hides that knowledge) • Give suggestions on the first steps to get started as it can support them in figuring out where they might be stuck. • Remind students (or reflect together) of what made them successful in similar situations in the past
Appears *stuck* on what to do next (so spends excessive time on a task that isn't as important)	• There is anxiety for many reasons that keeps them from engaging in the key tasks. Help students see how long they've spent on the task so far and what still needs to be done. Estimate time together on what it might take to continue. Plan out steps together going forward. (Perhaps it's necessary to tweak the expectations of the project as you see their ability and concerns more closely) • Use a visual timer to help show students how they are using their time
Appears *stuck* on taking action on an idea for a project (so ends up rehashing the same ideas with very little forward movement or making slow progress)	• Give a movement break to have students take time away from what they're stuck on • Provide examples or allow students to take time to check in and see what others are doing in order to generate more ideas
Appears moody, easily excitable or becomes emotionally flooded	• Give some space to think and regroup if they are upset. They may not have the words for how they're feeling. Look to other areas in their life that might be causing uncertainty at the time (social groups or family) • There may be a pattern to their moodiness, like tiredness because of a long week, hunger as it leads up to lunch, the longest break as a source of anxiety because of its lack of structure • Add practices of mindfulness throughout the day as a way to encourage students to begin recognising what they feel in their bodies
Struggles to make progress with a project or task as expected (as expected for themselves and/or the teacher)	• Review the expectations and outcomes of the task. They may have a specific idea of what must be done or how to do something that is much more complicated or bigger than is necessary

ADHD learners as twice-exceptional students

Both Henry and Emma might have been considered twice-exceptional (2E) students. These students have high academic and/or creative achievement (or potential), but also have learning disabilities. There are many different profiles of 2E learners because what can cause the differences in their learning abilities is incredibly varied. Not all 2E students are identified for their learning strengths or challenges either, and consideration for learning and organisational styles can also impact their achievement in a traditional classroom.

Some academically high-achieving ADHD students are easily identifiable. We can recognise they are capable of a lot more if they could only be a little less careless in their work, stop fidgeting in class or produce more of what shows us they know. Others have high academic capabilities seen through their insights, in-depth knowledge of a topic or their continually creative ideas and problem-solving. At the same time, they might "not achieve their potential", become the "class clown" and "act out in class". A common thread between these two profiles is that these students tend to be recognised for what they can't do. When we look at what students can't do, we miss the opportunities to nurture what they can.

Some ADHD learners (and more often those who are white), whose presentations are more noticeable because of their physical manifestations, *might* be recognised as 2E and therefore access support. But what about those students whose challenges aren't as obvious? They might have average academic achievement because neither their strengths nor challenges have the opportunity to stand out. They might also be the kids who use what strengths they have to compensate for or mask their limitations too. Their twice exceptionality only becomes noticeable when the workload or academic expectations overpower their coping skills and their academic performance begins to decline. We might find ourselves thinking or saying that they could be doing better if only they didn't have to do x or could just do y. You might hear about these students "not reaching their potential" and it's their own undoing too, rather than a learning challenge. For Black, Brown and Indigenous students, whose misbehaviour or lack of achievement is more often considered a character trait, they're even less likely to be recognised as twice exceptional.

It's not that twice-exceptional students have trouble understanding the concepts and gathering ideas about what they're learning; what tends to become a problem is how school expectations don't align with the ways they can show what they know. Demands such as to (legibly) write down their ideas in a specific way, complete calculations *correctly* (even when they show multiple times they know *how* to do them), stay organised (in specific ways, even if those expectations don't work for them) or follow instructions (that are only given in certain ways and might be challenging for them to understand) can result in additional barriers to expressing learning. Since these expectations can be impacted by invisible challenges that the students themselves may not be able to articulate, they find themselves falling short, especially when many measures of success are based on the areas of curriculum they can't do well.

As educators, we're often encouraged to focus on remediation as a way to support students. Due to the pressures from testing and the expectations placed on us over what children should be able to do in a specific amount of time and grade level, we focus on what students can't do. We need to see the whole child in order to support them. ADHD students, like many other 2E students, learn very quickly about what they can't do in comparison to their peers. They exhaust themselves trying to manage their limitations, all while being shown every day how they don't measure up in their areas of remediation. "Doubts of their ability begin to creep in, resulting in deteriorating feelings of self-efficacy" (Baum, Dann, Novak, and Preuss, 2011, p. 6). These students know that they are different and, as Silverman notes, "It's emotionally damaging to be unacceptable in the place you spend six hours of every day for 13 critical years" (Baum et al., 2011, p. 5). For ADHD learners, who often get a barrage of feedback over-correcting their behaviour, pointing out how they're efforts aren't meeting expectations, it only creates more barriers to their learning rather than reduces any.

Quick tip: Supporting twice-exceptional students

Ongoing (formative) assessments guide us in supporting 2E students in the classroom because we often have to accommodate areas of both challenge and strength. We can consider making adaptions to the content (what they learn), the process (how they learn), the environment (where they learn) or the product (how they express their learning) when we do (Baum et al., 2011). The key idea here is that we're not only focusing on a learner's weakness but also allowing them opportunities to develop in their areas of strength.

It was as if Henry became a different kid at break time.

His shrill voice and laughter carried over the air as he sprinted towards the action around the football.

"Pass … pass me the ball! Did … did … did you see that?"

He was louder and more energised as he spoke with his friends. One of the other students from the other form came running up behind him.

"No goal! No goal!"

"That went in!" Henry shouted back. He was visibly frustrated. The other student went on, "No, it didn't!".

That set them both off, arguing and shouting at each other. It was clear that the other kid was taking over the debate. They spoke clearly and confidently, stating one point after the other. Henry, on the other hand, being as excited as he was, struggled to get his words out coherently. His points could not be expressed quickly enough and that left him not able to say what he wanted. He became even more frustrated, making him less understandable to others. Henry ran off, tears in his eyes, with a friend following trying to comfort him. I considered going to him but noticed that his friend seemed to have it under control. I turned my attention over to the playground equipment area.

No sooner had Henry settled with his friend than Emma came running over, her eyes filled with tears.

"They … won't … let me … play …" I could finally make out through the sobs.

"Aww Emma …" It was always difficult to see a student so upset. Her two friends came running over as she tried to explain the situation from her point of view through her tears. "They said … that they… didn't want … to play with me …" More sobbing ensued, sounding almost uncontrollable at this point.

"No! No!" one of her friends interrupted. "We said that we weren't going to play her game because we played it yesterday."

"You said … you didn't like … my game …"

"Nooo … we didn't."

"You did!"

"We didn't!"

"You did …"

Emma struggled to get any more words out as her friends proceeded to explain the situation from their point of view. I glanced back over at Emma who seemed almost distraught over a situation that, after hearing more about it, didn't need that kind of response. This wasn't something that happened often, but it was something that tended to happen more to Emma and her friends than to others in the class. She was very quiet in the class but inside their friendship bubble I got the sense it might be a different story. It sounded as if Emma could be a bit overbearing or stubborn sometimes, not leaving a lot of space for her friends to make decisions too. Or perhaps she didn't understand that they didn't appreciate how she was playing with them. In the end, they agreed to try a new game for the next break, but I still wondered about Emma. It seemed as if she were the odd person out in this situation and I didn't think it was the first time either.

Both Emma and Henry had a couple of close friends and were quite talkative with them. Where Henry could be easily led by his friends into doing what they wanted all the time, Emma was more insistent on games being her way. These challenges with their friendship groups would provide me with clues as to what skills they may need to develop. The playground often provided a lot of information about students and social skills that I would never see in class.

Friendships and social interactions are areas where I'll observe students in order to better understand any possible neurodivergence. A lot of ADHD learners love to socialise, just like any other children. They can be very kind and quite fun to be around too. It's not surprising to see some of them easily making a lot of friends. They care a lot about fitting in and want to be liked too. But it's also not surprising that there are plenty of children with ADHD that struggle socially either.

I like to watch my ADHD students to see how well they interact with others. I watch for presentations of emotional dysregulation, cognitive inflexibility and impulsivity that might be impacting their friendships. I look to see whether they have a friend that's in or around their age or grade level and how others in the class interact with them too. These observations can inform my lesson planning, avoid any potential problems or even be topics to tackle within my morning meetings. I don't believe students need to have a lot of friends in order to benefit socially, but I think having one or two real friends matters.

As much as many ADHDers are social, being aware of using (or acquiring) better social skills can often evade their understanding. Social skills are not always taught directly, but we expect all children to naturally acquire them and expectations on how to relate and communicate with others can leave some students without the necessary skills to build friendships. Not all children play or socialise the same way when left to their own devices, which can leave some feeling excluded or struggling to make (or keep) friends. This can bring up a lot of anxiety in any child, but for ADHD children, problems with friendships can lead to a huge blow to their self-esteem.

The impact of ADHD on self-esteem

Self-esteem is a complex construct that can be defined as "a cognitive and emotional concept of an individual about themself and is a multidimensional construct involving different areas such as competence, achievement, and a judgment of self-worth" (Mazzone et al., 2013). It can also be impacted by having mental health challenges as well as difficulties with friendships. It's no surprise that ADHDers tend to have low self-esteem in comparison to their non-ADHD peers. Not only do many ADHD children have difficulty with co-occurring mental health neurodivergence like anxiety or depression, but they also tend to struggle socially too. Mazzone et al. (2013) also note how "the ability to successfully interact with peers, one of the most important aspects of social development for all ages, can also be impaired in ADHD children. This deficit in peer relationships can compromise interpersonal success and happiness thus leading to low self-esteem".

ADHD can make social skills seem non-apparent because of the lack of **perspective-taking** and self-management skills. A developmental delay in executive functioning impacts ADHDers' ability to "read the room" and see how their actions, badly placed humour or inability to compromise at times might be perceived and/or impact others (Wexelblatt, 2023). They can also struggle with self-reflection (meta-cognition), not remembering to assess and learn from their previous interactions. They might end up struggling to create or sustain friendships with same aged peers, have trouble with unstructured play, be controlling with their friends, dominate the conversation and play or obsess with their new friend, making it difficult for them to befriend others (Wexelblatt, 2023).

Social problems can become more significant as children get older too. What might have been easier to overlook when they were younger might not be as accepted by their peers when they're older. Scripts and social stories can be helpful in discussing dilemmas or social situations, offering suggestions of how they might respond in the scenarios, but for many ADHD children direct teaching of **perspective-taking** and self-management skills are necessary. This supports them in better understanding context in social situations and how to build reciprocity in relationships. Allowing them to practise (with guidance and support) through real-time socialising opportunities (like extracurricular activities or teams) or during free playtimes is essential for learning social skills too.

In the classroom, ADHD learners continually receive additional blows to their self-esteem too. It can make students look as if they're not as competent as they are, which leads to lower achievements and a lower sense of self-worth. For example, ADHD learners don't lack attention but have a surplus of it. It's not that they don't want to pay attention to the teacher, their friends or their peers when they're speaking, it's just that at any given moment *something* else can take their focus. Sometimes this *something* is connected to what's happening around them, but other times it's connected to something else that's on their minds or felt internally. This leads to dysregulation (intensified ADHD presentations, although not necessarily visible behaviours), as they try to make sense of what is happening. Only now, while they're trying to self-regulate, they've missed *something* in the conversation or instructions. By the time they've realised it, it's often too late to make it right. But that's when the reprimanding starts.

"Why aren't you looking at me when I'm talking?"

"Don't you care about what I'm saying?"

"Stop fidgeting and pay attention!"

"You can't repeat what I said because you weren't listening!"

ADHD students who are more visibly hyperactive hear even more reminders about what they need to change and fix about themselves in order to be successful. This doesn't just happen at school either, but at home, in clubs, sports teams and hanging out with their friends too. The message soon becomes clear.

Being themselves is not good enough.

A common story for many ADHDers in school is the continual correcting of behaviour that is outside their control. They're then given directives for how to fix things without being given any clue of what they mean or any practical guidance for how to do it. These phrases quickly become the soundtrack for most of their school journey too.

"If you could just apply yourself …"

"You're not showing your potential …"

"You need to try harder next time!"

"You need to be more careful!"

"You could do it if you tried, but you're just being lazy!"

There's nothing worse than being told that you could have done things differently, but not knowing how to do it. How do you try harder when you're already doing the best you can? What is this potential you're supposed to reach and how come you haven't reached it yet when you're trying so hard all the time? ADHDers learn to internalise these scripts as part of their own self-talk. Since ADHD brains have a strong negativity bias, these thoughts become easy to access and amplify, further decreasing their self-esteem every time they're repeated.

The thing is, ADHDers really do care – a lot – because they tend to have sensitive nervous systems alongside a smaller volumed amygdala that's quick to react to keep them safe. Upsetting or disappointing someone at the risk of being rejected themselves creates a lot of dysregulation, because to their nervous system, it's a threat, even if it's only perceived. At any given moment ADHD learners are trying their best too, even if sometimes it looks like they've "cared" on some days more than others. We don't often consider behaviour that is "zoning out", daydreaming or losing concentration as a sign of dysregulation, but it is and can happen quite quickly and without warning. This is usually a sign that they're experiencing something that is too much for their systems at the moment, but this reaction can be interpreted as something done to someone else on purpose. ADHDers can also be emotionally sensitive, not only to what they're told but also to how they feel in different environments, even if they can't always articulate these feelings.

ADHD students want to be seen as just like other students, only it often appears as if they're choosing to be careless, selfish, inconsistent and "lazy". This happens for a multitude of reasons, including impulsivity (acting out in the moment without thinking of others, the task or future consequences) or lagging executive functioning skills (creating inconsistency in achievement, "effort" and/or "motivation"). The consistent inconsistency of ADHD presentations makes it difficult to do the things they know they can do, but also attempt to change their behaviours in the moment when they're not acting or making decisions that best align with who they want to be.

Without adequate strategies and support in place, many ADHD children will continue to struggle with plummeting self-esteem. This can lead to problems with anxiety and depression can lead to problems with their ability to connect with others. These outcomes are even more prominent with ADHD learners from historically marginalised communities. ADHD students begin to dislike school, which just leads to more dysregulation, resulting in even more difficulties with ADHD. This in turn leads to lower academic achievement and increased school exclusions or school refusals. It's a cycle that continues until the appropriate supports become accessible to the student, including practices that support their self-acceptance, soften their self-talk and increase their self-compassion.

Reflect now

How are you recognising the natural talents, characters and uniqueness of your students? How do you model affirmations or positive self-talk to your students and encourage students in doing the same? How are you infusing representations of inspiring and influential role models from different backgrounds, races and genders, so all students can see more of what's possible for themselves?

Supporting Emma and Henry

It had been a few weeks since the incidents in the playground and I had integrated some stories and situations for the class to discuss and role-play solving break-time problems. I also took some time to connect with individual students during our silent reading times to update how they were doing in class and what they found helpful for their learning so far.

"I like how you read stories", Emma said shyly.

"I'm really glad. I love telling them." I smiled back and asked, "Did you use any ideas from them in the playground?"

Emma thought for a moment.

"Sometimes I guess. But I don't really remember ..." She giggled softly to herself.

I paused to think. "Maybe we can have regular class meetings before the break to remind us about our strategies and then we can share how we used them after?"

Emma nodded in agreement. "I think we all forget things sometimes ..." I nodded in agreement. Then the conversation went a bit quiet. Emma didn't have much more to say. A lot of inattentive ADHD students can be seen as the quiet or shy ones. If they're doing relatively well academically, then that makes it even easier to focus on the learners that appear to have more pressing needs.

When I spoke with Henry, he was a little more vocal. We had developed more of a relationship because I had recently spent time working with him on his writing needs.

"Sometimes you talk so fast, I can't remember what you said!"

I laughed and nodded. He wasn't the first student to tell me that.

"Would it help if I write the big ideas on the whiteboard so you can see them as I go along?"

Henry thought for a moment, "Yeah ... maybe ..."

"We'll try it and see how it helps", I suggested.

Henry nodded his agreement.

A difficult challenge with supporting inattentive ADHDers is that it can be hard to recognise their needs without insights from everyone that works with the child and even then, we all could miss it. Insight from those closest to them are important because they see the things that aren't visible at school. With classrooms being such structured environments, learners can mask the impact of inattentive ADHD until the organisational, regulatory and/or environmental scaffolds that schools create are reduced and the demands of higher education or adulthood increase. This leaves many inattentive ADHD students with problems they never realised they had and now feeling worse because they have no idea why they're struggling so badly now.

So perhaps it wasn't surprising that I didn't get as much information from either Emma or Henry through those quick conversations as I'd hoped. But I think something more significant happened instead. Maybe it was never about listing specific accommodations for them, but rather about getting the chance to be seen, heard and believed for the struggles they mentioned instead. Maybe in those short conversations, they felt like their ideas, concerns and needs mattered too, even if they weren't as disruptive for them as some concerns were for other students. We might not ever definitively know if any of our students are dealing with untreated inattentive ADHD, but we don't have to in order to still make a difference.

Key takeaways:

- Inattentive ADHD is difficult to notice in students and these students may try to cope with ADHD presentations by using their strengths until the school or life workload exceeds their capacity to do so.
- We miss ADHD in students when we interpret their behaviours through their assigned gender at birth without examining our **internalised biases**.
- Suggesting that differences in ADHD presentations are due to being socialised as different genders ignores the natural differences in people and creates the belief that masculinity and femininity are extreme opposites, rather than parts of a spectrum of behaviours in everyone.
- Low self-esteem is often a problem for ADHD children. They receive a lot of criticism for how different ADHD presentations can manifest.
- Many ADHD students are "twice-exceptional" students, meaning they have significant academic strengths alongside learning challenges (and often the challenges either become the focus of their learning or aren't recognised at all).

Resources to explore

Twice exceptional:

Teaching Gifted Students in the Regular Classroom by Susan Winebrenner
Teaching Twice-Exceptional Learners in Today's Classroom by Emily Kircher-Morris

Gender affirming:

Genderbread Person (a diagram to support explaining the differences in gender identity, sexuality and gender expression to young children) by Sam Killermann
Gender Spectrum: https://genderspectrum.org/
Mermaids UK: https://mermaidsuk.org.uk/

3

"She cries over everything!":

Ameera's story

This chapter asks us to reflect on:

- the significant overlap between ADHD and trauma presentations;
- working towards creating trauma-informed, equity-centred classrooms;
- supporting the learning, social and emotional needs of **emergent bilingual** learners;
- how we support students in managing their emotional dysregulation.

I couldn't understand what she was saying, but I knew that she was very upset. Ameera was a new student who started late into the academic year. When I first met her, I envisioned her inquisitive nature and friendly smile easily finding their place within our fairly racially diverse classroom school. But now, as we stood in the playground after the third altercation in as many days and only a mere month later, it was clear that Ameera was struggling. Not just in her friendships, but in accessing the curriculum too. Ameera's family left their country amidst rising political turmoil. Still awaiting the permanent arrival of some key family members, the stress of being separated had made things even more challenging for her family. The transition to her new home and school was no doubt adding more stress. Not to mention that having limited knowledge of the language of instruction only further complicated matters. Ameera was in a tough situation.

In my experience, that first year for many new students can be unsettling and overwhelming, even if they speak the instructional language. Moving to a new school brings up a lot of social-emotional challenges that we might not consider because we hear a lot about how *children are resilient and can bounce back quickly* from upheaval and upset. But how easy might it be to access resilience when we also consider additional social identity markers that further differentiate a student from the social norms of their peers? When these students are also navigating any possible neurodivergence (diagnosed or otherwise), while having communication barriers, their situation becomes even more complex.

Supporting students like Ameera with these transitions not only means language acquisition but also addressing their emotional and mental well-being so they can continue to learn effectively. Whether we have the information for any additional learning disabilities or not, most often we're left with meeting the needs as we see them arise. It's not as if we're playing detective trying to find the right label to what presentations we're noticing (although at times I know that helps), but more like figuring out what isn't working and noticing what is. We aren't always given access to the answers we might need, but it doesn't mean that we can't create classrooms and learning experiences that pre-emptively aim to feel safer for students to engage in either.

Meet Ameera:

- 7 years old
- West Asian,[1] Brown, Arab ancestry
- **emergent bilingual** learner, new to the language of instruction
- identifies as a girl
- outgoing, funny, imaginative
- loves: maths, PE, drawing
- detests: writing
- future aspirations: graphic book artist
- best known for: being physically aggressive in the playground, running from classes, wandering in classes, hiding under desks
- learning challenges: nothing diagnosed, but possible ADHD, dysgraphia
- additional information: new immigration status

---

1 The Eurocentric term of the Middle East was created by the British imperial government in the 1850s as a way to reference where this region was in relation to others in a scheme that included the separate regions of the Near East and the Far East. It included nations of Asia in relation to each other, British colonial India and the Ottoman Empire. We still use "the Middle East" today, but it's not geographically accurate; nor is it commonly remembered that it includes countries in North Africa and the majority of Turkey too. West Asian countries include Bahrain, Iran, Iraq, Israel, Jordan, Kuwait, Lebanon, Oman, Palestine, Qatar, Saudi Arabia, Syria, Turkey (part of both Europe and Asia), United Arab Emirates and Yemen.

"We were all playing, and then Ameera got angry and started shouting at us!"

"She pushed them down!"

"She never listens to us!"

"We tried to stop her!"

I shook my head in frustration. The onslaught of complaints against Ameera was becoming more common. I turned to Ameera who appeared to be more and more frustrated. Her broken English strained to be heard in the conversation, and when that was not possible she turned to Arabic to voice her own concerns. Then she started crying. Again. Ameera cried a lot or got very angry. Another Arabic-speaking student came forward with an offer to translate, which I accepted. It turned out that Ameera was trying to explain that they weren't playing fairly. They were running away from her and she never understood why. They were being mean to her (a claim vehemently denied by the other students involved). But all the other student witnesses saw Ameera push the other student. They all saw her shout at them too.

I glanced back over at Ameera, gave her my teacher look and thought to myself: *Why are you still fighting with everyone?!*

"Alright. That's enough." I stopped them all, while one of the students translated for me.

"We'll talk before lunch, but now it's class." It was too much for a quick chat. The problems Ameera was having at school seemed to be escalating and these kinds of conversations were happening more and more often.

Ameera's transition to the school was a challenge for all of us. Our language barrier made it difficult to effectively talk with her about all these changes she was dealing with in her life. I tried to keep in contact with her family to better understand how I could support her, but their English wasn't much better than hers. In fact, it was Ameera who often helped her family understand the emails sent from the school. It felt like no matter what I did, it wasn't working as I had hoped. I felt like I was at a loss in finding ways to help her.

Intersectional insight: Identity matters

Throughout the Middle East (West Asia and North Africa), there are different ethnic groups. It's important to remember that being Muslim is not synonymous with being Arab or Arabic-speaking. Islam is practised in many different countries (including outside the Middle East) and doesn't require one to be Arab or Arabic-speaking in order to do so. Arabs might make up the majority of the people in the region but not everyone uses the term Arab to identify themselves when in other countries. Many prefer to identify with their country of origin because identifying as Arab might feel ancestrally inaccurate or it holds negative connotations, either from their own culture or the interpretations of being Arab by the country in which they're currently located (Awad, Hashem, and Nguyen, 2021).

I tried to spend extra time with her, supporting her understanding of the class expectations, going over playground rules and planning with her how she might spend her break. I wanted her to feel like she belonged there too and even though

I had used all my usual tried and tested tactics, we were still struggling. I had tried pairing her up with multiple students inside and outside the classroom, including some who spoke Arabic, but nothing seemed to work for long. The disagreements and **emotional flooding** continued to happen regularly. Her lack of impulse control led to many altercations in the playground and caused significant challenges to building friendships too. During class, she was better self-regulated, but we still had plenty of moments of dysregulation. Although Ameera's understanding of the language of instruction was slowly improving, it continued to create significant barriers for accessing learning too, which I could only imagine left her feeling more frustrated and insecure.

As I shuffled the students back into class after the excitement of the morning break, we finally turned our attention to our literacy lessons.

"Arabic?" She turned to me, hopeful that what was pictured in the agenda meant a pull-out class for her **home language** instead. I gently shook my head. It wasn't an Arabic class. But I could see her resistance rising as soon as she saw my head start to move. Ameera's shoulders immediately drooped.

"No English", she protested before dragging herself over to her seat. I sighed.

Although not as common as it should be, some schools ensure that **home language** lessons are arranged for their students, either during school hours or after. We were fortunate to be in a school where there was access for Ameera to learn in her **home language** each week. UNESCO has found that "an estimated 40% of school-aged children don't have access to education in a language that they understand" (McConville, 2019), and this leads to millions of children all over the world ending up not being proficiently literate in any language they've attempted to learn in school. Studies have shown that having a foundation of reading and writing in a child's **home language** best supports their ability to transfer what they've learned to acquiring additional ones. Children use the languages they know to learn new languages, so developing their first language is an incredible asset and support for **emerging bilingual** and multilingual students. "When given the opportunity to develop all their languages, bilingual and multilingual learners can gain an advantage over their monolingual peers in terms of cognitive control, expanded communication skills, enhanced well-being and academic success too" (The Bell Foundation, May 2023). Ameera's ability to continue learning her **home language** was proving to be incredibly helpful in making the curriculum more accessible for her. Even though most of what I taught needed the language to be altered, engaging with new concepts and skills came a lot easier for all of us when introduced in Arabic first.

Reflect now

How has language played a role in fostering your sense of connection and belonging with others? How do you use language to build a classroom culture especially when multiple **home languages** are spoken? When have **internalised biases** influenced how you might have interpreted language and/or communication differently from what was intended?

Emergent bilingual students in the classroom

My experience in teaching English to **emergent bilingual** children made me feel fairly confident about my ability to incorporate support for Ameera's language needs in my lessons. I'd arranged an activity that included using some previously introduced vocabulary that I'd gone over first with her Arabic teacher and then sent home in advance. She was instructed to discuss the topic, words and images in Arabic with her carers. In class, Ameera started independently on a task I'd introduced her to in the last session. I'd check in with her for some one-to-one language instruction after I got the rest of the class settled into their work. Other ways I'd accommodated, modified or differentiated her work to support her language needs included:

- regular direct teaching of the parts of the English language in the classroom showing structures, phonetics, patterns, etc., with spoken and written scaffolding to support understanding or use of the structure (something all my students benefited from anyway);
- introducing new topics in the **home language** before the rest of the class and regularly repeating previously learned vocabulary;
- using images for instructions, daily agenda and new vocabulary;
- using audio and pictures for reading books not in the **home language** to support comprehension;
- providing hands-on learning and concrete examples aiming to connect to prior learning where possible;
- direct one-to-one teaching and modelling the use of language to start thinking about herself as a learner;
- maintaining high expectations for learning and assuming competence (supporting language to access curriculum meant simplifying it or using translation, *not* making lessons below grade level or doing the work for her);
- maintaining regular contact with her **home language** teacher and parents (to collaborate on lesson planning and support).

I looked over at Ameera to find her fidgeting with something she found in the materials box on her table. She was not getting ready for this class and I could tell that today was going to be the kind of day when getting her started would be challenging. She sat appearing uninspired, staring down at her task.

"Ameera?" I called over. "Ameera!" She looked up at me, somewhat startled, as if I'd caught her in a moment that she forgot where she was. I gave her a hand gesture that showed me using scissors. She gave a long, loud sigh as she stared down at the work.

"Teacher ..." she groaned. She pushed aside the work, refusing to engage in any of it.

"Look, Ameera. It's just like the other day. See?" I bent down and manoeuvred the paper within her vision to show where we'd done a few earlier. "Only do three more." I talked with hand gestures at the same time.

"Three, teacher?" She held up three fingers.

"Yes." I pointed to each question so it was clear. "One. Two. Three."

"Awww ... teacher ..." she complained, as if I'd asked her to write a five-paragraph essay. I giggled at the thought, which Ameera heard, and while grinning, proceeded to complain louder. Even with our language barrier, it was obvious to me that Ameera could be pretty funny. Sometimes breaking tense moments with humour was a good way to ease her stresses too.

I burst out laughing now and gave her a time out signal, "Alright, Ameera. Alright! I know it's not Arabic, but you can do it! You know this". I encouraged her, adding a thumbs up with a wide smile before stating, "I'll be right back". She glanced at me suspiciously, not entirely convinced of my claims of ease or of my return. I quickly backed away from her in order to get the rest of the class settled, realising I'd have to spend more time with her on this task than I'd initially planned.

It took Ameera a few more minutes to get started. She stared at what I was doing at the board for a minute. I caught her eye and gave a quick hand signal to get started. She complained again under her breath and eventually reached for her scissors. The paper slightly folded under the pressure of the scissors' hands coming together. The more cutting she did, the more frustrated she became. I glanced over again, coming to the end of my instructions for the rest of the class and watched as she pushed aside the scissors, having only almost completed cutting out one picture. She got up and wandered aimlessly to the back of the class, pausing to look at what I was doing at the board, then carrying on as she flicked the collar of a student's shirt in the process. They whipped their head back to glare at Ameera, who giggled at them before wandering off again.

"Ameera?" I gave her a puzzled look.

She looked up at me, shrugging incredulously before blurting out, "What, teacher?!", followed by something in Arabic to which my other Arabic-speaking students called out, "She's looking for a glue stick!". I looked back over at Ameera who smiled sweetly at me. I smiled back through slightly clenched teeth before reminding the other students, "Ameera knows where the glue sticks are. She doesn't have to touch *everything* on her way there to get them …". I looked back over at Ameera, who gave a quick wave of her glue stick and skipped back, unbothered, to her seat. I shook my head and made a mental note of how much effort Ameera put into avoiding or dragging out tasks rather than attempting to even start them on her own.

ADHD and complex trauma

ADHD can also co-occur with trauma. In *My Grandmother's Hands*, Menakem (2017) defines trauma as, "When something happens to the body that is too much, too fast, or too soon, it overwhelms the body". Trauma is a protective response that the body engages in when it's overwhelmed with that same felt sense of danger. This happens regardless of whether the threat is real or not or regardless of whether we know where the danger stemmed from or not, but this embedded trauma response is our body's way to keep us safe. Therefore it's help-ful to think of trauma not just as an event or a series of continuous or ongoing events, but something that happens in the body (see more in the Introduction). Trauma is the Greek word for *wound*, so if the *wound* stems from within the body then supporting its healing must include supporting the body too.

Early childhood trauma occurs in the same area of the brain, the prefrontal cortex, which means that "many people with complex trauma experience the same problems with emotional regulation, self-awareness and impulsivity" (Porteous-Sebouhian, 2021). The impact of either trauma or ADHD has lasting effects on the child but also "additional traumatic events can make the underlying psychological conditions worse, resulting in greater symptoms" (Siegfried et al., 2016, p. 6). Those children with ADHD that also have trauma show an increased severity in presentations which can result in poorer academic and social outcomes. Additionally, trauma presentations that also include the occurrence of general depressive symptoms "were the strongest mediators in the association between ADHD symptoms and trauma exposure" (Miodus, Allwood, and Amoh, 2021). But when a child (and particularly if they are Black, Brown or Indigenous) presents with particularly challenging behaviours, they may be punished rather than offered support, which can further impact ADHD and trauma.

Sometimes ADHD is noticed and treated, which reduces many presentations, but the trauma is still there and only amplified when met with harshness and criticism. This is why ADHD support should also consider the ways we're creating learning environments that are conducive to a felt sense of safety too. The root causes of the ADHD presentations are not always clear. Simply insisting on developing executive functioning skills won't be as effective as reducing ADHD presentations for long as the causes are rooted in insecurity or fear.

There are many ways that trauma might manifest in the classroom, and depending on the child's developmental age, trauma presentations look different too. Children with trauma and those with ADHD display similar behavioural presentations, albeit the underlying causes for them are different. Some similarities include the following:

- Agitation, nervousness and hyper-awareness of the environment (fidgeting, restlessness)
- Disruptive behaviour presentations (acting out, aggression)
- Dissociation that might look like inattentiveness (daydreaming, loss of focus)
- Sleep disruptions that can further impact presentations (making them more apparent in the classroom) but could be the result of intrusive thoughts or flashbacks
- Intrusive thoughts could also lead to agitation, with behaviour that looks like impulsivity (Porteous-Sebouhian, 2021)

We need to accept that not only will our students come to us with trauma but that schools traumatise students too. One-off strategies or 15-minute social-emotional learning lessons once a week aren't going to cut it in providing the support they need either. We need to create a culture in our learning environments that fosters belonging and connection which supports the integration of trauma, not simply react after the fact. The wellbeing of all our students, regardless of having ADHD, are at risk when we don't.

I walked over to Ameera to see that she'd started to engage with the task. Some pictures had been coloured rather than practising the writing, but she had since become distracted by something else she had found and had abandoned the task completely. The glue she had so painstakingly looked for earlier in the lesson hadn't been used. Once again, I gently suggested the writing practice that had to happen before the colouring and why. Ameera was not pleased. I watched as her eyes welled up with tears as she threw down her plaything and put her head down on the desk. She wouldn't budge. I knew there was nothing more I could do until she was ready. Ameera wouldn't be moved.

This was another thing that happened often. She would get easily upset over what seemed like the smallest redirections. Her reactions rarely matched the offence she accused the other person of either. It was challenging to coach her through these incidents. I went quiet to give her space to decide what she wanted to do with the work. When she calmed down, I'd speak to her again. But I knew she would say she didn't want to do the task because she didn't like it or something similar. We would then be at a standstill until I could come up with a compromise or decide if it was really worth her completing or not.

In the meantime, one of the other Arabic-speaking students in the class came over to see if they could talk to her. I agreed. I knew it was difficult to get used to a new school, a new country and learning a new language. I felt like I was at a loss for what to do next. Neither one of us was very happy in this learning environment at the moment.

I needed some more help.

Reflect now

What are the narratives you hold about why different students become emotionally dysregulated from being corrected on their work? How do you interpret and respond to emotional dysregulation from others depending on their age, gender, race, ability and socio-economic status? What beliefs do you have about emotional dysregulation or **emotional flooding** that might need to change?

ADHD Support: developing sustained attention and a felt sense of safety

Ameera was enduring some significant changes in her life due in part to having left her home country. It might have been tempting to think I could figure it all out on my own, but I only knew one part of her. Working with others would help create a fuller picture of her possible needs. Supporting Ameera meant focusing on cultivating connection and not just through building a meaningful relationship with me, either. Ameera would benefit from building stronger connections with her classmates, within the school community and the wider community she now called home. It would help her integrate into her new surroundings and feel she belonged. Although it wasn't clear whether Ameera was dealing with untreated ADHD or trauma, creating more opportunities for connection as a way to cultivate a stronger sense of safety could address some of the concerns for both.

Table 3.1 ADHD support: developing sustained attention and a felt sense of safety

Sustained attention The capacity to stay on task or follow a situation even when things feel difficult, boring, uninteresting or through other potentially dysregulating events

Possible ADHD presentations	Possible accommodations
Appears restless with their attention (going from task to task, resistant in starting or sustaining attention, or may need much more support throughout the task than usual)	• Depending on if the presentation is a pattern or out of character impacts the choice of support. Scaffold tasks with examples, one-to-one support or give tasks in smaller parts to complete. If presentations seem out of character, it might be necessary to prioritise emotional or mental support. Reduce the demands on the student and be flexible with what's being asked of them
Gets lost or confused with information in the classroom or during a conversation	• Shorten time for giving directions and/or direct teaching. Involve more students in repeating instructions or sharing they are learning
	• Include multi-sensory ways to teach and integrate new information
Interrupts others in conversation. Disrupts others learning while learning	• Use small-group and pair-work activities to direct teach specific skills that support their social skills and group work
Gets distracted by others or things in the environment (on the walls, something new in the space …)	• Have student work near the teacher or another student that helps them stay on task without necessarily having to remind them to keep going. This is **body doubling**
	• Choose seating where distractions are minimal, but also allow for other kinds of movement, whether it's fidgets or drawing, while listening to reduce anxiety and restlessness. If the student chooses something too distracting for them to use, reflect with them on how to choose something that might keep their focus easier
	• Give them some time before starting to look at any materials that they might need and discuss their uses if it's something new, rather than trying to start something when they're clearly distracted. Put a timer on so that they know how much time they have to look or explore
Loses focus in the middle of a task	• Schedule frequent breaks for students to process what's already been learned or done. All brains need a short time to process what's been learned after short amounts of time, whether it's through writing, discussion, movement or drawing about their understandings
Focuses on more enjoyable tasks only and avoids the other assigned tasks	• Reflect on what you've asked of them, whether there are skills that they might need to develop before they engage in the other tasks or what outcomes you're expecting. If there's something that you can do first to reduce the barriers to the task, it might make it more approachable

(Continued)

Table 3.1 (*Continued*)

	• Reflect with the student about their plan for completing the task or what is stopping them from engaging in it. "It's boring" is usually insecurity about something being too much, too long, or they can't see the importance of it. They might have other ideas of how to accomplish the task and could be more willing to engage if they had a say or were offered more options on how to complete it
Focus is varied even *on enjoyable* tasks	• Being excited or nervous about something happening later in the day often means a need for extra emotional regulation support in the present with multiple check-ins, more movement breaks or tasks that are more hands-on that allow students to become immersed in the project and less thought on what might happen later. Ensure physical causes that might bring up dysregulation are met (for example, hunger or thirst) • Look for patterns of lack of focus to see what might be causing more anxiety or discomfort. (For example: is it a particular environment, person, task or subject that needs to be addressed?)
Struggles to make eye contact when being spoken to	• Eye contact can be very overwhelming for many children. Allow students to look away, doodle or fidget if needed. Then have students repeat key points of what was said (in small chunks of information!) to double-check understanding if necessary
Talks incessantly when in a group or during instructions	• Make sure that the student knows what they are asked to do. They may not have a plan on how to start and need to talk out what they must do first (this might include needing to visualise what has to be done)

Emotional regulation: Developing a felt sense of safety Safety in the brain and nervous system comes from what is familiar, makes us feel good (calm, ease, content, neutral) and gives a felt sense of belonging (connection with others). Dysregulation is natural as we're all weaving in and out of our zone of tolerance. The key is supporting students to come back quicker to their zone of tolerance when they find themselves well beyond or frequently outside it. Supporting the development of a sense of felt safety comes from intentionally creating an environment that fosters belonging, is culturally responsive and makes time to build a relationship with the student

Possible ADHD presentations	Possible accommodations
Hides, acts out or runs away when upset	• Create a quiet, comfy corner with short activities to complete (if they choose) to redirect their energy • Some students prefer to hide under furniture until they feel calm again to discuss the problem. (I allow this and check in on them. I may bring over the activity if they decide to start working but still don't want to come out of hiding)
Very distressed (angry, frustrated or disheartened, saddened) when corrected	• Give consistent positive feedback too. Feedback should be practical and specific about the work rather than the student and given when calm.

Often dysregulated through zoning out, moodiness or excessive movement and fidgeting	• Intentionally choose frequent brain breaks, sensory regulation activities and movement breaks to help balance different neurotransmitters and regulate the nervous system. We want to support the student's ability to eventually engage with and choose alternative choices for self-regulation support by providing new options of strategies too
Is preoccupied with worries that may or may not be connected to the classroom or school	• Include other school adults in the student's circle of support when they needed a break (on difficult days give some freedom to sit with the counsellor or visit another space to do work)
Feels insecure about their ability, the process or skills necessary	• Catch them doing something well and tell them their specific actions (and often). "Good job" is not helpful because it's not clear what behaviours they were showing that were supportive in their learning
	• Give more flexibility to decide what work to do and genuinely praise and support any attempts or interest in completing a task. As the teacher, work to stay regulated regardless of the outcomes or process
Struggles socially to connect to others inside and outside the classroom	• Regular class meetings (guided and informal) to teach/discuss unwritten rules for the playground and in class. Discuss the impact these rules have on how we feel and behave as individuals, on others and on how they support our environment/learning. Students can make goals for their own improvement
	• Regular structured playtimes with activities for students to choose from (library open times, various activities led by teachers and/or older students during breaks) to help students connect with their interests and meet others
	• Find opportunities for students to make positive contributions to the school community and wider community where possible (being a reading buddy to a younger student, helping in the library or getting involved in community projects)
	• Direct teaching on how to work in small groups through fun, non-threatening tasks and games. Include scripts and body language prompts to develop an understanding of working with others. Students reflect on the process
Demands a lot of one-to-one teacher time or a lot more effort from teachers to stay regulated to support learning engagement	• Ongoing personal reflections of your own biases about what students should be able to do based on gender, race, class, etc. to reduce the dysregulation you might feel while supporting them
	• Reflect on the ways you might see yourself as being the only solution for your students' needs and how it's blocking you from seeing longer-term solutions and people to help them too
	• Assist students in connecting with others in the wider school community through different learning opportunities, clubs and other programmes

Creating a new classroom culture

We come to learning environments with our own cultural backgrounds, but we also exist in different cultures through our friendship groups, the wider school community and society. What we might forget is that every classroom has its own culture and we have a huge responsibility in guiding what that could be. But culture isn't something that we engage with our cognition, making it something we simply speak into existence and it happens. It's something that we feel and experience (Hammond, 2014). This is why it's never enough to just talk about belonging or spreading the message of "we're all different and that's OK". Culture is felt in our bodies (Menakem, 2017), so even though our students might cognitively *understand* what we're trying to convey as a classroom culture, it's what we do, show and express over and over again that allows them to eventually *feel* it.

For children like Ameera who have been unexpectedly transported from one familiar culture and made to cope with many new ones, it's not a stretch to assume that she would feel dysregulated more often as she adjusted to the new situations she was surrounded by. Nor is it a stretch to assume that for the body to feel belonging and safety it would take time. This makes it even more challenging for us to determine if we're noticing ADHD, anxiety, complex trauma or something else entirely. But luckily, within our role as educators there's a lot we can do to ease this transition and the dysregulation even when we don't know the root cause.

Menakem (2017) tells us that "cultural change takes hold through consistency and repetition. When enough people do the same thing, in the same way, over and over, eventually those actions become culture". This makes it even more important for us to be intentional about what kind of classroom cultures we want to create with our students. That's why trauma-informed and equity-centred spaces are essential to creating a classroom culture where all students (not just our ADHD ones) can feel safe enough to engage in their learning.

Trauma-informed and equity-centred practice

Alex Shevrin Venet (2021) defines trauma-informed educational practices as "responding to the impact of trauma on the entire school community and preventing future trauma from occurring. Equity and social justice are key concerns of trauma-informed educators as we make changes in our individual practice, in classrooms, in schools and in district-wide and state-wide systems" (Venet, 2021, p. 10). As teachers, we need to understand the intersection of learning and trauma, intentionally reflect on and check in with our own biases regularly, and learn about what and how we teach could trigger past traumas for our learners.

Trauma may be one of the most underexplored racial equity issues in education. This is why it's not enough to be trauma-informed, but also equity-informed as well. Venet notes, "the same factors that also cause inequity (like bias and discrimination) also cause trauma and we can't unlink the two" (2021, p. 12). When we don't actively do the work to learn **racial literacy**, "we don't prepare for the microaggressions that will happen in schools that leave our most marginalised or in-need students vulnerable and having to protect themselves". Schools become hazardous and traumatic environments where "issues of race and racial equity tend to be ignored or minimised" (p. 11). With school systems rooted in a history of sorting students, there is an "unexamined aspect of using trauma as an excuse to justify a deficit orientation of children" (Hammond, 2014) rather than realising that schools can both cause trauma and not respond to it effectively.

> ## Intersectional insight: A sense of belonging for marginalised students
>
> In order to thrive academically, the answer within all different marginalised groups is the same. Emotional safety and the feeling they belong are key. Teachers play a vital role in creating this for these students. For Black, Brown, Indigenous Peoples, Asian and other melanated students, this might look like including more chances to process learning in their **home language**, including representation within the curriculum and the school faculty too. For trans students (who are more than four times as likely to leave school if they encounter discrimination; Horton, 2020), this looks like teachers being more positive and accepting of gender diversity, moving away from victim narratives of trans people, and supporting them as they "navigate cis-normative institutional cultures and regimes" (Horton, 2020). Considering that the most marginalised communities tend to have higher rates of anxiety and ADHD often co-occurs with it (see Alex's story for more), the learning environment we create could play a bigger role in supporting the mental health of more students than we realise.

The education system has a long history of considering trauma as something that children from low-income communities (mostly Black, Brown and Indigenous Peoples) bring into schools, impacting their learning and well-being. This morphs into the belief that *a teacher can be that one special person to a troubled student that can save them*. It's a trap that all teachers can fall into, regardless of race, gender, class or ability too. This is called saviour mentality and engaging in it ignores the systemic problems that are impacting the student and their family. Instead, the person (often white) attempts to solve the problems of those more marginalised communities by deciding that their solutions are the best choice without consulting them to understand their real issues and what they might actually need. Often these solutions are based around an individual, non-sustainable act that can disempower the person they're trying to serve because they don't consider long-term needs and solutions.

But trauma-informed teaching practice isn't something that white educators must bring to (poor) Black, Indigenous Peoples and Brown communities in order to save them. How have they been able to survive through centuries of oppression and persecution for as long as they have? Where do you suppose the ideas of trauma-informed care came from in the first place? A part of **cultural humility** is acknowledging that (white) educators must be learning from Black, Brown, Indigenous Peoples, Asian and other melanated groups to understand the ways they heal and integrate trauma. It asks us to consider how we as teachers can be doing the same for ourselves within our own communities too. We are not meant to be a student's "only one". It keeps them stuck without other options and has us spiralling towards (or stuck in) burnout. Instead, we are there to support them in breaking barriers for more opportunities to genuinely connect with other students, the wider school community and within the greater community itself. Connection is what helps students heal.

Reflect now

How are you learning from marginalised communities about what healing looks like for them? What are some ideas and practices that you'd like to incorporate into your own life? In your classroom?

Strong, supportive relationships are important for healing and integrating trauma because building resilience happens within the context of them. Even though we wear many hats as educators, our primary one is still as teachers. Remembering the hats we've actually been trained to wear as teachers is important because relationships are rooted in reciprocity. This means we all have a role to play in the relationships we cultivate with others. If we want to build the kinds of relationships with our students that are rooted in reciprocity we need to stick to our job so they can build their capacity to do their part. We can support this by creating opportunities for authentic learning that foster connection and belonging to take place. Authentic learning opportunities mean we don't always create "filler work" for our learners when there are actual situations in students' lives they're trying to solve and better understand. It means we consider and build on their prior knowledge to help them do this (Hammond, 2014). Designing more authentic learning experiences placed within the context of students' cultures and their lives is how we connect with our students and foster their connections with each other and the wider community.

Quick tip

Venet (2021) plans and makes decisions for her classroom teaching, learning activities and the environment with empowerment, connection, flexibility and predictability in mind. Four questions she asks herself are:

- Is this predictable?
- Is it flexible?
- Does it foster empowerment?
- Does it foster connection?

These questions keep her proactively prioritising trauma-informed, equity-centred practice. For ADHDers who often struggle with too much rigidity in a classroom (but at the same time still need clarity on what to expect), or who want to be empowered and have meaningful relationships with others (but need scaffolding and direct support in doing this), every time we answer these questions we're keeping these students in mind too.

Supporting Ameera

One of the biggest lessons I learned as a teacher (and also one I wished I learned a lot sooner), was that I didn't have to do things alone. I never had to have all the answers and there were other people better suited than me to solve some of the challenges I was facing too. Many of us get the messages from others in our schools, from parents or our community that if we can't manage our classes or a student, then we are the problem. I felt like asking for help and admitting that not being able to fix the problems on my own meant I wasn't good a teacher. But it wasn't a sign of failing as an educator or failing the student, instead it opened the door to other possibilities I couldn't have found on my own.

Ameera needed a lot of support as she adjusted to her new life, so regular updates from her family and meetings with her Arabic teacher and the school counsellor were necessary. We pooled together our knowledge to create a plan for Ameera that centred on building connections (with others and the learning material), increasing her language acquisition and reducing triggers to her emotional dysregulation. I started by observing Ameera more closely in her learning and social behaviour, then slowly implementing lesson planning, environmental and learning activity changes while monitoring her responses to them. Regular check-ins with her Arabic teacher meant I could connect my class activities to ideas discussed in Ameera's **home language**. It helped make topics more familiar for her so she could connect her prior knowledge to them. This made her want to share more about her experiences with her classmates. Getting her involved in school-wide projects was important too. These opportunities made her feel more connected to her classmates and the school community as a whole.

As the school year progressed and Ameera became more settled with her new routines, I introduced more learning accommodations for her to manage the challenges she was having with writing. As her language developed, she connected more with other students and this helped reduce her playground altercations immensely. Although Ameera still had many ADHD presentations, including restlessness, task avoidance and emotional dysregulation, she had times that fluctuated to inattentive ADHD presentations too. The inconsistency in the ADHD presentations themselves is part of what can be so disabling when it comes to learning too. As educators, not only do we plan to pre-emptively manage dysregulation before it disrupts learning, but our willingness and flexibility to make changes when necessary are also invaluable supports.

Both ADHD and trauma experience a sense of disconnection. Trauma is rooted in disconnection between our mind and body, disconnection from others and from the natural environment. ADHDers can experience a sense of disconnection too. This disconnection occurs naturally due to developmental delays that make it more challenging to think first before reacting to the discomfort they feel. But I also think it happens when ADHD students are expected to override much of their body's protective reactions in order to regulate their responses in socially appropriate ways. If they can't perform these changes quickly and effectively they risk exclusion or rejection.

I think this leaves ADHD students caught between the threat of being disconnected from others and of becoming disconnected from themselves. Although both outcomes lead to more dysregulation, when made to choose between the two, self-betrayal will end up winning most of the time. But chronic self-betrayal leads to plummeting self-esteem, which only increases anxiety and/or depression, making them feel even worse and intensifying their dysregulation. Part of reconnection for ADHD learners means experiencing a felt sense of *belonging* in learning spaces so they can effectively acquire strategies to self-regulate in ways that respect themselves, others and the environment around them. They learn they can accept themselves as they are and thrive through interdependence, just like everyone else.

Key takeaways:

- All students need to feel psychologically and intellectually safe in order for real learning to happen in our classrooms.
- ADHD has significant overlapping presentations with complex trauma and many ADHDers have both (as well as other mental health neurodivergence like anxiety and depression that exasperate ADHD presentations too).
- A saviour mentality disempowers our students rather than supports their ability to build resilience.
- It takes time and consistency to build new cultures in our classrooms because belonging is a felt sense in the body, not a cognitive one.
- Being trauma-informed and equity-centred is ongoing work that isn't about dealing with trauma when we think it's happened, but about creating learning environments where we're preventing and actively responding to it.

Resources to explore

Trauma:

My Grandmother's Hands by Resmaa Menakem
Trauma-Informed Educators Network Podcast

Equity-Centered, Trauma-Informed Education by Alex Shevrin Venet
Minded: www.minded.org.uk/
Trauma-informed Schools UK: www.traumainformedschools.co.uk/

Social justice

Education Unfiltered Dr Sawsan Jaber, PhD NBCT: www.educationunfiltered.medium.com
Why Are All the Black Kids Sitting Together in the Cafeteria? And other conversations about race by Beverly Daniel Tatum
Social Justice for the Sensitive Soul: How to Change the World in Quiet Ways by Dorcas Cheng-Tozun
Social Justice Books: A Teaching for Change Project: https://socialjusticebooks.org
The Young Activists' Dictionary of Social Justice by Ryse Tottingham www.patreon.com/teachingwithmxt

4

"He never does anything you tell him to!":

Dhruv's story

This chapter asks us to reflect on:

- how ADHD presentations of demand avoidance are not the same as pathological demand avoidance;
- supporting the needs of demand avoidance students;
- increasing learner autonomy;
- how we build cognitive flexibility;
- the unique needs of **biracial or multiracial** students.

Dhruv and I were having a tough week and today looked like it was going to be a continuation of that. I hadn't even finished explaining the instructions for the first learning activity of the day when Dhruv started in with the silly noises, humming and nonsensical words that would eventually lead to fits of laughter from the class if I couldn't contain it. As the activity remained untouched on Dhruv's table, his attention instead turned to doodling on the mini-whiteboard in front of him. I tried not to get too frustrated about him not doing any of his lesson activities as this was becoming a common occurrence throughout all of his classes. No one had yet to figure out why. Even when I'd try to plan learning activities that I knew he'd love, there was no guarantee he'd engage in them either. He'd rarely say "*no*" to anything, but rather casually put them aside or take extra time with other tasks. Some tasks might get done with the bare minimum, but still plenty of others wouldn't be attempted at all.

But I should have known that if Dhruv was already avoiding activities so early in the day, there was a good chance this trend would continue. He sat at his table making comments with words I'd used in my instructions but not relating to the current topic. The class listened intently, trying to muffle their laughter as Dhruv looked around trying not to appear so surprised by the response as if he expected what he said to be that funny. I sighed and looked over at Dhruv. He looked straight back at me. And smiled. I took a deep breath and scanned the class using my best "*that's enough*" face, waiting for everyone to quieten as I calmly made my way over to stand unassumingly next to Dhruv as he sat at his table. Hoping to show that I was not fazed by Dhruv's interruptions in the slightest, I waited for everyone to eventually regain composure. I could sense that everyone was waiting on edge, eagerly anticipating what Dhruv might say next and what I was going to do when he did.

I had talked too long already. Dhruv wasn't the only one in class starting to get restless, so I changed course immediately.

"The instructions are on the page. Come up to the board if you want a little more time working with me. Otherwise start with what questions suit you." Dhruv said nothing and kept doodling on the board, only muttering a few words under his breath. By the end of the class, he'd completed a few questions. But not on the paper; he'd used the mini-whiteboard instead. I took a picture of his work to look at later and left it at that. Dhruv seemed anything but predictable and I hadn't figured out his pattern. Yet.

Meet Dhruv:

- 10 years old, European (father) and South Asian (mother) ancestry, **biracial/multiracial, white-presenting**
- identifies as a boy
- fluent in both the language of instruction and **home language**
- personable, insightful, creative problem solver and storyteller
- loves: drawing, reading, watching videos
- detests: writing, maths
- best known for: causing low-level disruptions during direct instruction and high-level disruptions during break times or in between classes
- learning challenges: ADHD, demand avoidant
- additional information: possible pathological demand avoidance (PDA), autism

---

Even when Dhruv and I had a good start to the day, it wouldn't be surprising if by lunch or late afternoon we'd be struggling to get anything done. A good day meant that he'd attempt to do something in class, would resist disrupting others who were on task or blurting out fewer random words or noises during instructions. Although we suspected Dhruv had ADHD because of his impulsivity, his frequent fidgeting with anything within his body's reach and his lack of focus or persever-ance towards completing most tasks, it couldn't explain the main challenges we were experiencing. Dhruv was an extremely charismatic student when he was at ease with a task, but quite often he would barely engage in the work at all. If he attempted to answer questions it could be considered a good day. Any insisting that he do more or even getting started would lead to him becoming agitated and making excuses as to why he was finished or what he couldn't do. It was becom-ing a constant battle between us. In the end, we were both miserable and anxious and I was no closer to understanding why he presented with so much resistance.

I wanted to build a relationship with Dhruv but I was finding it difficult to con-nect with him. The reactions I could get from him if I pushed him to complete something, especially if it was later in the day, kept me on edge. He could become easily frustrated, irritated and often appeared very moody. In the morning he might not do any of the lessons, but there were always reasons as to why he couldn't. In the afternoon the slightest question might make him argumenta-tive, inflexible or destructive. Occasionally he'd become emotionally flooded with anger and run from the classroom, leaving my TA to chase after him to ensure we wouldn't lose him hidden away somewhere.

The unique needs of biracial learners

Regardless of how Dhruv reacted, the school continued to give him as much leeway as possible and he was very fortunate for this. Other students behaving similarly would have been suspended multiple times, if not expelled by now. More so if they were Black. Even though Dhruv was **multiracial** with visibly light brown skin, it was clear that he wasn't Black biracial. This changed how many teachers interpreted his racial identity and therefore his behaviour wasn't automatically treated as if he were a Black student. But it didn't mean that Dhruv was seen accurately in his **biracial** identity either. During my time in the school I'd heard enough dehumanising questions asked about different multiracial kids like "What were they?" or "Where were they *really* from?". Questions like this were more often asked when the student didn't appear to have visible Black features.

> ## Intersectional insight: Biracial or multiracial students
>
> It's important to recognise the challenges that **multiracial or biracial** students bring to our classrooms. Often ignored in the curriculum, they experience unique racially motivated threats because they can "claim multiple racial ingroups that are simultaneously both negatively and positively stereotyped in the academic
>
> *(Continued)*

domain" (Rozek and Gaither, 2020, p. 3). They are often dehumanised (being asked questions like, what are you?), not recognised for their biracial identity (seen as a different race depending on how their behaviour is interpreted by others) or exotified. School staff need to engage in ongoing conversations, and self-reflection to focus on attitudes, beliefs and biases regarding multiracial students (Baxley, 2008). **Multiracial** teens report experiencing anxiety and depressive symptoms at higher rates than their monoracial peers (Fisher et al., 2014 in Campbell, 2020). Teachers can start supporting these students by reflecting on their **internalised biases** with questions like: How do I feel about interracial marriages? What perceived notions do I have about **biracial** people? What experiences have I had with **biracial** people and how have these experiences impacted me? (Baxley, 2008). We can also make a start to acknowledge and affirm the identities of these students by including **biracial or multiracial** perspectives from guest speakers and representation in our literature and curriculum.

Dhruv was getting frequent complaints about disruptions he was causing in other classes, and from his peers, that were increasing daily. As a **biracial** student, his carers wondered if the behaviour we were witnessing in school might be a manifestation of not feeling like he fitted in. Since he couldn't be easily placed within a monoracial group and the South Asian part of his ethnicity was rarely acknowledged, they were concerned it was affecting his mental well-being. Although it was unclear to say if it was contributing to what we were noticing in school, I knew I could do more for him in this regard. It helped students to see positive representation of themselves in their learning activities and to have space to talk with others that might be experiencing similar feelings. Perhaps changes like these might work towards helping Dhruv feel psychologically safer too.

All we knew was that we were all struggling (teachers and students alike), to understand Dhruv's resistance to everything. The more he acted out, the more difficult it got for me to support him and the worse his behaviours became for the school to continue to allow. With Dhruv's most recent meltdown resulting in him screaming slurs about other students in the class, things couldn't be explained away anymore. He was on the brink of expulsion.

Reflect now

What do you know about the needs of your **biracial or multiracial** students? How are you acknowledging the different racial identities of your **biracial or multiracial** learners? How do you think your interpretations of behaviour change depending on the lightness or darkness of their skin? How might the interpretation of a **biracial or multiracial** student's race change depending on who witnesses the behaviour and the behaviours witnessed? Where do you recognise **colourism** impacting how students are treated in your school?

Dhruv's parents were at a loss as to what to do, but meeting with them began to broaden my scope of what he was dealing with. If I felt like I was having a tough time of it, I soon realised he was struggling even more and so were they. They knew he had ADHD and even with medication making his behaviour less challenging than it was a year ago, they all still struggled significantly. Dhruv wouldn't do things that the school wanted him to do, but soon he wasn't even engaging in things he wanted to do either. Coming home from school would frequently lead to becoming overwhelmingly dysregulated at even the slightest hint of an insinuation of a request or question. Simple day-to-day tasks to take care of himself were becoming unbearable for him to attempt. He was becoming increasingly inflexible in what he expected to be done for him and what he would not participate in. Dhruv was also becoming more distressed about attending school and began arriving late or missing days altogether. It didn't seem like normal avoidant behaviour, and it definitely wasn't just ADHD.

ADHD Support: increasing cognitive flexibility and creating more autonomy

Not all ADHD students who avoid demands react in ways that are as extreme as Dhruv. He would consistently struggle to do anything no matter what I said suggested. The more I pressed the issues, the more his excuses could go from more socially acceptable reasons, to some that were nonsensical or ridiculous. If I kept pushing, he could become quite volatile or even aggressive. He challenged everything I knew and understood about teaching.

Traditional attempts at managing behaviour or engaging him in learning activities didn't work for Dhruv. Rewards and praise for his efforts or consequences for any issues arising from his refusal to engage only resulted in more resistance. Even trying to reflect on any outbursts with him after things had calmed down often found him denying the incidents completely. Dhruv's reactions could get so intense, I was becoming fearful that he'd re-escalate if I dared push any issues further. The only thing that seemed to work for us was finding ways to collaborate together on what he chose to do for the week, then leaving him to decide as to whether he would actually do any of the plan or not and hope he'd be listening during class as I taught.

Table 4.1 ADHD support: increasing cognitive flexibility and creating more autonomy

Cognitive flexibility Being able to change course or make revisions to an idea when there's an obstacle, change of plans or new information forces a re-evaluation of the initial plan or belief. It's about becoming more adaptable to changes around us and our environment

(Continued)

Table 4.1 *(Continued)*

Possible ADHD presentations	Possible accommodations
Needs predictability within the daily structure and the environment	• Having a personalised, pictured agenda of the day's activities to move around when needed • Model using future thinking skills to visualise the remainder of the current task and the ease or benefits of transitioning to the next activity • Including a transition activity (like a sensory diet) before the next activity to allow for time to feel better about going from one activity to the next • Regular enjoyable transition activities (like whole-class movement games) can also be something to look forward to, making the transition that much easier • Allow students to know when any fire drills or similar happen in classes, to reduce anxiety
Difficulty transitioning to a new task when not finished a current one or before something completely new	• Hyperfocus can be difficult to break from, depending on how the student feels about the task. There are many ways to approach it • Before you start: Model planning out breaking projects into tasks to support students in visualising natural starts and stops. Decide which tasks might take longer than others and why • Countdowns, familiar music and sounds that signal completion might work if they are doing something they can come back to later • Oftentimes ADHD students don't remember what activity is coming up next (or could be anxious about the next activity), so reminding them of this during the warnings to complete an activity can be helpful • Allow for extra time when necessary; it might take time to convince themselves that it's OK to change tasks
Struggles with changes in routine or expectations	• Grow capacity for flexibility in less-threatening ways like changing rules for games played in the class or finding multiple solutions to a maths problem • Give advanced warning of changes in schedule so enough time can be allowed to adjust to them (whether they must learn about where they're going or what's happening there, etc.)
Resists doing some classwork or homework	• "It's boring" or other refusals can be insecurity around their ability to do the task, not having the option to do things differently, or not understanding the point of a task, so discussing the reasoning for an assignment and being flexible in how it's completed might be helpful

Resists doing classwork that is of interest to the student	• Be open to changes in how the task is done or parts of the outcome. Quite often, resistance happens when they only see what they can't do. They might have other ideas for what they can do and some compromises could be made. Offer some alternative suggestions for getting started or achieving the outcome that can get them started or thinking of what options are within their control or capacity
Insists on not knowing anything or can't do the work because they don't understand	• Reflect on the instructions with them. ADHD students might say they don't understand *anything*. This makes them feel worse. When you can offer a chance to go back to the first step and ask them what they remember from there, it becomes easier for both of you to see where they got lost. It also supports them in seeing that there was *something* they understood
	• Talk it out with the student because when ADHD students are trying to organise their ideas in their heads, it's not always the most effective. Externalising their thinking (either verbally or otherwise) often makes visible where they're stuck and the best plan of action that's needed
Resists new ideas or opinions from others	• Provide students many examples and practices for thinking that goes beyond either/or thinking or "only one right answer" thinking through games that have multiple right answers, modelling decision-making skills that have more than one possible outcome
	• Model using *and* rather than *but* in thinking aloud in everyday situations or Philosophy for Kids that connects big questions and ideas to children's books

Emotional regulation: Managing the need for autonomy

As much as impulsivity can have ADHDers agreeing to anything in the heat of the moment, it's not always a guarantee that they will do what they agreed to when the time comes. Challenges with metacognition make it difficult for ADHD students to remember the last time they did something and it went badly. This makes it more difficult to reflect on and therefore learn from their past mistakes. They also may not realise that they have conflicting plans that day that are keeping them from completing the task, or that an event that drains their energy might make it difficult to do the task either.

Depending on their co-occurring conditions, the environment, their lived experiences or how they feel about their own ability to complete the task (even if they don't know how to articulate any of these reasons), ADHD can resist requests. But the end result, whether it's a lack of energy or anxiety stemming from a variety of reasons, avoidance has set in and often it's not usually clear for the ADHD student as to why. Offering more autonomy alongside guidance and support to make effective choices or manage the demands of the task, allows space for the student to decide what they can engage, while knowing what support is available to them as they need it.

(Continued)

Table 4.1 *(Continued)*

Possible ADHD presentations	Possible accommodations
Becomes agitated, or seen as aggressive or "defiant" when asked to do a task or participate in class	• Monitor your tone of voice when direct teaching, talking with students or giving directions in a raised voice, inflexions and how things are requested can increase anxiety in students • Refrain from phrases and requests that include "no", "don't" or "can't", yes/no questions, as commands and imperative language as it can contribute to raising anxiety and increasing the avoidance presentations. Try to use **declarative language** instead • Leave the activity options for the student at their table to choose from, allowing them to do as they wish (or not) without judgement or expectation
Avoids doing tasks and lessons they're asked to do (or not)	• Simplify the ways that the student can engage with the tasks. This helps reduce the demands. If it's something that they can watch rather than have to read (if they've shown proficiency in reading, for example) or a task they can use speech to text or type rather than write • Allow for flexibility for their own ideas and accept alternative ways for them to express their learning of the topic • Give them additional time to decide what they are going to do. They might complete the task in their own space with an advisor that they trust or in their own way. • If they already show proficiency, have a choice of independent activities to engage in that have been previously discussed and agreed upon with the student (not necessarily time-filler activities, but a choice of things they enjoy engaging in that also respect the culture of the learning environment)
"Low-level disruptive" behaviours in class: including chatting to friends, saying silly things and playing with materials or tech devices without permission	• Ensure that there are ways for the student to feel they have some autonomy over what is being done in class by using a fidget or drawing as you teach, engaging in their own task that they find interesting. Students listen in lots of different ways • Try not to engage in these interruptions, *but* at the same time know they're a sign that anxiety is rising in the student and adjustments to their situation (or what you're doing) like start the activity (direct teaching has been long), add humour to diffuse the anxiety, take a movement break, or ask students who are still struggling to stay longer while others can get started
Needs to have a say in what they do or they will not engage in the tasks at all	• Have thought processes modelled through stories, role-play and video, or "accidentally" overheard or left to be seen independently by the student. These reduce the demands by having the student choose to engage while allowing space for their autonomy

Arrives late, not always ready on time with transitions, always excuses for this and/or not caring about it	• Be flexible around attendance or coming to class late. It's difficult for some students to convince themselves to be somewhere at a specific time as it can become a demand. When a student comes late to class, privately welcome them with a smile and let them know you appreciate their arrival
	• With things they really need to be on time for, negotiate with them in advance or give a different time that makes space for later arrivals
	• There will be different accommodations for students with this need than the rest of the class so creating an atmosphere of acceptance without judgement is important. It's about everyone having access to support when they need it, even if it looks different for everyone
Unpredictable in what work the student decides to do in class	• Give some time before they transition to the task for a movement break or to the **sensory bin**, then check in with them to see where they are ready to start first. Sometimes reducing the anxiety means managing sensory needs first
	• Leave options of tasks in the eye line of the student to begin when they feel ready to engage
Emotional outbursts can be very jarring and might include physical altercations or verbal assaults. Might have meltdowns that can harm themselves and others or include destroying property	• Choose very, very few non-negotiable rules that are clearly understood for why they are in place. Make these rules around their safety and that of others
	• Be prepared to negotiate on task or project expectations and offer choices more often. This doesn't mean that you can't request deadlines or ask for specific things to be completed, but it'll be easier to do this while collaborating with the student so that they feel a sense of fairness and reciprocity in the process
	• Closely track their reactions. They might have their own unique pattern of emotional dysregulation that will tell you when they're approaching capacity. However, this can escalate at any given time and for any reason. It's better to notice the resistance and give them space to come to you while you self-regulate and decide whether this is worth pursuing when the student is more regulated
	• For some students with co-occurring conditions and neurodivergence, their capacity doesn't reset each day, creating cumulative stress. Monitoring ADHD presentations and emotional needs could suggest that other interventions might be necessary beyond what's currently available
	• Having a good school day doesn't automatically mean that the next day will be amazing and you've turned a corner. In fact, the next day might actually be even worse than normal. Be prepared for the days following that great one for the student to need more support than normal rather than less, as a way to recover

Table 4.1 (*Continued*)

Often becomes moody	• Track periods of moodiness to notice any triggers or patterns (times of day, week, certain people, situations, etc.). Consider if any physical needs (for example, tiredness or hunger) could be addressed and be in contact with their parents/carers for any changes in their day that might be impacting them
	• Humour and distraction can be used for managing tension with growing anxiety
Ignores requests and can become argumentative towards teachers or peers when asked to do something	• Include some *demand-free* time to help them self-regulate in order to handle more requests throughout the rest of the day. This might look like being in a space where they will not be disturbed for a certain amount of time and are allowed to do what they need
Can be "bossy" towards peers and appear unempathetic towards them	• Encourage learning about the needs of others through stories, watching others and role-playing – indirectly, but specifically about how to work with others and manage coping strategies to better interact with others
	• Model different responses to situations that are bringing up the bossiness. They may not participate in class discussions on the topic but it doesn't mean that they aren't listening either
	• Even when some students may appear to be more socially aware, it doesn't mean they are and can always benefit from direct teaching of skills and opportunities to practice them in real situations

When ADHD co-occurs with pathological demand avoidance

It was when Dhruv was coming off another school suspension in as many schools he'd attended that his parents were fortunate enough to finally find someone who knew about pathological demand avoidance (PDA). This changed everything we thought we knew about Dhruv's behaviour, because it became clear to us that it was the PDA presentations we had to learn more about supporting first. But in many ways, supporting Dhruv's co-occurring PDA would offer support in other areas he was struggling with too.

PDA is characterised by an intense fear of losing one's autonomy. It's so strong it overrides all other basic survival needs, which can include things like eating or hygiene, or even their own physical safety if they feel it's threatening their autonomy. What drives PDAers to avoid any and all demands placed on them (which includes demands that are implied, written or stated and internal demands they want or need to do for their own well-being), is finding a felt sense of safety. They spend their days constantly navigating what feels like threats to their lives

PDA learners experience demands in a cumulative way, so without effectively managing them, they start to have frequent meltdowns (or more accurately, panic

attacks) because they've become overwhelmed with fear. These can include saying or doing harmful and/or aggressive behaviours in order to regain the feeling
of equality and feel safer again. Over time, trying to navigate so many demands
leads to burnout, leaving them struggling to do anything for themselves (including
the bare minimum of self-care) until they begin recovering.

Ehrlich (November, 2022), describes PDA as "not behavioural or rooted in
demand avoidance, but about **neuroception** and the way the brain perceives safety
vs danger on a subconscious and automatic level". Essentially, the PDA student's
nervous system is extremely sensitive, and any perceived loss of autonomy or
equality sends them to react in a fight, flight, fawn or freeze response. Demands
feel that terrifying for them. Therefore, supporting PDA learners must include a
lot of co-regulation support to address their nervous system. They need to rebuild
capacity lost from dealing with the constant barrage of perceived threats to their
safety on a daily basis.

PDA and ADHD have many presentations that co-occur, including demand avoidance, but ADHD learners don't typically have *extreme* demand avoidance. Unlike
PDA children, ADHD children won't consistently avoid things they want or their
body tells them to do, like eat. ADHDers might get distracted and forget to eat,
but PDAers can "refuse" to eat even when food is directly in front of them and it's
clear they're hungry because they're haven't eaten all day. Although both children
might give a *socially acceptable* reason why they don't want to eat, the PDA child
won't necessarily change their mind because they're given what they want or their
favourite food. The same struggle could happen daily and at every meal too, even
if it's a food they know, love and eat often.

PDA also reveals more "typical autistic" presentations because they also
struggle with understanding social rules and expectations and cognitive inflexibility which often includes a need for routine. But unlike many autistic students,
PDAers can be very charismatic when you meet them, making it even more difficult to notice the gaps in their social understanding. It's when you start seeing
the challenges they have in maintaining relationships that their social struggles
become more apparent. PDA learners need some of the same support you might
give to ADHD and/or autistic students, but I think the focus on supporting their
neuroception in order to increase their sense of safety takes priority.

Although PDA is considered a profile of autism, recent studies have suggested
that it also might be more predictable to find PDA if someone has ADHD too. This
suggests that "personality constructs such as low emotional stability, behaviours
associated with personality disorder, and ADHD predict self-reported PDA better than
do measures that broadly screen for autism" (Egan, Bull, and Trundle, 2020). For
PDA students, having unmanaged and unsupported ADHD could easily present as
an additional barrier for their access to learning. The impulse to avoid demands
would be very quick, distracting them from internal sensations that might provide
clues to meeting any biological need. But these discomforts when not initially met
would only return later, adding more anxiety and intensifying their demand. Supporting co-occurring ADHD would reduce some of the internal reactions created to avoid
demands, but not necessarily address the root of their problems. Quicker access to
the frontal lobe could help access more cognitive flexibility to interpret and respond
to demands, rather than avoiding because they're reacting through a limbic response,
but accommodations within their external environment would still be important.

In retrospect, it wasn't surprising to see that by mid-morning Dhruv was often already overwhelmed. His humming, singing and blurting out random words and phrases during direct teaching time encouraged me to quickly change to small-group instructions instead, thus giving him space to start the activities as he needed. By lunch, his head could be stuck to his desk because his eyes hurt. He might remain unmoved by any choice of activities to participate in, even though in previous classes deciding between activities worked fine. But I'd leave them there all the same for him to decide what he wanted to do. Towards the last lessons of the day, he'd give an excuse like his legs hurt so he couldn't move, making it impossible to go to music class. I'd sigh to myself as Dhruv stayed at his desk with me while my TA took the rest of the class to their lesson. I wasn't sure if what I was doing was helpful or not, but in time it occurred to me that if Dhruv was using made-up ailments to avoid something, it was often just best to let it go. After all, if more *socially acceptable* avoidant strategies weren't accessible to him at that moment, then he must have been terrified.

Reflect now

Think about some students you've worked with who weren't easily engaged in learning and you found difficult to connect with. How did that impact you emotionally, physically and mentally? What people, practices and beliefs did you have in place to support you to stay grounded and offer yourself grace through the most challenging moments? What do you tell yourself when you're struggling to connect with students? What systems and supports are (or could be) put in place in your school or learning environment to help foster more connection with learners who are struggling socially and/or emotionally?

A pervasive drive for autonomy

PDA students don't necessarily consider their need for autonomy and perceived equality over their environments and outcomes as pathological. For them, this can feel like life or death. Their fears of demands are rooted in their survival. This is why many PDAers don't consider themselves as being *pathological demand avoidant*, but rather have a *Pervasive Drive for Autonomy* instead. In order to keep their autonomy, PDA students utilise many social strategies to limit and avoid demands. These include procrastination, making excuses (some that can be nonsensical or very imaginative), ignoring requests, creating distractions and disruptions with noise or saying random words or changing the subject in conversation. They can be so masterful at this you might not catch they're avoiding demands at all.

Every PDA learner is different and shows their PDA presentations in a different way depending on their capacity for demands at the time. Demands accumulate, so keeping a close eye on how fast and intense their PDA presentations escalate is really important. We might interpret them as trying to control or manipulate a situation. When there is a threat to their autonomy, their PDA presentations help them equalise (or often referred to as leveling, a term, coined by Kristy Forbes) it so that their percieved sense of autonomy being equal to those around them is restored and their sense of safety returns. If we miss the signals that they are becoming more dysregulated through their subtle signs of equalisation and choose to engage in them because we are becoming upset with what we interpret as disruptions or attempts to "challenge our authority", their PDA presentations can quickly escalate and the subtlety disappears. This is when the situation can spiral into unmanageability. The more dysregulated (including unclear and inconsistent) we get, the more panicked they can become. They perceive through *our reaction* that their autonomy really *has* been taken and therefore they must equalise with us in order to have the same autonomy as us. If they perceive that all autonomy is lost, they react as if their lives are in danger and they will go into fight, flight or freeze in order to do whatever it takes to get it back.

In schools, demands are everywhere, from everyone and written all over the place, so these students are constantly under threat. They stay hypervigilant about their autonomy by trying to avoid demands. PDA is often described as an "anxiety-driven need for control", but when we consider it from a lens of just anxiety, we're missing how disabling PDA actually is. Ehrlich (2022) suggests that when we look to just reduce anxiety, we're not considering the way that the nervous system is wired to find a loss of autonomy threatening. This isn't just something that is happening in their head. If it was, then they wouldn't automatically react to any demand they're presented with. They are experiencing these threats in their bodies and that experience is stimulated by what the PDA learner perceives from the environment around them. It is extremely difficult to learn in an environment where you constantly feel under threat, which is why many PDA students end up school avoiders or simply being excluded altogether because they are constantly acting out.

Even when as educators we can't see or understand the threat of a loss of autonomy for these students, it doesn't make it any less real for them. Traditional ways of managing behaviour don't work for these students because they're based on our attempts to modify their behaviour, thus taking away their autonomy when we do. Giving rewards and punishments or complimenting the behaviour we want to see are all subtle ways we condition students to abide by our rules of the space too. They take away students' autonomy by implying what they must do (which is a demand), in order to fit into our expectations. We need to build learning environments that reduce the PDA students' demands by giving them more autonomy over the space they learn in, what they learn and how they learn it. This doesn't mean that they don't have any rules, but rather that rules are limited to a few non-negotiables that ensure their safety and that of others, rules that they can understand the need for and agree with too. We also can include regular "demand-free times", which is a place for our PDA learners to do whatever they want in order (and often with someone they trust to stand by as co-regulation support) to rebuild some capacity from the cumulative demands. This can support their ability to engage in the classroom a little easier later on in the day.

But a bigger shift needs to happen in the way we think about teaching and learning too. One that is in collaboration with students and fosters autonomy.

Developing learner autonomy

Schools were never designed with children's needs in mind. Initially, education was aimed at communal socialisation as dictated by people in authority. This meant encouraging attitudes, behaviours and habits that worked towards communal survival during difficult times when there were few resources, all while never having to rationalise the decisions taken (Bangera, March 2017). With the Industrial Revolution in the nineteenth century, education aims changed but still in response to what society needed at that time. It wanted children who would grow up to be adults that could do what they were told and have predictable skills that would continue to serve society.

Much of education is still the same today and yet the world children are arriving in is nothing like the eighteenth century. Education was never about the needs of the children. In order to meet the demands of a world that is constantly changing, education needs to "to producing individuals who demonstrate independence in thought and action, think rationally, and are capable of critical participation in the societies they live in" (Bangera, March 2017). This happens when we create learning environments that foster autonomy.

Learner autonomy is characterised by students taking more responsibility and ownership over their learning. Rather than the teacher or curriculum driving education experiences, students partner in the learning process with the educator, having a say in what to learn and how, and the speed at which to learn it. It forces teachers to rethink their role in the classroom by creating learning environments and giving access to learning experiences that facilitate more student input. Educators consider how they can guide and support students in finding resources while developing the skills and attitudes they might need to further take more responsibility for their learning. Autonomous learning isn't about students being free to do nothing or having to teach themselves all the time. It's about whether learning is controlled by the learner. Teachers do this by helping students to "develop the ability to have certain control over their learning, through modelling and providing practice, and by boosting their feeling of motivation and self-confidence to engage successfully in its process" (Djoub, January 2022), through providing "wise, actionable feedback" (Hammond, 2014).

Intersectional insight: Eurocentric education

Many schools are impacted by education that's been "founded on principles of **colonialism** which continue to centre on Eurocentric knowledge and theories of teaching and learning, leaving out the diverse knowledge of Black, Indigenous, and other marginalized communities" (Ugwuegbula, 2020). This looks like centring the history and knowledge of whiteness while excluding Black, Brown, Asian, Indigenous Peoples and other marginalised communities. This perpetuates racism and **white supremacy culture** and creates a lack of belonging and connection for these students in their learning environments. "Feelings of isolation, shame, and disconnection ensue, leading to significant detrimental impacts on their future social, economic, and political opportunities" (Ugwuegbula, 2020). These feelings and learning outcomes can only be increased in the populations of marginalised ADHD students. They are continually reminded how they don't truly belong in most classrooms and must always emotionally regulate this understanding in ways that don't result in further consequences for them.

ADHD students learn in ways that are rarely conducive to contemporary education practices. Executive functioning developmental delays make it more challenging to access the skills necessary for learning within these linear expectations of time and achievement. But that doesn't mean that these students don't work well with more autonomy or that it isn't necessary either. On the contrary, ADHD learners achieve very well when given the opportunity to work on meaningful tasks and learning experiences with flexibility to engage in ways that work for them. These students need carefully facilitated learning experiences to feel willing to learn. This supports them in developing the skills to grow into lifelong learners who understand how to collaborate with others and develop strong problem-solving and critical-thinking skills – tools that will help them in today's society.

Like all students, ADHD students need to discover what effective learning looks like for them. They need support in developing the confidence to be who they are while learning what tools or resources they need in order to be at their best. ADHD children can't grow into the adults they want to be by being told what they are doing wrong all the time and how they must change who they are in order to be *acceptable*. Instead, they need to learn in trauma-informed, equity-centred, culturally responsive learning environments. These are the spaces that foster belonging and collaboration, encourage empowerment, allow for flexibility and provide predictability. They give students the chance to learn what it means to be themselves through building meaningful connections with others.

Reflect now

What beliefs, fears or possible misconceptions do you have when it comes to understanding learner autonomy? How does your comfort level of being a collaborator with students change based on their race, gender, ability and socio-economic status? What kinds of changes in your beliefs, skills, organisation and planning would have to be made in order to move your teaching practice towards more learner autonomy?

Although I was still quite anxious about Dhruv's well-being, at least now I had something of a plan. If I truly believed that his need for autonomy was about survival, then I had to give him autonomy over what and how he learned too. In short, I needed to completely back off of my expectations for his learning and be flexible with how he saw his learning to be. I could collaborate with Dhruv on what we felt might be important to learn and how to share his learning. I could still introduce helpful skills, model my thinking, observe what he was studying and share social stories to support him, but I had to trust that together we could help him learn what he felt necessary to learn.

Dhruv had finally managed to come to school for the first time in weeks but arrived a lot later than start time. He came in making silly noises, which made some of the students giggle, but I had learned by this point to ignore it. Although the rest of the class could get easily caught up in the distractions, I noticed my own ability to quickly disengage from it and continue with the task at hand was helping the rest of the class do the same.

"I'm glad you're here", I told him as he came in with his bag and placed it by his chair. He completely disregarded the pegs where students were normally expected to hang up their belongings. Instead, he placed it on the floor in between two tables, making it difficult for me to manoeuvre to get to another student. He kept his jacket on. I smiled at him as I gently attempted to move the bag aside.

"Let's just move this over –"

"I need it" he abruptly cut me off. I could sense the anxiety in his voice and felt my own anxiety already rising, but something in me knew that this wasn't worth fighting over. The class fell silent as they looked at me to see what I'd do next. I took a breath and looked over my shoulder to the other students.

"There's no need to stop what you're doing", I reminded them, "You know what you've planned for today." They proceeded to whisper quietly amongst themselves as they continued their tasks. They knew that he had different needs to feel comfortable in the class and were learning to accept that. I quietly dropped the bag and continued to my final destination. When I came back, the bag had been moved aside.

I said nothing but breathed a barely audible sigh of relief as I placed the task in the centre of the table, leaving Dhruv to engage if he chose. After mentioning to the students at his table that I would be around to check in on them or at my desk if they needed me, I went to the next group of students. Dhruv took a few minutes to look around the classroom before reaching towards the middle of the table. He already knew what we'd be doing this week and might not engage with it, but even looking at it was a start.

Intersectional insight: PDA or oppositional defiant disorder?

There isn't a lot of data on Black, Brown and Indigenous children with pathological demand avoidance (PDA). Instead, these children have disproportionate rates of oppositional defiant disorder (ODD), conduct disorders or anti-social diagnoses over white children who exhibit behaviours similar to PDA. Baglivio, Wolff, Piquero, et al. (2016) suggest that "Black males are 40 % more likely, while Black females are 54 % more likely, to be diagnosed with conduct disorder than white people, even upon considerations of trauma, behavioural indicators, and criminal offending. Black and Latine males are approximately 40 % less likely to be diagnosed with ADHD than white males". With assessment criteria for both ADHD and autism initially normed for white, male-presenting children leading to their disproportionate diagnosing, perhaps it's also no coincidence that Black male-presenting children were disproportionately diagnosed with ODD without ever any thought of PDA either. I often wonder how many Black, Brown or Indigenous PDA learners have developed what Sally Cat has coined as Internalized PDA so that they can move safer in society (see the Resources to explore after this chapter).

Supporting Dhruv

Dhruv was slowly coming out of the challenges he'd found himself in earlier during the school year. With a parent who could work from home and permission from the school, we were fortunate enough to begin a flexible schooling timetable. Dhruv would come to school most mornings with the freedom to decide what lessons he'd engage in or whether he'd attend any classes beyond my own. He came to school with the food he liked and allowed me to put it on his table for easy access to reduce some physical demands. Some days he'd even do it himself. The more we both learned about how his brain worked, the easier it was for us to collaborate on what was most helpful for him.

Break times became a choice of staying indoors alone on his iPad or outdoors with a couple of trusted friends that he seemed better able to manage being around. It was still delicate work for all of us, but I can imagine it was even more challenging for Dhruv. We never knew how anxious he'd feel each day or what learning activities he'd be capable of doing. I'd closely monitor his PDA presentations, watching for any sign of his equalising or levelling reactions. I knew that the more I could reduce the demands (those were his main barriers to learning), the more he came to classes, the longer he'd stay in class and the more he would find his own way to engage in learning.

Dhruv still hadn't gone to many classes outside my own for over a month. The option was always available to him, but he just didn't have the capacity for it. During those times we sat in silence, each working on our own things. Sometimes Dhruv would chat with me about things he found interesting or funny. I would stop what I was doing and talk with him; sometimes I could mention things that I did to solve learning or social problems he was dealing with but through stories that connected to myself or someone I knew. It was important that I remained calm and thoughtful with my choice of words and tone.

Careful to keep the topic to what he wanted to discuss.

Careful to engage as authentically in the conversation as I could.

Careful to follow his lead on how little or how much he wanted to engage.

When I got the chance to talk with him I recognised that whether he was doing what I invited him to do in classes or not, he was still learning. It was clear that Dhruv was listening when given the space to work as he needed. His learning needs asked me to rethink everything I thought I knew and understood about teaching and learning. Some days when he seemed more at ease, you could see glimpses of the kid he really was – the one that was curious, insightful and eager to help when he could. It reminded me that Dhruv belonged in the learning environment too just like everyone else.

And he belonged there exactly as he was.

Key takeaways:

- **Biracial** students have their own unique struggles to the classroom each day including experiences of microaggressions, discrimination and erasure of parts of their racial identities. They then attend lessons where they experience being made invisible in the curriculum, impacting their mental health and well-being.
- Pathological demand avoidance (or pervasive drive for autonomy) is often considered a profile of autism that can frequently co-occur with ADHD. It is characterised by an intense fear of losing one's autonomy over any other basic need and results in fight, flight or freeze responses in order to avoid any and all demands (including their own).
- Cognitive flexibility is about being adaptable to changes that happen in the environment and ADHD learners typically need support in feeling safe enough to deal with change effectively.
- Developing learner autonomy doesn't mean allowing students to do whatever they want or nothing at all, but how much of the learning is controlled by the learner.
- The education system is based on Eurocentric ideas of **white supremacy** and was never made with the needs of children in mind. Instead, it aimed to train children to grow up to take a role in the survival of society and within it these ideas.

Resources to explore

Pathological Demand Avoidance (PDA):

The Educator's Experience of Pathological Demand Avoidance by Laura Kerbey and Eliza Fricker

PDA Society: www.pdasociety.org.uk/

At Peace Parents Podcast by Dr Casey Ehrlich: www.atpeaceparents.com/

PDA by PDAers: From Anxiety to Avoidance and Masking to Meltdowns by Sally Cat. Website includes resources on Internalised PDA: www.sallycatpda.co.uk/

Declarative language

Declarative Language Handbook: Using a Thoughtful Language Style to Help Kids with Social Learning Challenges Feel Competent, Connected, and Understood by Linda K. Murphy

Biracial/multiracial

Biracial Britain: What It Means To Be Mixed Race by Remi Adekoya
The Mixed-Race Experience: Reflections and Revelations on Multicultural Identity by Natalie Evans and Naomi Evans

5

"He can't do anything by himself!":

Simon's story

This chapter asks us to reflect on:

- the overlap between inattentive ADHD and "sluggish cognitive tempo";
- how writing challenges and dysgraphia overlap with ADHD;
- inattentive ADHD and its interpretations for **whiteness** and male-presenting students;
- supporting ADHD (and) dependent learners by decreasing learned helplessness;
- moving through a blame culture learning environment to one of radical responsibility and community care.

"I want to be able to do my homework myself, but I'm afraid that I won't be able to without help … again." Simon sighed after hearing my suggestion that we start to attempt some homework soon. We were chatting together briefly while I was on break duty, reflecting on the progress he'd made over the year and how he demonstrated those changes in a recently completed project. It was one that he not only did independently but that also showed his developing problem-solving, planning and task-initiation skills. I knew he was anxious about the impending possibility of doing his homework independently and yet desperately wanted to know he could.

Quite frankly, I was nervous too. I knew the last thing either of us wanted was to go back to where we started when no learning activities were being attempted without continual prompting and check-ins by the closest adult to him. We'd come a long way since then and Simon's confidence as a learner was growing and it had taken lots of patience, calculated risks and resilience to get there. Initially, Simon struggled with the weight of the labels placed on him about who he was a student, but he was finally at a place where he could see himself very differently. The question was whether Simon was ready to trust the abilities he'd recently rediscovered in himself now too.

Meet Simon:

- 9 years old, white, European ancestry
- identifies as a boy
- **emergent bilingual** with stronger communication in the language of instruction than his **home language**
- easy-going, insightful, imaginative
- loves: drawing, video games, travelling
- detests: maths, writing, being put on the spot
- future aspirations: anything to do with animation or designing buildings
- best known for zoning out in classes, being a slow-working, dependent learner
- learning challenges: handwriting difficulties
- additional information: quiet and agreeable

At the start of every school year, I always find myself awkwardly straddling a fine line between how much I need to learn about my students from the previous year's teacher and taking time to get to know them on my own first. I always wonder how long I should wait to give them a chance to settle into their new class with me versus how much I should learn about them before the year starts. It can be a very precarious balance. Ideally, I want to allow every student a fresh start and offer them the benefit of the doubt from anything that might have happened the previous year. I don't know what they've gone through over the summer, how they've changed or grown. I don't know how any learning challenges have changed how they see themselves either. I want to see them as they are now, without the filter of someone else's experience hanging over them and any biases that come with it.

When they come to me with labels placed on them by others, I know it can influence how I see and interact with them, whether intentional or not. But I don't know what labels they're hoping to keep themselves, new ones they're hoping to adopt, or the ones they want to transform or desperately hope to throw away either. It doesn't help me if I'm completely lost about a student, but it also doesn't help to decide who they are before we get to know each other either. This year with Simon started with me being overwhelmed as a new teacher to a new grade level and I needed all the help I could get. Unfortunately for him, I found myself taking on all the information about my students I could without stopping to question any of it. Especially when it came to those children whose teachers had a lot of concerns about.

Simon was at the top of the list.

The overwhelming consensus about him from all his previous teachers and support staff was pretty much the same,

"He can't do *anything* on his own!"

"He's never paying attention …"

"You *always* have to sit with him or he won't do *anything* you give him …"

"It's because his parents do *everything* for him …"

"He's got *the worst case* of learned helplessness I've ever seen …"

It was clear to *everyone* that it was either Simon's and/or his parents' fault that he couldn't do what was expected of him. But with the blame placed squarely on his shoulders, it initially felt like there wasn't much that I could do for him either.

Blaming someone can insinuate that now that the "*blamed* person" knows what they've done, they'll know how to do better next time (or they'll do what they've been told in order to solve it). But it can also insinuate that the "*blaming* person" doesn't have a role in the situation and therefore no responsibility in changing it. We have a responsibility in how we choose to respond to being blamed but I think we have to consider when we find ourselves using it too. Blame is easily weaponised depending on who's using it and who it's aimed towards; it can disempower us and others while hiding the real problems that need to be addressed instead.

Living in a blame culture

It's no accident that blame is used in school when things aren't going as expected and students aren't achieving as we've been told they should. We blame teachers, the parents, the administration or the school district or the school system itself. We blame ourselves too. But quite often the blame falls squarely on the struggling student. When they're not "putting in the effort", or being over-reactive or repeatedly not meeting expectations we set for them, they become the problem, and we're not. Blame is everywhere in this society and with it comes a lot of shame and guilt. These are two emotions that (even when hidden under other emotions like anger or frustration) can keep us stuck, feeling disempowered from taking actions that are within our capacity towards making change.

We live in a world where the messages we receive from our families, our schools, our friends, our jobs and in the media tell us that when we can't live up to the demands of the social norms and if we can't do so perfectly, it is our fault and therefore we're not worthy or enough. This leaves us fearful of making mistakes because of what they might mean for us if we're seen as being the problem. To protect ourselves, we learn to see others as the problem rather than risk being seen so ourselves. But blame helps to hide the real problems we're all facing too.

The problems in school aren't necessarily the teachers, the administration, the parents and certainly *not* the students, but are rooted in the oppressive culture that underlies our school systems, the **dominant culture** of **white supremacy**.

With so many messages in society blaming us, shaming us and telling us why we're inherently a problem when we *do* mess up or we don't perform perfectly, we learn there's no both/and of a situation. Therefore, we can't see failure as stepping stones to success, or lessons we could gain from making mistakes. The message becomes: "If we can't succeed, then we fail. And if we fail, we're not enough." Either we risk being thrown away or (in an effort to save ourselves), we must throw away others. Our experiences are simplified into either/or, right or wrong. Good or bad. Worthy or not.

And we risk rejection any time we can't conform and do so exactly as expected.

Our school systems breed environments where everyone's worth is on the line, and for ADHD learners the risk feels particularly high and they can struggle to regulate it. The "consistently inconsistent" challenges in school with attention and focus, movements that aren't socially appropriate to the task they're working on or communicating in ways that aren't socially acceptable have them constantly at risk of being blamed for their behaviour and then risk rejection or exclusion for it. ADHD learners often struggle to regulate emotions, but the emotion that tends to bring up a lot of dysregulation is the real or perceived feeling of rejection. When the threat of rejection happens, ADHDers can easily become **emotionally flooded**, which is usually seen as *socially unacceptable*. But avoiding the threat of rejection could also look like shutting down or procrastinating, both of which carry meanings about our ability be a productive member of society that could lead to rejection too. Depending on the social identity markers you hold, all of these reactions can have varying consequences for how you're accepted by others, or not.

As teachers, if our students don't perform well on the standardised tests or achieve the magical, forever changing, arbitrary goal of potential (that in actuality is some version of perfection that no student could actually touch it, let alone achieve it – nor could we as educators ever teach well enough to have them meet it), we risk rejection. Parents, who if their children don't come to school as absolute perfection, are not parenting well enough. Admins who don't listen enough, discipline too much or not enough, and demand too much or not enough will inevitably fail too. The list goes on and on. School systems are designed to ensure that none of us truly stand a chance of being successful as we are because the aim is for us to change to conform to the expectations of the **dominant culture**. There will always be someone else doing things better than we do, and when things don't go as expected, there will always be something or someone that can be blamed, all while the oppressive systems created by the **dominant culture** remain the same.

The threat of blame influences the ways that our actions as teachers are interpreted too, depending on the social identity markers we carry and the kinds of environment we're working in. As a Black teacher working with a predominately white teaching staff, it's important to remember how closely Black, Brown and Indigenous Peoples are monitored in workplaces for mistakes and how quickly we're blamed and punished when they happen. These kinds of situations mean we regularly work under extra pressure to be *beyond perfect*, because we have spent our whole lives being closely watched in schools while being allowed much less grace for our mistakes than the white people around us. But if we make changes and things go well, the praise is often given to the individuals in charge (who are predominately white men or in schools, white women), rather than groups more marginalised too. These dynamics make school environments inherently unsafe for marginalised teachers.

White supremacy culture conditions us all to believe that if we just did everything right (read: perfectly), as teachers, students, administrators, parents/carers and support staff, we'd be considered good enough and wouldn't be rejected from the group. If we can't prove that we're enough, then we find others that we consider as "less than enough" and therefore should be rejected instead of us. When we as teachers are already blamed for every failure that happens in the classroom, while being overworked, undervalued and juggling excess demands like social-emotional needs, well-being, career counselling, coaching and mediation (many of these jobs weren't even part of the job description when we signed on to be teachers), the options to avoid blame feel very limited. We're already doing as much as we can and addressing specific needs like ADHD become an additional task to an already overwhelming workload.

Blame also tries to tell us that when we make mistakes or do harmful things towards others, we must independently work to make things right. Since we must be the singular problem, we must be the singular solution. We don't learn about how being in a community can support us, including being held accountable when we make mistakes. Accountability is how we support each other to be our best selves. Our work as educators is not easy and we will mess up (and mess up often) and so will those people we choose in the community with us. We can't be at our best when we're forced into rejection and isolation. We are interdependent and need each other. It's in our communities that we don't need to have all the answers, we get support in learning from our mistakes and it's safe enough to acknowledge where we can do better. Blame insists that our safety means keeping ourselves far from those who have done wrong, but community care teaches us the compassion in realising that we don't automatically need to be thrown away or throw others away when mistakes are made. Blame tries to tell us that it's either them, or us, but interdependence and community shows us that we can all be better when we work together.

We teach within the **dominant culture**'s realms of all or nothing and either–or thinking, all while the roots of the problems in schools remain hidden. Problems like the inequities of the systems that show up as racism, sexism, **transphobia** and transmisogyny, classism and **ableism** amongst others all create varying degrees of barriers to education. People focus on their own challenges within the system (remember, not all oppression has the same weight when considering a person's proximity to power in society), and tightly grip hold of the privilege they have while fearing how it could be taken from them. White guilt in having unearned privilege keeps people from using it to support those who are more marginalised. Blame makes sure the problem doesn't have to be us and ensures that we see ourselves *completely* separate from it. Then we don't have to take any responsibility for how we're causing harm (either intentionally or not), while remaining disconnected from our communities that could help us work towards any accountability to do better. Then nothing around us truly changes – just as **white supremacy culture** intended.

It wasn't surprising that blaming Simon hadn't worked to support him. It also wasn't surprising that the strategies that had been used for him in the past weren't very effective either. Neither option considered other possibilities that might be creating barriers to his learning besides himself. When a student becomes labelled as "the problem", the solutions revolve around trying to get them to change their behaviour. But expecting a student to change themselves when they fear any mistake they make can only bring further humiliation, criticism or rejection (all of which the ADHD brain interprets as a threat, causing more dysregulation), is not going to be an easy change to make.

Reflect now

Where do I find myself using blame towards myself and others in my learning environment? What solutions might I be missing or not willing to engage with because the real problems can stay hidden under the blame? How am I learning to take responsibility for what is mine that I can control while remembering not to take on what isn't and ask for help or simply let it go? How am I learning to build and/or lean more into the support of a caring community when I struggle in my classroom or learning environments?

Simon and I weren't having a great day.

We were just over a month into the school year and I was already worn out. Although something in me knew that in order for Simon to even *attempt* any of the set tasks, I needed to get him to trust me, I wasn't always exuding calm and patience. On good days, I could work within his capacity (which was him doing next to nothing as he stared into the void, oftentimes fighting to stay awake), while trying not to feel *too* anxious about it.

But today I was impatient. I'd been working for weeks on Simon and we weren't connecting at all. In fact, I'd say that it was becoming a power struggle. The more I tried to force him to do things, the less he did.

I wasn't just losing, I was also losing him.

I had already been through these interactions enough to know where things were going. But on this day, I couldn't let it go. I should have asked him what made it difficult for him to do this activity. I should have given a couple of suggestions for the kind of help I could give him. At the very least, I should have apologised for my impatience. I could have done almost anything else that would have been much better than what I actually did next.

But I didn't.

Learned helplessness as a trauma response

Simon had a history of difficult experiences from his previous school. Often feeling humiliated by his teacher and unable to communicate his needs as effectively as his peers, he slowly began to retreat into himself. School expectations became too much for his nervous system to handle and he was most likely traumatised by school because of it (see Ameera's story for more on trauma). Learned helplessness "exists when individuals believe that their own behaviour has no influence on consequent events" (Seligman, 1975). What behaviour we noticed in Simon was not a choice, but a reaction his body created in order to survive what it perceived as a threat. Simon wasn't able to access many of the executive functioning skills necessary to learn at the moment because he needed to *feel safe* first. Even the idea of attempting any learning in school felt threatening to his body and dysregulated his nervous system enough to repeatedly shut down. The learned helplessness had taken over and the executive functioning developmental delay with ADHD (alongside some other co-occurring conditions he might have had) only added to the difficulty he was experiencing engaging in lessons.

Students feeling helplessness are frequently depressed or anxious because of how they witness their attempts to make changes to their situations always ending in failure. Soon, they don't believe they are capable of getting anything right, no matter what they try. Since the repeated efforts to achieve keep resulting in disappointment, it only adds to their evidence that what they believe about themselves and their powerlessness in the situation is true. At the same time, if they stop trying to change things, they continue to fail, becoming more anxious or depressed. This ends with the student feeling even more helpless and even less driven to make change. It gives them a continued reason to believe that their efforts will never be recognised and therefore they have no power to change their cycle of failure.

At school, the *important* learning activities are often not chosen by the students but by the adults around them. This adds pressure on the student to find success in the task and can lead to them feeling worse if they believe their efforts will never be considered good enough. Ross Greene (2021) says, "children will do better when they can" and that "behaviourally challenging kids are challenging because they're lacking the skills to not be challenging". There are many different reasons why a child can't do what is expected of them, whether it's cognitive, emotional, social or physical skills lacking or a need that hasn't been met. When we can isolate those skills or unmet needs, we open the door to locating alternative possibilities for support.

There's also the added sense of threat for students if they feel they can't do what's expected. For ADHD learners, whose focus is naturally drawn to what they sense is threatening in their environment, their ADHD presentations can become even more prominent. When they sense the possibility of failure (even if it is perceived), restlessness, distraction, zoning out or shutting down completely become protective mechanisms. This makes it more difficult to access the thinking part of their brain necessary to make different choices in the face of feeling uncertain or worried about a task. Failure often comes alongside feelings of blame and shame that could lead to a threat of exclusion or rejection too. The brain, particularly an ADHD one, wants to do anything it can to protect itself from those threats.

We have expectations of students for the kind of behaviour that doesn't always come easily or naturally to those who might have developmental delays in executive functioning skills. These are the skills needed for children to become what educators have learned to perceive as "good students". They help learners self-regulate in ways that are expected and allow them to reflect on the different perspectives that could influence their actions to better align with what's expected. These skills helps students control their initial reactions and respond to *doing what they're told*. They build the self-directed behaviour necessary to complete what students have been told are "important" activities, efficiently, accurately and within the allotted time. But for many ADHD learners, until these skills are directly taught and modelled, and support is scaffolded and done over a significant amount of time, they're not going to regularly choose to utilise them. At least not until they remember them and then feel safe enough to try them in the moment. That's where I was mistaken with Simon. I'd interpreted his behaviour as something he chose to do and could change if he just tried hard enough. I never understood that he was already doing the best he could.

Looking beyond the learned helplessness

Simon and I went outside the classroom for a chat. I felt my voice getting more and more animated with every sentence.

"Simon", I began. "We've been working for 15 minutes now and you haven't written or drawn a thing!" His head went down as I continued. "In fact, you never write anything. You barely do anything! How does it feel to have people do your schoolwork for you? All. The. Time."

He looked straight up at me and spoke without a single hesitation. "Terrible. I feel terrible."

That stopped me in my tracks and it was at that moment that I found him again.

This worn-out, fed-up, dark-haired, little white boy was hidden behind all these ADHD presentations. He let out a barely audible sigh like he had the weight of the world on his shoulders. As if I was just another teacher who put it there. He had given up on me and I had given him every reason to. At that moment, I knew I was completely and utterly wrong. Wrong about what I thought I knew about learned helplessness. Wrong about what I thought when I observed Simon too. Learned helplessness might have been a huge barrier to accessing learning, but it was also his body's way of protecting him.

Simon's inattentive ADHD presentations were making it incredibly difficult for him. His inability to access more of his thinking brain to regulate himself in the ways he was expected to appear in class (alert and calmly engaged) were being blocked by his body's instinctive reactions to manage his discomfort. This is why he would automatically zone out, daydream and repeatedly shut down (seen in his drowsiness) instead. Engaging in any ADHD regulation strategies that might support his learning meant not only supporting his learned helplessness but also introducing him to other self-regulation strategies. The ones he currently used kept him closed off and waiting for the nearest adult to step in, set lower expectations and then do the work for him. They were continuing to destroy his self-esteem and confidence. He wasn't effectively learning anything.

This is what kept him safe in the classroom and anything beyond that was way beyond his current comfort zone. I needed to help him break his cycle of learned helplessness by designing more learning activities where he had some choice and could see himself completing them. It would take baby steps, he would definitely do less than what others would, but it didn't mean that he would do less challenging or thoughtful work. He needed to believe again that any attempt he made, no matter how big or small, would always be enough, and that he could trust in that too.

Otherwise, all I was doing was creating another dependent learner.

Dependent learners and ADHD

Although the term *dependent learner* comes from describing the achievement gap, it also became evident to describe some of what Simon might have been going through. The achievement gap comes about from educators having lower expectations for what their most marginalised students could achieve – they rely on lectures, textbooks and worksheets to drive their curriculum without considering their students' differences, needs and interests. It creates a situation where those with unequal opportunity to access high-quality curriculum, more experienced teachers or having to learn in larger class sizes end up becoming dependent learners. These learners lack higher critical thinking and reasoning skills for deep learning and depend on their "teachers [to] do most of the heavy intellectual lifting, and through direct instruction, tell students what they need to know" (Haberman, 1991).

These students become trapped in a cycle of busy work with little intellectual or personal satisfaction attached, leaving them unsure of how to tackle unfamiliar tasks or problems. They're also continually underestimated in their abilities. Without engaging in learning that creates a productive struggle, they don't develop the skills and brain power necessary to become independent learners. Essentially, they don't learn how to learn. Over time the gap between learners increases, creating more frustration and shame for the students who see that they're falling behind. This leads to "behaviour problems" in class, which means for the predominately Black and Brown students who are the most impacted, more trips to the administrators' office, further taking away their learning time. It's the process of creating dependent learners that starts the **school-to-prison pipeline**.

Being a dependent learner doesn't necessarily mean a student can't learn to do high-level thinking tasks if given the chance to learn how to engage in them. In fact, learning gaps start off quite small when all children start school. It's the educator's beliefs about the student's ability that widen them by keeping these students from being introduced to higher-order intellectual tasks. Instead, they teach easier and more repetitive tasks, which reduces academic rigour (Hammond, 2014). Simon might have dealt with lowered expectations but I can see how many ADHD students would end up in this situation too. In fact, I'd bet that a lot of ADHD students end up with lowered expectations and start to experience (learned) helplessness simply because of all the ways their efforts to change go unnoticed because their ADHD presentations are used to define their efforts rather than a sign of needing support.

Emotional dysregulation and the intensity of their emotions would make it more challenging for ADHD students to regulate feelings of helplessness, depression and anxiety too. With the added complication of delayed executive functioning, trying to pause and consider alternatives to their familiar reactions (that are also ADHD presentations) would also require additional support. When working with dependent learners to develop their capacity for independent learning, Hammond (2014) suggests that we need to be building a partnership with our students, creating a plan with them while providing actionable feedback and understanding where they're starting from and what they want to be as learners. ADHD students need the same sorts of support because engaging in higher-order thinking means scaffolding in using executive functioning skills too. ADHD doesn't impact intelligence, meaning these students have the capability to learn how to learn. We just have to provide opportunities for them to practise engaging in higher-order thinking skills alongside the necessary support.

ADHD Support: working memory and reducing learned helplessness

If anyone were to tell me that Simon had ADHD, I wouldn't have believed them. Simon was nothing like the white boys who couldn't sit still, interrupted lessons, talked non-stop and ran around the classroom without a care for others. Simon was gentle and quiet. You could forget he was in the class if you weren't careful. He was *nothing* like what I thought ADHD looked like. Considering the additional presentations that I noticed, but didn't know what caused them, I thought it best to focus support on an area I'd noticed him struggling with most: working memory.

Like many ADHD learners who manage co-occurring neurodivergence, their energy can be easily drained when the cognitive load is too high. Supporting working memory is one way I could help manage energy. This decision also allowed me to help Simon through the learned helplessness too. Since I was making intentional choices about where I needed most of his energy, that meant making sure that the more challenging activities for him were highly scaffolded and planned during his best times of the day. Coupled with more flexibility and time with learning activities he felt most confident with or could help others, it would allow him to practise where his natural talents could be of use in the more difficult tasks he did too.

Table 5.1 ADHD support: working memory and reducing learned helplessness

Working memory The ability to hold key information in our mind to be used to complete more complex tasks. We can also retrieve learning experiences from the past to inform what we do in the present and in the future. Supporting a student with working memory challenges would include compensatory and recall strategies as well as utilising external aids

Possible ADHD presentations	Possible accommodations
Struggles to follow a sequence of steps, verbal instructions (even when reminded multiple times)	• Giving instructions simply, step by step, one material at a time, with visual aids and examples when possible • Have students reflect on what they heard in the instructions while you fill in any missing information • Present smaller parts of the project or learning at a time. Allow for self-regulation breaks and processing time in between each part or new knowledge • Allow for extra time to review
Needs more repetition and time for processing information	• Include opportunities to engage in various memory games to provide access to more memorisation strategies • Introduce new topics in advance. Include visual ways to learn • Reduce how much the student must learn at one time and repeat using a multisensory approach
Gets lost in one detail of the instructions	• Keep instructions clearly ordered and always accessible in the same places (both, in class or in assignments) so they're easy to refer to • Reduce the amount of work that would impact the working memory
Struggles to infer or make connections to prior knowledge	• Connect to the learner's prior knowledge and consider their cultural background and lived experiences when doing so • Teach concepts in multisensory forms and including using visuals that support a student's ability to correlate to the new information
Misses steps to a project or not showing the work done to complete a task, skipping words	• Give students the bare minimum work necessary to show their understanding. Being overwhelmed with too much information at once makes it that much more challenging to get work started, much less completed • Break down tasks and allow students flexibility in not having to depend only on their working memory – offer time to write things down and don't necessarily expect memorisation to be the sign that information is learned

(Continued)

Table 5.1   *(Continued)*

Needs wait time before answering a question	• Give time to think by offering questions in advance so they know they'll be answering them, taking time to listen to others share first (or discuss in smaller groups first), or writing down their thoughts before sharing in order to give space before expecting an answer
	• Using mini-whiteboards to give students a chance to write down thoughts before sharing them with others
Has trouble starting tasks independently	• Use external aids like graphic organisers, checklists and planners
	• Focus on completing what is absolutely necessary (quality work over quantity)
	• Check in with students to reflect with them on their time usage and make adjustments to workload as they go along when necessary
Struggles to remember what they heard, read, want to say or were told to do	• Give visual and audio support when teaching new concepts (the more culturally congruent, the easier it could be for them to connect to prior knowledge)
	• Review new learning often
	• Break down instructions, have them repeat and clarify expectations and needed materials as they begin them
	• Use external aids like graphic organisers, checklists and planners
	• Have reference tools easily accessible or visible
Has trouble remembering facts and procedure knowledge and transferring that knowledge to other study areas	• Direct teach about how concepts connect to previous knowledge
	• Give students the chance to repeat tasks and add more detail (like using their pre-assessment mind map and then adding details, during and at the end of the unit to make their learning more visible)
	• Teach information in a variety of ways, including modelling thinking and problem-solving
Struggles to remember their materials and belongings	• Work with the student to create a routine for starting tasks, organising materials or transitioning between tasks. Scaffold support so it can eventually be done independently. Make it visible and be flexible with making changes as you go

Emotional regulation: Reducing learned helplessness

Seligman (1975) suggested learning helplessness consisted of three different parts: "an undermining of one's motivation to respond; a (reduced capability) of one's ability to learn that responding works; and an emotional disturbance, usually depression or anxiety". Supporting our students means finding ways to help them break the cycle and see that their efforts can create change. For Simon that meant meeting him where he was at by not treating him as if he couldn't do anything independently, but focusing on what he was doing and building on that. At the same time, we needed to reduce the barriers that were impairing his ability to access the skills he had that could support effective learning too

Possible ADHD presentations	Possible accommodations
Feels disheartened in attempting tasks that are typically difficult for them	• Create a plan with them that would support their ability to engage easier (this is looking at one outcome at a time. If they can tell stories well but struggle to write, then grade the content while allowing them to share it in a medium that best supports them) • Find areas where they shine no matter how small and let them know it often (and in ways that allow them to feel like they offer a valuable contribution to the classroom)
Becomes restless or disengages when trying to engage in learning activities and won't attempt them	• Check in regularly to model thinking aloud on strategies for completing the task on time (to become confidence in sharing their planning with others) • Pair students with a trusted friend who allows them to do some of the work but also doesn't mind taking the lead in completing it
Becomes dissociated or gives up easily	• Break down instructions into smaller tasks and model self-talk on how to work through it (modelling how this can be done also encourages different ways to complete tasks). • Smaller tasks or steps forward to reduce the overwhelm
Allows others to lead and complete the task with little additional input from themselves	• Be mindful of who they are paired to work with and allow more choice in work partners. Their closest friends could provide more support and encouragement while also not expecting as much from them in areas that they are too nervous to engage with, while still including them in the process
Needs frequent encouragement or reminders to continue	• Any attempt to do something independently is accepted and appreciated, no matter the size or significance. Find something very specific to praise and that is *genuine* • Give meaningful and actionable feedback without expecting them to change things in a specific way (like allowing for verbal reflection if writing is too much for them)
Struggles to start or persist in completing them	• Allow space for them to work at the pace as they need without expectations for what they should complete. Meet them exactly where they are • Offer specific examples of how you could help (or they could get support from others) and let them decide, without shaming or judgement

During times when writing was expected was when Simon seemed most stuck. He was never disruptive or argumentative, he just couldn't get started. At. All. When it came to writing, his tasks would remain untouched in front of him until someone urged him forward. It was as if he'd become accustomed to starting only when someone was hounding him. Simon had also developed the routine of ensuring others volunteered to be writers in any group work too. But for us, I soon found ourselves in what was becoming a very familiar cycle:

1. Simon would be staring off into the distance.
2. I'd ask him what he was doing.
3. He'd say, "Nothing".
4. I'd ask, "Why not?"
5. He'd say, "I don't know".
6. Frustrated, I'd grab his pencil or materials and point it to the page, then to the board/book/activity/task and back to his blank page again.
7. He'd finally start to do *something* (*something* meaning: write a few words).
8. I'd walk over to help another student.
9. Less than two minutes later, I'd come back to find him staring off into the distance again.
10. I'd become exasperated and grab his pencil, repeating myself.
11. Then I'd scribe as he told me what he wanted to say (on a good day, I'd even wait for him to answer first).
12. I'd walk away frustrated, completely fed up.

This obviously wasn't getting us anywhere. For Simon, the bare minimum necessary to complete a written task wasn't even a possibility on his own. His writing was very laboured. The letters, though neatly formed, often appeared thick and dark on the paper. He took his time to focus on each letter as if searching his memory for the one he needed to write – every time he wrote. Until I could implement ways to simplify writing for him (meaning: reducing the amount of writing necessary or completing it with technical support, rather than reducing the cognitive challenge), I'd never be giving him a chance to see that he was capable of expressing himself through written expression, let alone see progress in it.

ADHD and the complexities of writing

Dysgraphia impacts a person's handwriting and their ability to express their thoughts in written language. ADHD can co-occur with dysgraphia, creating additional challenges with their writing and written expression. A student with dyspraxia has handwriting that is often illegible, yet still takes an enormous amount of effort to produce. There can be many reasons for handwriting problems: motor difficulties, spatial and visual processing difficulties, or difficulties visualising the appearance of letters, so dysgraphia isn't as widely recognised as dyspraxia or dyslexia (both of which can also cause handwriting challenges but for different reasons). But since our present education system still insists on handwriting as a medium through which evidence of learning is produced, it's expected that by around 10 years old that children will have mastered handwriting to write quickly, efficiently and legibly. But in order to get to this point, learners need "to have well co-ordinated motor skills, intact visual perception and good kinaesthetic sense and a sense of fluency and rhythm while writing" (Addy, 2004).

Students navigating dysgraphia often can't effectively process information and write at the same time. This can keep them from expressing themselves when writing as dysgraphia impacts their ability to write quickly, fluently and effortlessly. With schools focusing heavily on written tasks as a way to show knowledge, dysgraphia takes a toll on a student's self-esteem too. When teachers and peers make comments on a learner's handwriting neatness, writing speed and the amount written on a topic, these students often learn to equate their intelligence to the quality of writing they can produce. They often learn to see their struggles with writing due to a *lack of effort* or *laziness*. But dysgraphia doesn't impact intelligence and effort isn't determined by how much or neat a student's handwriting is, so where might they get that message? As teachers, we have our school experiences and beliefs about what it meant for us to be good writers. Our own **internalised ableism** can show up through the expectations we set on our students' handwriting and writing abilities too.

Reflect now

How do I define "effort" and what do I think it looks like for a student to give their best effort? How have my expectations around "effort" been defined by my experiences? How do I notice and interpret "effort" depending on the different students I teach when I consider what I've learned to believe about race, gender, class, different neurotypes, ways of communication, physical ability, etc.?

In addition to the physical act of writing itself, ADHDers often have a significant amount of challenges with written expression too. Some studies suggest that working memory and attention may play significant roles in this "because writing composition is generally more complex than reading and/or calculating. It also entails a higher cognitive load on the working memory of a person" (Tindle and Longstaff, 2015). ADHD students would likely benefit from a step-by-step method of instruction to support their writing skills alongside learning specific writing procedures. Re and Cornoldi (2010) suggest that "at early stages of development, both declarative knowledge (knowing what has to be done) and procedural expertise (being able to actually perform the task) have to be addressed. A special focus needs to be given to procedural expertise because it directly relates to executive functioning difficulties". With the additional complexity needed to express ourselves in writing, "it's more likely that children with ADHD are more prone to fail in a writing task than a reading or mathematics task" (Mayes and Calhoun, 2007). It's not surprising that for many ADHDers writing in schools is fraught with so much anxiety and resistance. How much do we miss in a student's understanding when writing becomes the sole or main source of expressing it?

> ## Quick note: ADHD isn't always simply brain-based difficulties
>
> As many as 50 per cent of ADHDers (Fliers, Franke, and Buitelaar, 2011) have problems with coordination and can be quite clumsy. They might bump into things, have difficulty tying shoelaces or using cutlery or struggle with sports and games that require balance and coordination. There could be many causes for this, like lack of focus, hyperactivity or impulsivity. But they might also have a co-occurring neurodivergence called development coordination disorder (DCD) or also known as dyspraxia. This impacts the planning of motor skills movements, since there is also an impairment in balance and increased postural sway, which is the movement of our centre of gravity when standing still (Hove et al., 2015). Dyspraxia can have an impact on sensory needs too, so support might also include working with an occupational therapist. ADHD–DCD students might benefit from additional instruction and practice in learning physical skills along with activities that support the vestibular and proprioception systems and activities that engage the core muscles and practise balance like yoga.

Supporting students with writing challenges

Depending on the kinds of challenges that you're noticing, any combination of support may prove helpful. Writing support can look like this:

- Using writing frames, storyboards or pictures to support the planning process. Writing that starts from a blank page can be overwhelming for many students, not just ADHDers, but allowing time to draw, use and move post-its and pictures can help build ideas and provide a starting place.
- Allowing for time to talk about the topic or share ideas before the writing starts (many ADHD students need to organise their thoughts outside their head because of their executive functioning skill development delays).
- Consider scribing key ideas and vocabulary for them or helping them get very specific on each portion of their writing (sometimes too much at once can be a lot for ADHD learners, so consider their capacity for information or instructions at once).
- Providing sentence starters to help guide the writing process, especially if it is a particular writing style.
- Giving plenty of extra time for the whole writing process.
- Infusing movement breaks or allowing flexibility for students to take breaks and do their **sensory diet** when needed. Sometimes a change is necessary, especially when ADHD students get stuck **hyperfocusing** on the wrong things.

- Sometimes ADHD learners can work well with a writing task and then struggle next time, so allow for flexibility for the consistent inconsistency these students deal with.
- Remembering what your outcomes are for the writing and assess accordingly. Comments and corrections on grammar and spelling might not be necessary if you're only interested in the content of the writing piece.
- Considering the quality of the content of writing over the quantity. An ADHD student might only write a short amount but could also express a lot in other ways when given the chance.
- Allowing for flexibility in how students show their learning, especially when handwriting is an issue. Can they use other technology like typing or speech-to-text?

Reflect now

What does success look like in your classroom? How does the definition change depending on what students show they achieved in a certain amount of time, their social identity markers, etc.? How much does a student typically have to complete in order to prove that they've understood what was expected?

"Sluggish Cognitive Tempo" or inattentive ADHD

There could be numerous reasons why Simon was struggling with attention and energy levels that impacted his ability so badly to engage in learning or even attempt it. ADHD was one idea, but what made it puzzling was the degree to which he found himself lost in daydreams and drowsiness on a regular basis. It could have been because of sensory overload, physical symptoms that we were unaware of or even just a bad night's sleep. But one theorised co-occurring neurodivergence in approximately 30 to 63 per cent of people with inattentive-type ADHD (Barkley, 2018) is "Sluggish Cognitive Tempo" (SCT), or as Barkley has coined it (which might sound nicer to some than sluggish, I suppose), Concentration Deficit Disorder (CDD). According to Barkley (2013, accessed in 2018), SCT (or CDD) is marked by these presentations:

- daydreaming (staring out into the distance);
- trouble staying awake/alert (even appears drowsy/sleepy);
- feeling mentally foggy/easily confused;
- appearing/feeling foggy, like their mind is elsewhere;
- is lethargic (appearing apathetic/withdrawn);
- appears underactive;
- doesn't process questions or explanations accurately;
- appears lost in thoughts.

But what makes SCT/CDD separate from ADHD is its lack of visible hyperactivity or impulsivity and how it internalises presentations of depression and (most likely) anxiety. Although there are inattentive ADHD presentations that overlap with SCT/CDD which also include being slow to start or complete a task and a lack of taking initiative or fading of effort, studies have shown that the challenges faced with SCT/CDD don't typically include executive functioning. Instead, SCT/CDD challenges tend to centre around early information processing or attention, spatial memory, organisation and problem solving, and motor speed problems (Barkley, 2012, 2013; Garner et al., 2010; Huang-Pollock et al., 2005; Skirbekk et al., 2011; all accessed in Barkley, 2018). They also contribute to significant social challenges due to more frequent social withdrawal. People who are thought to have both SCT/CDD and ADHD have challenges with both too. Whether SCT/CDD is its own neurodivergence, a type of inattentive ADHD or the result of different causes altogether, the fact that these presentations are visible should be an indicator that the student, for whatever reason, has reached capacity for what's currently happening around them. And therefore, they need some support.

When it came to Simon, I wonder if regulating a nervous system that became so easily overwhelmed within our learning environment quickly became too much for him. In order to protect him from the onslaught of information, sensations and sensory stimuli, perhaps his nervous system resorted to shutting down instead. Since these reactions were occurring a lot more frequently as the days went on, it might have indicated that Simon was trying to work so far beyond his capacity that he was approaching burnout (if not enduring it already), which takes a lot longer to recover from. When overwhelm and overload build up without reprieve, many ADHD students display more presentations. Noticing when our ADHD learners' behaviours become more intense, more easily dysregulated or more frequently dysregulated, meeting their needs at the moment can help them function better later on. Depending on any co-occurring neurodivergence, our ability to scaffold support can reduce the possibilities of them succumbing completely to burn out and needing days, weeks or longer to recover. When we recognise some overwhelm in the moment this is when we might:

- reduce demands and requests placed on them;
- give some time alone, suggest they rest their head on the desk or go to the quiet corner;
- decide whether there's another way to complete the work or whether it's even that important;
- let them go for a walk to get some water;
- give them a break to fidget, stim or move as needed.

Without time for a reprieve, our ADHD learners' constant efforts to regulate and engage "appropriately", but to no avail, might begin to feel fruitless, frustrating and inevitably exhausting for them. The more they try to make things right, the more difficult it feels to accomplish and the worse things get, which only makes them feel even worse about themselves (often making the presentations worse too). Careful observation of our students can reveal their increasing overwhelm, irritability or even zoning out as signs that perhaps whatever's happening around them is becoming too much to effectively function under the sensory stimuli, demands or expectations. Their reactions are telling us that they might need us to chat or sit with (for co-regulation) or give them the space and time to self-regulate and rebuild some capacity to re-engage in their learning.

I finally understood why Simon felt helpless.

Supporting Simon

As we continued to discuss the possibility of him easing into completing some homework again, in the playground that day, I could sense the concern in his voice.

"Do you think I could do it without my dad's help?" he asked me. "I'm just afraid I won't be able to."

I knew he considered it as a huge risk. He could finally see he was capable, but would a missed assignment, requiring help sometimes or watching someone try to take over the work he had to do mean he wasn't good enough again?

"You know, it's OK to ask for help. It's also OK to experiment and see what helps you best with the homework too", I suggested. He thought for a moment before finally nodding in agreement.

"Well … Maybe if it's something really small …"

I smiled. "Definitely! And nothing will go home unless you can tell me how you're going to do it."

He paused again. "Maybe we can record myself saying the instructions, so I can watch it at home again too."

"That's a good idea, Simon. Let's do that."

He smiled shyly and ran off to join his friend for the remainder of the break. I started to think about what might be most helpful to him to take home. Maybe something he could get started on ahead of time for class but only on the week-end. I knew I'd have to meet with Simon's carers so they could learn what we had decided and how best to support him. It was important that Simon saw that he could handle the consequences of his decisions if he made mistakes too and that he could have the chance to make things right if he chose to.

Learning demands that students be vulnerable. They need to make mistakes in order to engage in the process, but everywhere they look, students get the message that they can't. If they can't learn in the ways that are expected, they learn that they must change themselves for fear of not fitting in, or worse, being rejected altogether. The further learners appear to be from what's ideal or expected of them, the worse they start to feel about school, learning and eventually, themselves. For ADHD students particularly, this increased dysregulation makes it more challenging to connect to their frontal lobe and decide what they need in order to get on with the business of learning. Schools are not immune from causing some dysregulation and discomfort, as these are a natural part of the learning process; but schools are not immune from causing trauma either, and that should never be forgotten.

Key takeaways:

- *Learned helplessness* is often talked about as a behaviour that some students do, caused by their parents or by choice. But often it is a reaction to trauma that can be further compounded by ADHD.
- Inattentive ADHD students can easily become dependent learners because of the cycle of repeated failure, leaving them struggling to regulate the emotions of it and finding no other solutions to being blamed for their ADHD presentations.
- Blame is a tool used by *white supremacy culture* to protect from being seen as not good enough and rejected from the group, while simultaneously hiding the societal problems that cause us to resort to blame in the first place.
- Writing can be difficult for many ADHD students. Some students may struggle with the process itself while others find expressing themselves through writing more challenging.
- "Sluggish Cognitive Tempo" or "Concentrations Deficit Disorder" can be seen alongside more prominent presentations of inattentive ADHD. It's not considered a type of ADHD because of its lack of visible impulsivity and hyperactivity.

Resources to explore

Executive functioning skills

Social Thinking by Michelle Garcia Winner: https://www.socialthinking.com/
The Pathway 2 Success (SEL and EF Skills): www.thepathway2success.com
The Autism Discussion Page on the Core Challenges of Autism and *The Autism Discussion Page on Stress, Anxiety, Shutdowns and Meltdowns: Proactive Strategies for Minimising Sensory, Social and Emotional Overload* by Bill Nasan
Zones of Regulation by Leah Kuypers: https://zonesofregulation.com/

Dyspraxia

Dyspraxia Foundation: https://dyspraxiafoundation.org.uk/

Mental health wellbeing for young people

The Autism Workbook by Romy Worthington: www.ticcersunite.com/
Young Minds: www.youngminds.org.uk/

6

"She's the ideal student!":

Ji Yeon's story

This chapter asks us to reflect on:

- the overlap between ADHD, maths learning disabilities and dyscalculia;
- the ways we can be more culturally responsive;
- how we develop meta-cognition in our ADHD learners;
- how we support ADHD learners who struggle with perfectionism;
- the needs of the new student;
- the impact of the model minority myth on our Asian* students.

***Please note**: The term Asian, which makes up roughly 50 ethnic groups, doesn't automatically refer to all 50 ethnic groups when used, which erases the cultures and experiences of the various groups. Depending on where you are in the world, you might interpret the term Asian to refer to different ethnic groups than I do. My interpretation of Asian (listed below) hints at where I've been most influenced by **white supremacy** when using Asian to refer to people whose ancestry is these countries:

Southeast Asia: Brunei, Burma (Myanmar), Cambodia, Timor-Leste, Indonesia, Laos, Malaysia, Philippines, Singapore, Thailand and Vietnam.

East Asia: China, Hong Kong, Japan, Macau, Mongolia, North Korea, South Korea and Taiwan.

My interpretation of Asian excludes those whose ancestry are also in the same
   regions:
South Asia: Sri Lanka, Bangladesh, India, Afghanistan, Pakistan, Bhutan, Nepal, Maldives
   and Iran.
West Asia (commonly referred to as the Middle East): Georgia, Armenia, Azerbaijan, Turkey,
   Cyprus, Syria, Lebanon, Israel, Palestine, Jordan, Iraq, Oman, Yemen, Kuwait, Bahrain,
   Qatar and Saudi Arabia.
Central Asia: Tajikistan, Uzbekistan, Kazakhstan, Turkmenistan and Kyrgyzstan.

As I knelt down at Ji Yeon's desk to chat with her about our most recent writing project, I was amazed by the number of details she had added in her most
recent edits. She had a strong vocabulary in the language of instruction.
Ji Yeon was new to the school (but not the country), and she was settling into
her new class well. She had already caught up with a writing task that others
had started the week before and was doing edits and revisions without a problem. Ji Yeon was very meticulous about her written work, making it very detailed
and insightful to read.

   After completing a small-group writing workshop, I liked to do short check-
ins with individual students. Some days, I'd have students write their names
on the board as a way to make an appointment with me. But other times (like
this day), I would wander from workplace to workplace, just to see what students had been up to since our last meet-up. Meeting with Ji Yeon was always
an easier check-in to do. I listened as she shared where she currently was
in her editing and was planning on doing revision. We referred to the goals
of her writing and I modelled how I might review if I was remembering them
as I worked:

   "Hmmm ... I wanted to add more adjectives and speech to my story. Did I
do that? I can see that I added more adjectives because of the purple pen.
Hmmm ... but I've only gotten one conversation though. I wonder if there's a part
of your story where I can show what's happening through a conversation rather
than just telling it?"

   Ji Yeon thought for a moment but didn't respond with anything. I waited for a bit
longer, but she only smiled wider, giggled a bit and still added nothing.

   "Nowhere? There's nowhere else you could add some dialogue to your story?"
I gave a sideways glance, jokingly hoping to reduce the growing discomfort I could
sense rising in her.

   Ji Yeon shrugged again, "I don't know ..." she admitted as her smile faded and
she looked down sadly at her work.

   This was something I was beginning to notice with Ji Yeon. She produced huge
amounts of work (particularly with writing), but she struggled with handling actionable feedback or reflecting on where she could improve. It was quickly becoming clear to me that Ji Yeon was used to getting a lot of praise for her efforts.
I couldn't help but wonder if she was used to her work being considered perfect
as soon as it landed on the teacher's desk. If this was the case, maybe she
wasn't used to having her work returned with actionable feedback given to build
on what she's shown she already knows. I was going to have to tread very gently
to get her used to the idea that it wasn't a character flaw to be corrected and
certainly not one to make mistakes.

Meet Ji Yeon:

- 10 years old
- Korean ethnicity, expatriate parents
- identifies as a girl
- **emergent bilingual** with stronger communication in the language of instruction than her **home language**
- enthusiastic writer and learner, artistically creative, friendly
- loves: writing stories, listening to stories, drawing pictures
- detests: being corrected, making mistakes
- future aspirations: writer
- best known for: working intently, never causing a scene
- learning challenges: none
- additional information: not as academically capable in maths when considering other academic strengths

It was no surprise that Ji Yeon came with so many glowing reviews from her previous school. She was extremely enthusiastic about learning and had high academic outcomes. From the moment I met her, I realised that Ji Yeon had high expectations for herself too. All she had experienced was praise, performing exceptionally well on her first attempts at learning activities. But I could see it might be difficult for her too. Since she was rarely corrected she never got the chance to see that learning happens through making mistakes and is always ongoing. Without having accessed learning activities that allowed for depth and complexity in their exploration to extend her understanding, Ji Yeon wasn't used to having to persevere through an appropriate levelled challenge to stretch herself. She would need support in integrating into her self-image as a learner that she didn't have to be perfect to be successful.

New students and the nervous system

Ji Yeon was fortunate to be a new student who was familiar with the language of instruction, but not all children have those added supports. For many students, a new move might include a new country, a new language and also new cultures to understand. Not to mention the many intersecting identities a new student has that can impact their ability to seamlessly integrate into a new educational experience. At any time we could be teaching children who are refugees, asylum-seekers, or children whose parents are there for a short period for work or study, all of them with needs that will vary depending on their language, socio-economic background, educational background and more. These experiences add another layer of challenge for the student who's trying to adjust not only to everything that's new but also to the loss of what they've left behind.

Changing schools calls for a lot of support from teachers, parents, other students and the wider school community to ensure that this transition happens as smoothly as possible. It can be an intensely emotional time for students, even when they've not left their home country. Change brings up a lot of discomfort and dysregulation in the nervous system. Even a welcomed change is still a signal of unsafety to the brain, so it's natural that students would be dysregulated from it too. Unfamiliarity, even when welcomed, can still be seen as unsafe in the body. Depending on how sensitive a student's nervous system naturally is (whether they have ADHD, another neurodivergence or a history of trauma, for example), a new school environment itself becomes an additional challenge for regulating alongside the dysregulation that learning demands of students.

Remember, dysregulation is noticeable behaviour that shows the child isn't alert and ready to engage in the task at hand. But the body's nervous system can't determine whether a sensation would be "good" to feel. It also can't decide to only feel what the brain has labelled the "good" feelings and ignore the "bad" ones either. It has no judgement on any emotions, it simply becomes activated by something that then sends a sensation through the body. All emotions have a charge (or sensation) too and the nervous system is simply concerned with whether it has the capacity (or the space) to regulate or integrate it. The body can't just change its ideas of safety because our logical brain tells it to. Building a felt sense of safety in the body takes time.

For a new student, surrounded by all these new people and experiences, it's not surprising that it would be very uncomfortable for any brain and body to manage. But for an ADHD brain, which is naturally quick to leap to its alarm centre (the amygdala) and protects a body that stays hypervigilant of its surroundings (even in an environment it's familiar with), imagine the possible heightened sensations it might have to regulate when everything it knows changes. Then, since ADHD brains have delays in executive functioning, it might struggle to recall how these changes might connect to what's familiar so they can feel safer sooner too. To varying degrees, all new students need support that is centred on how we build psychological and felt safety. Creating learning environments and experiences that connect to prior knowledge of their culture and lived experiences is a good place to start.

Reflect now

How are you intentional about the ways you support your new students or those transitioning on to new places? Where do you think your **internalised biases** may impact the ways that you interpret their behaviour as they adjust to their new learning environments? How do you support the students who are left behind after a classmate moves on?

Cultural-responsive teaching: an introduction

Ji Yeon didn't come into classes as if she was an empty vessel just waiting to be filled by her teacher's knowledge. She was a whole person, influenced by her own culture and with it the values, beliefs and lived experiences that guided how she saw herself as a learner and what she expected of me as her teacher. This cultural lens wasn't left at the door the moment she stepped into our classroom. As her teacher, my cultural lens and influence weren't left at the entrance of our classroom either. The way that I saw Ji Yeon as a learner would also influence my expectations and how I taught her too. I would have to intentionally be checking my **internalised bias** about East Asian learners. Gaining more understanding and awareness of Ji Yeon's culture meant that I could support her in connecting and integrating the new knowledge and expectations she'd experience in her new learning environment.

Learning environments centring white mainstream, Eurocentric ideas for students, especially those who are from different cultures, make it significantly more challenging for them to feel like they belong. In order to feign fitting in, they are expected to put aside their own cultural lens and still learn as expected of them. These students learn they can't object to their names being mispronounced or laughed at or to being given nicknames by their teachers or peers. Or they might get so used to having their names pronounced incorrectly, they end up learning to prefer it in order to fit in. It's also how some students learn to hide parts of their cultural identity (like changing their clothing) and others decide they must stay isolated from their peers in order to protect themselves for refusing to fit into these expectations. How can we expect students, within education systems not made for their safety in mind, not to become dysregulated? When their belonging is risked over not fitting in, they must learn to change who they are instead.

Fitting in does not equate to belonging and the belief that it could goes against everything we know about the brain, the body and how we learn. It essentially suggests that historically excluded student populations should feel *just as safe* as white students in a learning environment that could be unfamiliar in terms of its content, cultural expectations and/or expected skills development. They are expected *to feel safe enough* to learn in an environment that's not created *for* them or even *with* them in mind. Not to mention they must learn in an environment that is rooted in racial biases and inequities designed to exclude them from the start. Then, if none of this were enough, we incessantly police some marginalised group members for excelling in their learning, while expecting others in different marginalised groups to excel in specific subjects, refusing to support them if they can't. This is why culturally responsive teaching matters.

Designing a culturally responsive learning environment

Culturally responsive teaching is an asset-based pedagogy that works to see how we can increase the engagement and motivation of our Black, Brown, Asian, Indigenous or other melanated learners "who have historically struggled in schools or are often socially alienated" (Vargus, 2008). It is "based on the assumption that when academic knowledge and skills are situated within the lived experiences and frames of reference of students, they are more personally meaningful, have a higher interest appeal, and are learned more easily and thoroughly" (Gay, 2002). It also asks us to pay attention to how we're privileging white, middle-class values and expectations in our classrooms and how we're ignoring, devaluing and discrediting the wealth of knowledge, histories and values that come from our Black, Brown, Indigenous, Asian and other melanated students. Without acknowledging and affirming the cultural resources that come with these students, we can't effectively use their knowledge, or build on it and their experiences either. This eventually leads to detrimental outcomes for the academic achievement, self-concept and self-esteem of historically excluded learners.

The classroom environment we create with our students needs to build social, emotional and intellectual safety so that students can collaborate and learn together while building strong, confident learner identities. This is essential for all learners, but for our ADHD students (and especially depending on their marginalisation by society) this is crucial. Being intentional about the messages we're sending through our classroom decorations and set up matters. What we choose to include as the decor goes beyond simply what looks pleasant (although this is important). It also becomes additional regulatory support for learners' nervous systems because of what it suggests about what matters in the space and the learners within it. Hammond (2014) suggests that as culturally responsive educators, we acknowledge "the classroom environment as a powerful container in its own right that reflects, communicates and shapes values".

What we put on our classroom walls and how we organise our learning spaces need to be reflective of what matters to the collective values of everyone who learns in it. Our brains are continually scanning our environments for what feels safe (especially as ADHD learners) and that means every choice we make in creating our environment matters. When considering that safety to the brain also means seeking what's familiar and what feels good, adding familiar objects and colours for learners in our spaces helps the brain go into a state of relaxed alertness. This state is conducive to learning.

When new students (or anyone who visits our learning environments for that matter) come into our environments we need to be asking ourselves what is important to our learners. We want to reflect on the messages about learning we hope they'll understand when they look at our classroom walls and around the space. How can we transform the values of our students into images, symbols and objects in our classrooms? This is how we begin to create spaces that the brain recognises as familiar and safe.

Hammond (2014) mentions a few ways that we could do this, including:

- Finding or borrowing (from families) authentic artefacts that represent the different cultural backgrounds of your students rather than multicultural posters that don't show the value of the various cultural influences that your students bring to the learning space
- Rather than using common cultural heroes posters or pictures, include rotating artistic works, engineering diagrams or tiles as accents pieces from different cultures

- Rotating using colour schemes or artistic styles on bulletin boards that are significant to different cultural groups in your class
- Adding nature and natural elements

As for considering how we can support new students in cultivating more safety and belonging within their first days and weeks of school, we can include the following:

- Pairing the new student with two existing students and if one speaks the same language as the new student that is helpful too. (Having two students initially to support the new student keeps pressure from just one student needing to have all the answers or be the only playmate. Pairing students is important to the nervous system for co-regulation too. Remember, just because they speak the same language doesn't mean that they'll automatically like each other or should do all the translating in class either.)
- Ensuring that they understand the importance of the classroom routines and rituals (our class routines should be thought through very carefully because they are ways that we not only organise our classes but also show what values are most important to the learning space, help foster community and belonging and support learning experiences).
- Finding robust ways to communicate when experiencing language barriers. Being misunderstood or unable to effectively communicate creates additional stress for the new student.
- Observing the new student at break times to see how they are integrating with their peers. Support them in getting involved in a break-time activity and understanding the social dynamics of the school. (I do this with all my students at points throughout the year because building friendships supports connection and belonging).
- Supporting new students in catching up with any academic work (even if it is done through their **home language**) and integrating more culturally relevant learning experiences into planning.
- Having regular one-to-one check-ins with the student. They don't have to be long and detailed, just getting to know them better.
- Finding a safe adult in the school they can go to who speaks their language where possible.
- Having regular contact with carers to monitor the student's transition and address any concerns as they come up (changing needs or habits their family would be more aware of that can impact their child's learning).

Culturally responsive teaching is much more than just representation in the curriculum, adding some books in the classroom library or learning about a festival, holiday or tradition. It's about recognising that "learning stems from a complex relationship among social, biological, and emotional elements in which intersections with an individual's cultural orientation must be taken into consideration" (Vargus, 2008). For ADHD students (and even more so when considering those most marginalised) – who in addition to the typical ADHD challenges of self-regulation and executive functioning skills delays, also experience much higher rates of anxiety and depression – culturally responsive teaching adds to creating welcoming learning environments. I suspect that the stronger sense of familiarity we can create, the better chance we have at reducing or managing ADHD presentations in our classrooms too.

Intersectional insight: Sensing belonging in individualist and collectivist cultures

Understanding the **individualistic** and **collective** cultural influences of our students can give us a good starting place when planning learning activities that consider their prior knowledge and learning experiences. But it might not be the best way to ensure we're creating a learning space that provides a sense of belonging though. Cortina, Arel and Smith-Darden (2017) found that when it came to predicting stronger belongingness, power distance (the psychological distance between social ranks) would be a better measure. They found that regardless of cultural background, teacher–student relationships that were learner-centred, emphasising care while downplaying extrinsic rewards, created more student engagement which in turn increased their sense of belonging. They also discovered that learning environments that encouraged cooperation over competition also had a positive impact on students' well-being and achievement too.

Within a few weeks of Ji Yeon's arrival, I'd noticed the learning gaps in her maths skills. They were subtle, but her ability appeared vastly different when I compared the outcomes she achieved in other subjects. I found myself often correcting her work; where at first I thought they might be careless mistakes, the frequency of their occurrence made me wonder if there were some skills or knowledge that she was missing instead. I wanted to find a way to gently approach her about it but I knew it wouldn't be easy.

"Ji Yeon ... do you want to explain to me how you solved this? I'm just trying to understand this part here." I pointed to the paper while kneeling next to her to hear what she had to say. While working with her partner, I had recognised the repeated error I'd seen earlier in Ji Yeon's work.

Her friend spoke up. "See, Ji Yeon. I told you to try this way ..."

But Ji Yeon didn't look up, at all. Instead, she quickly grabbed an eraser (which was fortunate, because I rarely had any out in the classroom) and attempted to erase all her calculations before I reached over and gently placed my hand on the page.

"No, no, no. Don't erase them! It's not the whole question. It's just here." I pointed to it in the remaining responses, before I continued: "Why don't you tell me what you were thinking and we'll figure out together where it got tricky ..."

I paused for a moment to see how she'd answer, before I realised that she wouldn't. Ji Yeon's head drooped to hide the tears welling up in her eyes. I leaned closer and whispered that we'd take a moment in the hallway together to chat (what I maybe should have suggested from the start). I grabbed her book on the way, knowing that when she was calm I could show her how common the errors were and how she could make them right.

This would be the start of building trust with Ji Yeon around learning maths. It was important that she learned that it was OK to make mistakes without the added fear of what she thought it might mean if these mistakes were about something wrong with *her*.

The complexities of learning maths

Maths learning difficulties (MLD) become noticeable when students show deficits with number sense, calculation, memorisation of number facts or maths reasoning when considering the abilities of their same-aged peers. Approximately 35 per cent of people have a maths difficulty and 6.4 per cent of them have dyscalculia or another kind of maths learning disability (Kennedy, 2020). So to put it plainly, not only is having a maths learning difficulty about as common as having ADHD, but maths learning disabilities are about as common as dyslexia too. But in order to understand how ADHD and maths learning disabilities overlap, it helps to understand the brain a bit more because two cognitive processes support our maths learning.

The first is domain-specific processes which deal with how the brain solves maths problems. It's naturally wired to work with numbers, recognise many from few, compare amounts and do things like order items from least to greatest. The second is domain-general processes, where we access executive functioning skills and language. The thing is, being "good at maths" isn't just about the way that we solve maths problems with domain-specific processes, but it's also about the language too. Maths is its own language and it's not easy to express. Plus there are multiple ways to express the same mathematical concepts which are often challenging for students with language disabilities. Add ADHD alongside it, which is predominately about delays in executive functioning skills, and maths learning becomes that much more difficult. "Mathematical language and executive functioning skills seemed to be the strongest and most consistent classifiers of low performance. Both of these domains have been reported to be foundational for early mathematics development" (Purpura et al., 2017)

"Nearly a third of children with ADHD also have a math learning disability, and 25 percent of children with MLD have ADHD" (Kennedy, 2020). When ADHD is added to the equation we know we'll see additional challenges with general-domain processes and that means executive functioning skills like:

- working memory: problems memorising maths facts and remembering the steps to solve problems;
- processing speed: although this has nothing to do with maths ability, our schools often assess students on their ability to retrieve facts quickly, which leads to more maths anxiety for all children, not just ADHDers;
- attention difficulties: struggling with keeping focused in order to complete the calculations, or not getting distracted by other thoughts and what's happening

in the classroom (which expends more energy to stay focused on the task at hand);

- trouble task switching: stay focused to complete the task or notice when the questions have changed and demand a new kind of calculation (which again takes energy to switch to new tasks because of what it takes to keep focus);
- low frustration tolerance: when working so hard to keep focused and remember the calculations, persevering when calculations increase in difficulty can become challenging;
- emotional regulation: having to use extra energy to regulate any emotions around not making mistakes or being considered "good at maths".

Sure, there are plenty of ADHDers that really struggle with calculations, maths language or conceptual understanding, but there are plenty more that do really, really well in maths too. These are the ADHD learners that catch on to new concepts quickly and race to complete their work (and often do so before their peers). They might have had a stronger foundation in numerical language or their executive functioning challenges may be more prevalent in other kinds of tasks. They may also be quicker to see patterns involved in maths that other students can't see. It's also not surprising that many ADHD learners do well in maths, especially in comparison to writing. There is a higher cognitive load that's involved with writing that maths doesn't have. These ADHD students may make errors in their calculations, but the root cause of them could be traced back to executive functioning skills delays, more so than cognitive, language or mathematical ones.

Decreasing maths anxiety

It was becoming clear that in addition to some of the calculation issues I saw in her work, Ji Yeon (like many students), had some maths anxiety too. When the nervous system interprets something threatening, learning becomes difficult and for ADHD learners (or any student whose system feels unsafe) this would mean experiencing more "ADHD" presentations (whether visibly or internalised). Since maths can be very anxiety-inducing for so many students, supporting their dysregulation around the subject becomes essential for their learning and well-being. We need to create the conditions necessary for the nervous system to become more relaxed and alert in order to engage in effective learning. Some things I've found that help me reduce anxiety for all my students, while gaining more confidence in their maths ability include the following:

- Talking about the anxiety: sharing stories about my own maths (or other school subjects fears), discussing and practising what we can do when we feel that way helps (whether that's deep breathing, affirmations or positive self-talk during challenging bits, knowing how we can ask for help or that mistakes are natural).
- Starting with small, simple tasks: to build perseverance towards doing more complex tasks and allow students to feel successful regularly throughout their learning journey.

- Modelling positive self-talk: choosing phrases to talk to yourself through persevering through a difficult problem.
- Normalising using manipulatives, resources and maths dictionaries at any age: it encourages students to slow down and see that there are multiple ways to solve and understand problems.
- Planning relevant maths activities: I think this encourages students to do calculations naturally in their own way, recognising that there could be many ways to solve the problem. When activities are culturally congruent, they support students in connecting concepts to what they innately understand from their own schema. This allows them to access the task more effectively, thus building confidence too.
- Reducing rote learning and pages of maths problems: I think these create the conditions for students to equate completing maths quickly to mean being "good at maths". It can also take away from the creativity of maths.
- Doing more small-group and partner work: I rarely have students working alone in maths class. It's a language too, so communicating and working together is essential. It encourages feedback and more problem-solving, and adds co-regulation support.
- Giving clear, prompt feedback: it's actionable, adds clear examples of what is needed for growth, and when given kindly and respectfully allows students to correct with the co-regulated support of a caring guide and see progression right away, which helps build confidence.
- Using frequent, ongoing formative assessments which help me check knowledge in non-threatening ways and consistently design learning opportunities that meet them where they're at.

Even though I knew Ji Yeon didn't have dyscalculia, it was clear she needed some support and still struggled with anxiety around maths. I wondered if part of using perfectionism or being fearful of making mistakes was a strategy to deal with the expectation for her to be a talented mathematician simply because she was Asian. But Ji Yeon was just like any other average maths student who understood some concepts and procedures and struggled with others. Much like any other student, she would need some additional guidance and support at times too.

Reflect now

What makes a student "good" at maths? What messages did you receive about the importance of maths growing up? How do you think they impact the ways that you teach now or your expectations of your students' abilities? How are they further influenced by **internalised biases** of different cultures, gender or socio-economic status?

A note on dyscalculia

Dyscalculia is an unexpected difficulty in understanding numbers. These difficulties are thought of as a continuum, not a specific category, and have many factors that cause them. What sets dyscalculia apart from other maths learning challenges though is "the severity of difficulties with number sense, including subitising, symbolic and non-symbolic magnitude comparison, and ordering" (Sharma, 2022). It often co-occurs with other learning challenges, neurodivergence and mathematics anxiety. Since maths is a subject where there are foundational understandings and skills that must be developed in order to progress, students that struggle in their early years of maths learning will tend to have more difficulties later on. Supporting students with dyscalculia means helping them develop their internal visual representations of numbers by making connections between mathematical symbols and maths language. It's not enough for them to see the digit number symbol; these students need additional visuals, manipulatives and hands-on ways to develop fluency when working with numbers. We need to help these students find meaning in the digital symbol rather than teach them procedures to solve problems that lack the understanding behind them.

Intersectional insight: To ask for help or not?

There are many reasons why families wouldn't know about, actively seek out or understand how to navigate what social, emotional or mental supports are available to help their child. Many Black, Indigenous and Latine families have endured histories of medical racism and lack trust in health systems. They may also find it difficult to find time from work to take their child to appointments or with renewing prescriptions. Many immigrant families from marginalised communities also endure language barriers that keep them from accessing support within the systems. (Schmengler et al., 2021) For Asian immigrant families in particular, having their needs ignored for so long means they may not engage in seeking out support or have very little experience of doing so.

Many Asian students tell stories of not being supported in maths classes while watching their peers get support for the same challenges they had. This sends the message that they aren't allowed to receive support. It leaves them with no choice but to figure out what they don't know by themselves or not at all. This could create gaps in understanding that force many students to use different coping strategies in order to hide or compensate for them. With perfectionism as a coping strategy, the hope can be to produce work done so well they won't be discovered for what they don't know or believe they don't know well enough, especially when the message is clear that they should already know the topic perfectly and know it without additional help. Many ADHD students use perfectionism as a way to over-correct something that they've been continually reprimanded for or think they should be able to do without support too. It makes it more difficult to determine whether the learner is impacted by untreated ADHD or whether they are doing something that comes naturally to them without feelings of dysregulation because of it.

It took a minute for Ji Yeon to wipe her eyes and feel ready to chat. I waited for her, bending down to her level, maths book in hand for when she was ready. It's not always easy to adjust to a new school, and additional challenges with learning only just add to the uncertainty. I could feel her anxiety through the words she tried to get out in between all the sobs:

"I'm ssssorry ..." she stammered. I reached inside the classroom for a moment and brought out a tissue for her. When Ji Yeon finally calmed enough, I began to speak.

"There's nothing to be sorry about ..." I paused for a few moments before I continued: "I know this maths stuff feels big sometimes, but I promise you, it's really going to be OK."

Although still not saying anything, she began to breathe a lot easier and I could see her focus coming back to me again.

"Look, Ji Yeon ... I know it's not easy being new to a school. There are a lot of different things. Maybe you could tell me a little about maths in your old school. Why don't you show me how to do this over here?" I pointed to a question she'd solved in a way I'd never seen before. She nodded as she shared a little about some of the things she did in her previous school. We'd had conversations like this before, especially when I was explaining some of the routines and rituals we had in the class. It also gave me some insight into what she might have expected from me as a teacher and how I could bridge some of her prior knowledge and experiences with what she was doing in class now.

Sharing about her previous maths experiences also provided the opportunity to see if there might have been some processes or terms that she was more familiar with using that I could incorporate and support her understanding better too. Learning together seemed to be a lot less threatening for Ji Yeon, who loved to teach me her method of solving the problem. It made it a lot easier to help her get more comfortable being corrected by me too.

"Well," I said triumphantly, "this is a good day. I learned something new."

Ji Yeon gave me a slight smile as I told her to take an extra moment to go to the bathroom and just take a break. We had made some steps forward towards getting more comfortable with making mistakes. It's difficult to unlearn the need to be perfect, even more so when everywhere you look, the message is that perfect is not only what's expected of you, but also all you're ever seen to be. But for Asian students, being successful and achieving high academic outcomes while never requiring assistance, isn't just a message within the education system. It's everywhere.

The model minority myth

The model minority is built on the belief in **white supremacist culture** that Asian people are inherently more talented and have a stronger **"pull yourself up by your bootstraps" mentality**, making them more successful. It's an anti-Black, racist illusion that if other non-white people "worked as hard as Asian people", then "they could be as successful too". But there can't be a model minority unless there's a lazy, unintelligent other. This is how the model minority pits marginalised groups against each other because the lazy, unintelligent other is usually Black.

It suggests that if Black people worked harder and had stronger ties to their communities, they could overcome oppression, just like Asian people have. However, it disregards the centuries of oppression and all its societal systems that create barriers for Black people to thrive. For Asian communities, their culture, knowledge, values and lived experiences, alongside all the racism they endure as well as their advocacy work towards liberation, are erased.

The model minority myth has a very sinister way of playing out in education. It often leaves Asian students who don't fall neatly into its assumptions missing out on learning support because they are blamed for not succeeding, all while watching their non-Asian peers get support for the same challenges. Many Asian students must balance the expectations of their families alongside the school's expectations to be extremely high academic achievers. For some, being unable to meet them can lead to questioning their social identity, leaving them feeling never good enough or embarrassing their family (Wong, 2015). When high grades are seen as normal for these students they may receive less recognition or praise (e.g. from teachers or parents) for their achievements. This creates additional stress for low-/lower-achieving learners as their accomplishments may be downplayed. Not to mention that low achievement in a subject area is more often explained away or not seen as irreversible by teachers when compared to how they interpret the same achievement levels of Black students. It leaves those students who are struggling and in need of additional support without any, because it is assumed that they will catch up since they are hard-working, and their families will ensure their success. They won't wish to disappoint their families so they will sacrifice more and eventually earn their academic achievements (Wong, 2015).

In many schools, we tend to record the results of our Asian students as one data set.* We use this data to further perpetuate the model minority stereotype by assuming that all Asian students are "successful" while only a small amount of Asian communities actually are (Talusan, 2022). Academic achievements by those considered model minority students can also be delegitimised because it's assumed that they've had outside influence to do so (like having additional family support or being pushed "too hard" by their family to succeed) and therefore it's not been naturally acquired or done "the right way". Since white dominance is central to **white supremacy culture**, "gains are only made when they serve white interest" (Bradbury, 2013). This doesn't take into consideration the different

---

* Another way Asian countries are grouped together is when using the term Asian American and Pacific Islander (AAPI), which was created to be more inclusive of Pacific Island countries within Asia. However, this is also a hugely diverse group of cultures. Much like our data sets that group Asian students, the AAPI term hides the specific issues that Pacific Islander communities face separate from Asian communities too. Not all people agree with the use of AAPI or even Pacific Islander as their identity, so as always check with how they wish to identify.

The Pacific Islands generally include countries whose origins are the original peoples of Polynesia, Micronesia and Melanesia. Polynesia includes Hawaii (Native Hawaiian people only), Samoa, American Samoa, Tokelau, Tahiti and Tonga. Micronesia includes Guam, Mariana Islands, Saipan, Palau, Yap, Chuuk, Pohnpei, Kosrae, Marshall Islands and Kiribati. Melanesia includes Fiji, Papau New Guinea, Solomon Islands and Vanuatu.

cultures with varying histories and systemic, financial and economic barriers that impacted their ability to become successful (including academically successful) too. It's true that some East and South Asian communities might score better on certain school subjects than other groups – including white students (Talusan, 2022). However, when we assume that all Asian communities do, it erases the struggles of those Asians groups who consistently don't show these kinds of results and creates barriers that keep them from achieving higher.

Intersectional insight: Who's the model minority?

It's important to note that depending on where you're located in the world, those Asian communities who are considered the model minority vary. It's also a very fluid status and can be taken away when the Asian community doesn't adhere to the expectations of **whiteness**. For example, in the United Kingdom, Indian and Chinese students are often considered as the model minority, but other Asian groups could be seen as the model minority depending on factors such as classism or having behaviour that maintains the status quo (like appearing submissive or docile in school, for example). Bradbury (2013) notes: "Although it (being considered the model minority) may offer some benefit to some students who have access to high expectations and positions of success (however temporarily), it principally serves to maintain the status quo in terms of White dominance in education."

Education is not a neutral practice. When we don't consider the unique identities of our Asian students we don't have to reflect on how we might perpetuate the model minority myth in our classrooms. We don't see how our actions influence how our Asian students learn to see themselves. We also miss opportunities to ensure accurate representation of different Asian communities within our classrooms and curriculums too. When we don't take steps towards understanding the influences of our most marginalised students' social identity markers on how they learn and see themselves as learners, we perpetuate the racist, patriarchal systems in society designed to dehumanise and exploit them. Our inaction can do a lot more than simply impact a student's academic achievements.

Reflect now

What Asian groups would be considered the model minority in your teaching area? How do these beliefs impact the ways that their behaviour is interpreted in your school environment when compared to other students? How are you learning about becoming more culturally responsive to these students' needs? What have you been doing to challenge the pervasive stereotypes of the model minority myth in your education setting?

ADHD Support: meta-cognition and reducing perfectionism

It's easy to reason away difficulties when a student appears less impacted by them. With marginalised groups that are typically seen as either never causing disruptions or always causing them, their barriers to learning can be interpreted as expected behaviour for their group and therefore they remain unsupported. For ADHD presentations that aren't easily identifiable or don't appear to interfere with their academic outcomes, this is when changes we make in our learning environments for some could benefit everyone. For example, the decision to focus on Ji Yeon's meta-cognition allowed us to slowly introduce more opportunities to reflect on and learn from mistakes for all our students. It also meant that any learner that used coping mechanisms like perfectionism or harsh self-criticism, or had times where they might struggled with a poor learner self-image, could learn alternative strategies too. The challenges Ji Yeon faced, although seemingly not as impactful to her as compared to what others might be struggling with, were still barriers for her to effectively engaging in her learning. They deserved to be addressed too.

Table 6.1 ADHD support: meta-cognition and reducing perfectionism

Metacognition Includes the ability to reflect on what's been done and what's needed. It allows a person to self-evaluate and self-monitor their effort and social skills as well as supports problem-solving.

Possible ADHD presentations	Possible accommodations
Unsure of what's necessary to complete a task (time, effort, what the finished task looks like...)	• Model language for reflecting on work: What does complete look like? What will help me get done on time? • Visual timers for reminders of ongoing evaluation of their work progress and what's impacting their effort (e.g. tiredness, worried about something, needing to learn a new task, redo a task, finding a task easier than initially thought)
Struggle with evaluating their work or effort	• Be specific with feedback (make it clear and actionable, not just "try harder" which is vague and assumes they haven't been making an effort) • Model language for evaluating work or effort that offers practical solutions rather than blame and shame, which keeps learners stuck with what to change. (For example, "I was tired today, so I felt distracted. I need to go to bed earlier, or have my friend check my work before I hand it in next time." Rather than, "I need to pay closer attention") • Help students avoid self-criticism by modelling and/or providing questions for evaluating their task work (before, during and after). Ensure that questions consider the environment and/or skills that might need altering or developing in order to complete the tasks more successfully

	• Give homework (it if must be given) feedback as a few specific items that went well and one specific way that the student can improve their work, with guidance on how
Not aware of how their actions impact others, struggles with perspective taking	• Find or create games and activities that help students practise recognising meaning with different facial expressions and tone of voice and seeing a problem, event or situation from various points of view
Difficulties in solving problems (including social skills)	• Involve the class in practising to solve everyday social problems
	• Suggest questions for students to ask themselves like: What did I do when I had this problem before? What people or strategies helped me before? Who or what might be helpful for me now? What are three possible solutions?

Emotional regulation: Reducing perfectionist tendencies

Perfectionism compounds the underlying anxiety an ADHD learner might have. It keeps them "trying harder" but often without a clear understanding of the impact of their ADHD on their efforts, maladaptive coping strategies emerge. Strategies like overcompensating on projects to prove their worth further impacts their time management when they unknowingly get stuck in the details. Using perfectionism as the standard by which to measure themselves by their own and others' expectations keeps them from seeing themselves realistically. Addressing perfectionism in ADHD learners means offering positive reassurance to help them see themselves with more compassion, and setting achievable goals while supporting their prioritisation as they learn to accept making mistakes and see their abilities more realistically. Then we can show them that like all people they have areas they can develop and strengths to capitalise on too.

Possible ADHD presentations	Possible accommodations
Become upset, disheartened or unable to progress in work by feedback that requires corrections (or hesitant to mention ways to improve their work)	• Acknowledge their feelings about receiving the feedback or corrections; it's not easy to hear even if your intention is to help. Learning is still a vulnerable act. Give bite-sized corrections at first and scaffold the ability for them to correct it themselves
	• Model receiving corrections in class and positive self-talk while making changes. (I regularly skip words when writing on the board, forget the date, or even make mistakes on purpose so that I can model how they will help me in future)
	• When giving feedback, keep the focus on the work, not the student. Ensure that the actions are specific and helpful

(Continued)

Table 6.1 (*Continued*)

Want to know exactly what's expected, not easily willing to take risks in learning for fear of making mistakes	• Have other students repeat the instructions and give examples of how they might start a project. Use examples to give clarity on what is expected or to encourage students to build on it
	• Reflect with the student on times when they knew exactly what to do. When they recall a time, ask them how they knew what to do. What helped them remember or feel confident they could do it? What did they feel in their body that told them they understood correctly?
Takes extra time on tasks (may want to add every little thing they can think of)	• Check in with students to ensure that they know exactly what to do. Review with them the time they should spend on the different tasks in a project. It might be helpful to adjust production expectations as they go so that there's a focus on quality over quantity
	• Review their work plan together with a focus on estimating time and what ideas are following the instructions or not. Break down bigger tasks into smaller chunks and provide more time estimates. Be flexible with students' ideas and provide clarity on what needs to be completed and why so that they can better understand the bigger picture of the project
Voices frustration about how much they work but are disappointed when comparing results with their peers (this happens in younger grades too)	• Regular check-ins with students give clues to what they are doing with their time and what might be hindering their progress. Talking with parents/carers about their study process can also help us see where there might be gaps in their skills or knowledge that could be supported
	• What kinds of expectations does the student have for themselves or do their parents/carers have of them? Observing how they handle disappointment, feedback or their interactions with family and peers gives us clues to how realistic they might be about their expectations and what support they might need
Frequently asks questions to check their understanding (but show they already know the answers every time this happens)	• Include an "ask three then me" rule in the classroom for some tasks to encourage students to find ways to trust each other
	• Offer scaffolded levels of guided support to give students a chance to become more comfortable with deciding what they need: "If you're ready to get started, go now. If you want to do more examples with me, stay seated. Feel free to leave quietly to start independently at any time you feel ready. If today you just want to follow along with me, that's OK too"

Supporting Ji Yeon

Ji Yeon and I continued to build on from the maths lesson incident. That also included working with her family to better understand her previous learning experiences too. Ji Yeon needed to experience making low-risk mistakes within a safer environment. She also needed to believe that when she did get things wrong she had the chance to make things right without being defined or reduced by it. This is where strategies like giving feedback based on "what went well" and "even better if" come in handy, because they give me the chance to show learners that:

1. Nothing is perfect and it never has to be
2. There are outcomes they achieved
3. There is one thing they can do that could help them improve
4. They're given the time to make the suggested change

One of the most important parts of this practice is giving students the chance to reflect on their work and make changes. I intentionally list something very specific, with clear steps or instructions on how they might make the corrections when needed. It also allows me to correct homework a lot quicker because I can scan through what's been completed without having to correct every last thing (which can also be demoralising to students). Since the feedback is personalised, I've found that this practice can give students more ownership of their work too.

Ji Yeon, like other ADHD learners, could easily focus on all the mistakes she made. This made it challenging for her to take more risks in her learning. Being intentional about reflection and its purpose in learning was helpful for her. It reminded her of successes in other areas of their life that she could use in times that were challenging too. Some coping mechanisms might initially hide ADHD presentations (where other strategies might be more beneficial), but they can easily become ways they learn to see or define themselves too. Our ADHD learners can quickly hyperfocus on and internalise the messages that dehumanise them, impacting how they show up in learning spaces. I've found that the more our ADHDers are seen and accepted as they are, the easier it is for them to accept themselves and the more aware they become of the kind of support they need too. Their lived experience acts as an additional expert in finding solutions for their learning barriers leaving them more empowered to ask for support and advocate for their needs in the future.

Key takeaways:

- New students have lots of transition needs, which are made more complicated if they have ADHD.
- Maths difficulties and disabilities are very prominent in ADHD students. Both domain-general and domain-specific procedures are necessary to build a strong foundation in maths and ADHDers could struggle with either.

(Continued)

- The model minority myth is a part of **white supremacy culture** that perpetuates the idea that Asian learners are more successful than other marginalised students. This often impacts if they're seen or supported while struggling academically.
- Meta-cognition supports students' ability to reflect on their learning, their thinking and supports social skills development.
- Culturally responsive teaching is based on the belief that students learn best through their own cultural context. It considers the roles that the brain and body take in learning.

Resources to explore

Cultural-responsive teaching:

Culturally Responsive Teaching and the Brain by Zaretta Hammond
Start Here, Start Now: A Guide to Antibias and Antiracist Work in Your School Community by Liz Kleinfield: www.teachandtransform.org/
Unpack Your Impact: How Two Primary Teachers Ditched Problematic Lessons and Built a Culture-Centered Curriculum by Naomi O'Brien and LaNesha Tabb

Wellbeing for adults:

Permission to Come Home: Reclaiming Mental Health as Asian Americans by Jenny Wang
Decolonizing the Body: Healing, Body-centered Practices for Women of Colour to Reclaim Confidence, Dignity, and Self-Worth by Kelsey Blackwell
This Pain We Carry: Healing from Complex PTSD for People of Colour by Natalie Gutierrez

Holistic Life Navigation Podcast with Luis Mojica

The Myth of Normal: Trauma, Illness & Healing in a Toxic Culture by Gabor Maté and with Daniel Maté
Living Resistance, An Indigenous Vision for Seeking Wholeness Every Day by Kaitlin B. Curtice

Dyscalculia

British Dyslexia Association (Dyscalculia): www.bdadyslexia.org.uk/dyscalculia

7

"He just won't sit still!":

Diego's story

This chapter asks us to reflect on:

* the overlap between ADHD and sensory sensitivities;
* meeting sensory needs with culturally responsive teaching;
* building a felt sense of safety by remembering how the brain and nervous system work;
* initial considerations for creating flexible learning spaces and why this matters;
* how scarcity impacts what we believe we can change within the physical learning environment.

Diego stood motionless, overlooking his table in the centre of the classroom as he sobbed unconsolably. His chair was knocked over and the work he'd been given was now on the floor, alongside his table's class materials that were piled at his feet. What I assumed would be an engaging maths station activity had somehow turned into something quite distressing for him. He was still screaming when I quietly approached the table to see what was happening, ensuring he could see me. The other students at the table looked up at him in alarm, some covered their ears and others just looked puzzled. This wasn't the first time we'd seen Diego like this; it was just that we were seeing it happen more often and with more intensity.

   "Teacher!" one child volunteered. "I think he's sad because he couldn't use the markers very well …"

"No …", another student spoke up, "he doesn't like this game."

"No, it's the scissors –"

"Thank you!" I stop them quickly. "This is all very… helpful …" I glanced over at my TA, hoping they saw something, but they simply shrugged. Diego continued to sob, his screams getting louder the longer we watched. He was not happy about something and one thing I was certain of: he wouldn't be saying much about it. I was learning a lot over the last few months since we began to suspect that perhaps Diego was more than just a kid who didn't speak much of the language of instruction and ran throughout the classroom at every opportunity. Or that he only wanted to do what he liked and could be disruptive much of the time. When it came to understanding Diego, we were still only at the tip of the iceberg.

Meet Diego:

- 6 years old
- Latine ethnicity, light brown skin
- identifies as a boy
- emergent bilingual, but minimally speaking (including in his **home language**)
- outgoing, energetic, sensitive
- loves: being read to, drawing pictures, break time
- detests: writing and using scissors
- future aspirations: a palaeontologist (he appeared to love dinosaurs)
- best known for refusing to engage in learning activities, frequent meltdowns
- learning challenges: social-emotional-behavioural challenges, suspected sensory processing needs, suspected ADHD, suspected autism
- additional information: doesn't always play with others

I asked my TA to oversee the class so I could try to help Diego calm down. As the meltdown continued, I did the only thing I could think of which was to gently guide him to the quiet corner. It was a simple space in our class, where I had a small basket of fidgets and soft toys, things I knew he really loved. There were a few pillows and a little play tent the children liked to snuggle up in when they had any free time or needed a quiet space. I knew he'd eventually calm down there.

"Diego? Diego?" I crouched down to his level to talk with him. He kept crying and sharply turned away from the table when I began to speak with him. I backed up, kept my stature low and attempted to reach out to him again, but was sure not to touch him as I noticed that he often recoiled from any gentle touches to his hand or shoulder.

"The quiet corner. Let's go to the quiet corner …" I motioned with my hand for him to come towards me as I backed away from him and closer to the quiet corner. All I kept saying to myself was, "Stay calm … stay calm … Stay. Calm. It'll be OK".

"I know it's tough … It's OK … you're safe …" I said softly over and over again as I crept towards him. Diego slowly moved towards the tent and crawled inside. I left his favourite dinosaur toy within reach in case he needed it. Eventually, the uncontrollable sobbing turned to quiet sniffles and then finally nothing.

He'd fallen asleep. It was doubtful that Diego would talk to anyone or engage in any more activities for the rest of the day. I knew that much about him now.

As much as I was getting used to Diego's reactions and meltdowns, I was still very nervous around him. I was learning about what might upset him, but throughout this process I'd been hit and scratched, and watched as he hid under tables refusing to come out; he would often scream, cry and a few times tried to run from the classroom altogether. There were also many times, like today, when after a meltdown he'd just stop talking altogether or simply fall asleep. All I could think about was how much more unmanageable Diego's behaviour was becoming and I was struggling to figure out some root causes of it. All I could think of was how could I change him or how could he change himself, never considering that there might be many other triggers or reasons for the behaviour in the first place. This thinking was limiting the scope of solutions I believed were possible for Diego. It kept me doing the same things over and over, expecting that eventually he'd behave how I wanted him to, but it wasn't working.

I finally reached out to Diego's parents, who were as supportive as they could be, but to them he was just an active, quirky little boy who could be sensitive at times. Although they couldn't see what I considered as challenges, they tried to share what they felt worked to help him feel or stay calmer in the different environments. Even if there was some sort of learning challenge, they wouldn't agree to any formal assessments or medical interventions. Of course, they would support him however they could at home, but I knew that it might be limited due to their own language barriers and time constraints because of their work. Still, I hoped to use the insights I'd gained from them to bring some practices that were more familiar to Diego into the classroom. I thought it might make him feel more comfortable in the space.

Intersectional insight: The family's persepctive

How parents interpret their child's behaviour is as influenced by their own culture, environment, financial status and history as much as teachers are influenced by theirs. This can impact what they would consider as being a need or barrier to their child's learning and whether they would seek out support. For example, one US study suggested that Indian parents would be more concerned about social difficulties with their children than white parents, who are more likely to be concerned about language delays (Schmengler et al., 2021). Latine parents were seen not to identify symptoms that others would consider to be incredibly prominent and were similar to Black parents, who preferred behavioural support over medical interventions for their children. This differed from white parents who were more apt to choose medical interventions over behavioural support. Many other studies have shown that immigrant parents were also more unlikely to identify ADHD presentations in their children. This could be for various reasons, including how different cultures viewed typical ADHD presentations stemming from social or spiritual problems rather than medical ones. The way that we approach learning challenges and classroom behaviour with parents needs to keep their differing interpretations in mind.

Besides having frequent meltdowns in the classroom, Diego really didn't enjoy being in the lunch room either. Like many school dining halls, the acoustics were loud and echoey. Each day was becoming more of a mission to get him there, let alone stay to eat. Waiting in the line-up to get through to the dining room was also causing problems. I'd hear about how sometimes he'd finally sit down, with his hands over his ears, staring at his food at the same time. Most of the time, he refused to eat anyway. But this would only lead to him acting out later in the day, so the expectation that Diego ate in the dining hall needed to change. To make matters worse, the lunch room was where we'd have our school assemblies too and Diego didn't like them either. I couldn't get him to stay at one beyond a few minutes before my TA or I had to leave with him. But I soon noticed that there were many things in the school environment that regularly caused Diego a lot of discomfort and dysregulation when compared to his peers.

My learning support teacher suggested that Diego might have some sensory needs and asked that I list what I had noticed so far, doing so through simply noting what I saw, *not* what I thought the behaviours meant. So, I witnessed Diego run around the class and eventually sit in a chair when everyone was asked to sit on the carpet. What I didn't see was Diego refusing to listen to instructions by running away from me and using a chair while refusing to sit on the carpet when asked. Keeping to the facts would help me consider other outside causes or triggers of Diego's behaviour. I needed to observe what I saw while keeping my own biases and beliefs about him or his behaviour out of the picture.

What I noticed was that Diego had a whole host of reactions to everyday materials, places or activities that seemed more intense than those of most other children in the class, like:

- not putting on some PE equipment or dress-up costumes;
- covering his ears to loud sounds;
- going to the tent when he got extremely upset;
- turning off the lights unexpectedly;
- frequently tripping over himself and bumping into others in line-ups;
- running around the classroom unexpectedly;
- ripping papers and breaking pencil when attempting to write more than a few words;
- chewing on the ends of pencils when attempting to do longer tasks;
- shutting down in class with challenging tasks or during social problems;
- displaying anger or other strong emotions when experiencing social problems;
- resisting using some of the art supplies because of texture;
- using scissors with support on how tightly to grip the paper;
- often becoming distracted and daydreaming, especially by the end of the day;
- becoming unsettled with unexpected changes to the week's agenda;
- wanting to lean against the wall or sit in a chair when asked to come to the carpet.

I also wrote about the triggers for the reactions, the responses from those around him and how he eventually calmed down. In fact, any details I could think of around the incidents could be influential in noticing some patterns to his reactions.

If I realised he was tired, if there was a change in the schedule or if he wasn't eating, this all could become data for better understanding him. If he was hampered with unmet sensory needs, it meant I would have to look at what stimuli were specifically causing him distress and from there I could create a plan of support.

> ### Reflect now
>
> What sort of assumptions do you carry about what students should be able to manage or handle when it comes to sensory input in the learning environment? How do you think these assumptions and expectations might change depending on your students' race, gender, age, economic status or other social identity markers?

Sensory processing needs 101

I don't think we realise how much our senses impact the way we think about, feel and experience the world around us. Anyone can become dysregulated because of a sensory experience. Think about when something is too loud or has a strong odour, or notice when we become more irritable when we're tired or hungry. These can cause some dysregulation in our nervous system, but for most people, their brains can quickly filter through the stimulus and regulate it, bringing them back to feeling alert and ready to engage with the world again. For others however, it's not always that simple.

Most of us learn that we have five senses but actually we have eight:

1. Visual: how the brain processes recognising, differentiating and interpreting visual stimuli through comparison
2. Tactile: how neural receptors that are generally found in the skin, process different kinds of pressure
3. Auditory: how the brain interprets, recognises and differentiates sound stimuli
4. Gustatory: detecting the taste of different substances
5. Olfactory: the brain's process in detecting, interpreting and differentiating scent stimuli
6. Interoception: how the brain interprets different sensations within the body
7. Proprioception: the awareness of the position of different parts of the body and the strength of effort being used in movement
8. Vestibular: the perception of our body in relation to its movement and balance

Our senses take in information from our surrounding environment and a part of our brain filters through it so that just the right amount of stimulation comes through. Then our brain can decipher what's necessary information to focus on. For some ADHD children and those with other neurodivergence (including trauma), there could be various difficulties that keep the brain's sensory input "filtering system" from working effectively. These children must now expend additional energy to find ways to process sensory stimuli, by using strategies to either avoid them or seek out additional stimulation (Nason, 2014). This can be exhausting for a child, creating an unrecognised energy drain that also impacts their readiness for learning.

Being regulated is the ability to appropriately engage in the task at hand (Nason, 2014). So, depending on what the child needs to accomplish, they would have to be appropriately activated for it. Our learners can be hypersensitive to the sensory input (the stimulus overwhelms any one of their multiple senses and they become over-stimulated) or they may be hypo-sensitive (they seek out the sensory stimulus because they are under-stimulated). Quite often, having sensory processing needs means experiencing a bit of both. It's difficult for children to gauge the amount of stimulus needed in order to optimally self-regulate, so finding the delicate balance of activation necessary uses up a lot of their energy too.

Quick tip: Supporting interoception

Interoception is our ability to recognise and interpret the sensations we feel in our bodies. When we can better regulate the touch, proprioception and vestibular senses, we gain a stronger connection to our interoception sense. This means that as educators when we consider activities that support the regulation of these senses then we could help students in better accessing their interception. With that, they can better attune to their bodies need when they become dysregulated.

Although it's natural to have extremes of stimulus that we must regulate daily, problems arise with the inability to regulate effectively. When that happens for a prolonged amount of time with no space or time to reorganise and regulate the input, the student goes into sensory overload. This becomes an emergency state for the brain. It understands that the body doesn't feel safe and therefore it must prioritise regulation over all else, including learning. It will do whatever it can to regulate the body so that it is safe again. If this happens a lot and consistently, the system can experience burnout which can take much longer to recover from than simply reducing the affecting sensory stimuli in the first place.

Many of the behaviours that we might witness when a student is over- or understimulated look very similar to ADHD too, only their causes and triggers might be different. There is still an underlying sense of anxiety that comes with a disorganised and overwhelmed nervous system when the cause is due to problems with sensory processing. Anxiety is uncomfortable and discomfort is dysregulating for the body. When a body is dysregulated, it feels unsafe. Therefore, the brain reverts to what it knows will quickly bring it back to a felt sense of safety, whether it's the best choice for the environment it's in or not.

Our school environments are an onslaught of sensory information and much of it can be unfamiliar, especially at first (new people, materials, timings, smells, sounds, lighting, skills and information). There are different activities or ways we can set up our environments that can help our students to self-regulate sensory information. Being intentional about how we organise and manage our physical environment (see Ji Yeon's story) includes integrating sensory regulation tools and strategies. Even new sensory regulation strategies work best when connected to their prior knowledge, experiences, cultural beliefs and histories. This not only helps learners have a much better chance at accessing new self-regulation strategies because they connect to what is already familiar, but also cultivates more belonging.

We need to get a better understanding of what sensory processing needs are impacting our learners and what the resulting presentations are telling us. Hyper-sensitive students may become overwhelmed easily because of all the information they cannot filter through. This is when we might see them become distracted, even more sensitive to their environment (covering their ears, running from the room) and losing focus. They might become frustrated, irritable and angry, start crying or have frequent meltdowns. They would avoid the stimulus if they can. These students would need access to activities and strategies that calm the nervous system. Hypo-sensitive students struggle to receive enough information to process and seek out more stimulus if they want to stay activated, becoming more restless, hyperactive and fidgety. Or they can become so under-stimulated that they appear drowsy, sluggish and slouchy (Nason, 2014). These students would need access to appropriate activities and strategies that activate their nervous systems. Most students would need access to activities for both options throughout the regular school day, especially if they display multiple presentations.

Depending on what senses are activated, a variety of different strategies to either activate or calm the nervous system can be used. With students like Diego, working with an occupational therapist, learning support teachers and paraeducators in understanding their sensory processing needs and getting suggestions for accommodations is important. That will help you better design a **sensory diet** that is personalised to their sensory processing challenges. Keep in mind that depending on the capacity of their nervous system at that time, students might only be able to engage in certain strategies too. This means that even when they're being taught new more effective or appropriate self-regulation strategies, their systems still won't naturally utilise them in distress. Instead, they will continue to use their go-to automatic strategies until their bodies build the capacity to slow down enough in order to think of using new ones. That takes time with modelling, practice (when not distressed) and getting to know their sensory needs. At the same time building a stronger connection in order to enhance your ability to co-regulate with them when needed could prove helpful when having to de-escalate any reactions.

Quick tip: Integrating sensory processing strategies

Some strategies can be used for both calming and activation depending on the behaviours you're noticing. These should be practised often and not when the student is in a crisis state. It's helpful to engage them in reflecting on how the strategies made them feel (you might think about modelling how to describe the sensations in your own body) and what strategies they've enjoyed, found most helpful or are starting to use in different places besides the classroom.

Table 7.1 Self-regulation and co-regulation

Self-regulation	Co-regulating (done as a teacher or with other students)
Take ten deep breaths	Model calm behaviour
Count to ten	Model how to use a fidget toy or a
Squeeze a stress ball	self-regulation strategy
Give yourself a hug	Offer choice
Use the swing	Offer a snack or drink
Spin in a circle	Do a movement break
Jump on a mini-trampoline	Read a story
Draw something that makes you happy	Use a timer
Lay on an exercise ball	Ask, "What can I help you with?"
Balance on a stool	Go for a walk together
Go to a quiet area	Offer positive, actionable feedback
Eat something crunchy or chewy	Keep your voice calm
Go get water	Keep from talking or making demands
Read a book	Stay calm while saying "you're safe"
Rock gently on a ball	Use **sensory bins** with others
Relax on pillows	Take a walk together
Listen to music	Give them space from others watching
Do wall push-ups	Practise mindfulness activities
Use a fidget toy	Take a brain break
Jumping jacks	Do yoga poses
	Do push and pull exercises
	Hand out materials for others
	Remove triggers

Since up to one in six children have sensory processing needs, not just sensory processing disorder (Child Mind Institute, August 2021), creating a sensory-friendly learning environment would support more students than you might realise. Not to mention that it's something that all students can benefit from because becoming overwhelmed with sensory information can happen to any student at any time. Providing a sensory-friendly learning environment should be an essential strategy we implement for creating a safer learning environment for our ADHD students. Accommodations can start with a few physical classroom changes and some thought towards integrating regulating materials and activities, and creating purpose-designed spaces, into the learning environment.

Building a culture in our classrooms

All humans long to feel like we belong and we feel this through the cultures we belong to. There are many different cultures around us, including clubs, sports teams, and even our families have their own culture. Schools have their own culture too. This culture is based on white, Eurocentric expectations of education. That culture make schools inherently unsafe for many children, particularly those from historically excluded communities. Our ADHD learners are no different when it comes to not fitting the culture of many school environments. They are hypervigilant to threats to their belonging because of their emotional dysregulation, especially when it comes to fears of rejection, real or perceived. Their need for belonging might be heightened, but so too are the challenges to regulating their nervous system.

It's vital that we're intentional about the culture we want to create in our learning environments. Those students who fall outside Eurocentric expectations will find it harder to feel like they belong. It means they will feel a lot more dysregulated too (whether it's always visible or not), so as teachers we've always got to be doing the work to build our own capacity for difference to better co-regulate with those marginalised students. We need to have regular practices of learning to calm and regulate our nervous system, using more self-compassion and creating communities so we can talk about and integrate any challenging classroom situations keeping us feeling unsafe or dysregulated around certain students too. The changes we need to see in our classrooms are often reflected through the work we're putting towards ourselves first.

We can't change the systems that exclude and marginalise our students overnight, but when we can create a space that "offers people better ways to belong, and better things to belong to … we can belong to a culture" (Menakem, 2017, p. 148). A culture takes time to build but they are incredibly important to all humans. They "create belonging and make our bodies feel safe … because it's not something that's experienced in the mind, but in the body" (Menakem 2017, p. 252). We all have the ability to build our capacity to belong, even our students. The ways that we continually repeat the use of rituals, songs, stories, mentoring, the rules and the codes of behaviour we follow in our classroom are some of the ways that we do this. The choices we make in learning materials, the design and decor of the space, the inclusion of our students and the wider community, the ways we speak to each other and work together also signal to learners the kind of culture we're trying to create.

When I met with Diego's parents again, I knew I needed to learn more about his home and what sorts of things Diego would be familiar with that they noticed left him feeling at ease and what energised him. They smiled as they shared how Diego was fortunate to have a lot of extended family around him. Together, they would spend a lot of time eating, chatting or being outdoors. It made me think that Diego might enjoy having an adult near him or working with others, even if it was just a partner. He also loved music and listened to some songs on repeat, so activating activities for him might also include opportunities for songs, call and response, dancing and movement. Calming activities might include stories, listening to quiet music or time in the garden area. Finding activities that were more familiar to Diego meant we were building on his prior knowledge with new learning experiences. The best part was that addressing Diego's sensory processing needs would also support many of his possible ADHD needs too.

> ## Quick tip: Avoid dysregulation because of "physical" needs
>
> I like to have a small collection of snacks and cups for water for those children that need them. I let students have water bottles at their seats and get a snack when they want for longer or independent stretches of work time (as long as they follow our class agreements). I'd rather they eat and drink when necessary than be distracted by hunger or thirst. School days are long and people get hungry or thirsty at different times for various reasons. Even something like a student's ADHD medication wearing off could mean a sudden increase in their appetite and a change of mood towards the end of the day.
>
> I also allow students to use the bathroom whenever they need (including when I'm direct teaching), so I leave bathroom passes that are easily accessible for them to carry or wear. If students haven't had this option before, the first week of school feels a bit like a revolving classroom door. But being crystal clear about the purpose of this arrangement and discussing the consequences of potentially abusing it helps students utilise it more wisely and support others in doing the same. A bathroom pass is mostly to allow my students to be in the hallways without being questioned by other teaching staff. It also helps me keep from having my whole class in the bathroom at once. I used to have them labelled by gendered bathrooms, but now I have a certain number of passes and keep them gender-neutral.

ADHD Support: reducing impulsivity and managing sensory anxiety

An area that Diego was noticeably struggling with was impulse control, which meant that direct teaching and in-the-moment support would be necessary. Sometimes you can't get away from that fact when working with much younger ADHD children. Expecting a child as young as Diego, who was being taught in a learning environment where he was culturally and linguistically different from his peers and with additional communication needs, to be able to stop being impulsive independently was just not realistic. I knew I needed to plan very carefully for him and ensure that he always knew what to do if he needed a break or had finished a task a little earlier than expected.

I wanted to integrate new strategies in a learning environment that helped him feel safer within it. This meant getting closer to his zone of proximal development by gathering information about his sensory triggers and how he had learned to manage them. I also needed to track signs of when he was approaching sensory overwhelm and into sensory overload. I couldn't do this alone and often had my TA or learning support teacher to observe for me when I was in circle time or in small groups with other students. Then we hoped over time that we could intervene sooner to reduce the amount of meltdowns he was having. We also hoped to build on the tools he was already familiar with and eventually support him in incorporating additional strategies that might be more effective for him.

Table 7.2 ADHD support: reducing impulsivity and managing sensory anxiety

Impulse inhibition The ability to think before acting, control the urge to do or say things that might not be necessary at that moment and have the ability to see how your behaviour and actions impact yourself, others and how they see you

Possible ADHD presentations	Possible accommodations
Desire to touch and grab materials without pausing first (theirs or other people's)	• Introduce more weight bearing, jumping and pushing activities (like wall sits or wall push-ups) to support proprioception sensory needs during transitions • Break up instructions to reduce overwhelm and anxiety (which may be causing the restlessness and grabbing for materials) • Keep hands busy with drawing or fidgets or include a "while listening" task for direct teaching or group work • Model thinking and showing the consequences of touching other people's things without permission and not putting things away • Introduce the use of different fidgets and teach how they are used. Allow students to choose which ones work best for them. Let students use as needed
Constant need to move through the class or move in seat	• Teach students how to use flexible seating and learning spaces. This includes considering the why for the different options, what effective use of the space looks like and the cause and effect of not using the space well on themselves and others • Include a **sensory diet** • Include regulating brain breaks and movement breaks throughout the day and in between transitions (add music or call and response to signal transitions) • Provide choice for where to complete school work (whether standing, sitting, under the table, in the hallway…) • Plan more active and/or preferred tasks for the end of the day or week when tiredness most impacts learning • Utilise chair bands and other types of foot fidgets. Provide wedge cushions to sit on • Introduce "*chewlery*" toys and have parents include crunchy snacks or even a water bottle with a straw (for proprioception regulation, especially if students chew on materials)

(Continued)

Table 7.2 *(Continued)*

Starts right away without considering instructions or materials (especially when given tech devices)	• Give access to materials for the task as needed • Allow access to materials for an experimental time before giving additional instructions, if necessary • Materials are clearly accessible, organised and labelled so students know where they belong and can practise finding and returning material when completed (allow time in the activity to get into the practice of doing this)
Makes noise during direct teaching (blurts out answers or other noises)	• Consider whether direct teaching has been happening for too long. If you're spending a lot of time communicating but your students aren't, then effective learning isn't taking place • Movement might be necessary to either reduce anxiety or to activate them (depending on the situation) • Provide various options on how students answer or feed back, especially within a whole-class discussion (mini-whiteboard, drawing names from a jar, thumbs up or down, turn and talk, post-its, one to one, small groups) • Mini-whiteboards help to get down ideas before they're forgotten (and also double as a way to listen and doodle)
Talks incessantly or plays around when working in small groups or with partners	• Reduce the anxiety (especially if it's a lesson they feel less confident in) by giving topics in advance, providing a clear role for each student in the group, using talk structures and collaborative learning practices so students have step-by-step instructions on how to engage • Be flexible with seating so that students can engage in their groups while moving as they need

Emotional regulation: Reducing sensory anxiety

A body with sensory processing challenges struggles to regulate sensations that they know, but also finds it difficult to become accustomed to new sensory information (Dillon, n.d., accessed 16 June 2023). At any moment, the environment can change sensory input, so there's often anxiety anticipating this. Modifications to the environment to reduce troubling sensory input aren't always possible. Having access to materials like fidgets and noise-cancelling headphones, or doing sensory regulation activities beforehand, can help prepare the body for what it might encounter

Possible ADHD presentations	Possible accommodations
Resists engaging in un-preferred tasks or changing to certain tasks unexpectedly	• Give an advanced look at the material or of any changes in agenda • Decide what outcomes are most important to complete or if there are other ways that the competency has been met in other lessons • Work one-to-one or with a friend if it's absolutely necessary to do the task. Allow flexibility and choice where you can, including where they work and how they access or express learning
Becomes "aggressive", disruptive or frustrated when misunderstood or unable to communicate needs	• Use robust and effective ways to communicate, whether that's through a combination of pictures, translation with technology or giving access to an augmentative, alternative communication (AAC) device – include vocabulary that supports expressing discomfort (body parts, emotions, illnesses) and any special interests they might have (sharing special interests can be soothing) • Track patterns of disruptive behaviours during the school day to create a **sensory diet** to better support the ability to self-regulate • Reduce disruptions due to tiredness, hunger or thirst by providing easier access to students' snacks, water and the quiet corner. This can help eliminate wondering whether physical needs must be met or not
Becomes agitated and upset with changes in adherence to classroom expectations or inconsistencies in managing consequences	• Be very consistent about what is expected of students in the classroom and the natural consequences for breaking these expectations • Clearly label areas of the classroom and their purposes. (This creates more consistency for the student and therefore builds a sense of safety)
Continue to use self-regulation strategies that disrupt the class environment even when they're learning new ones	• Choose the most disruptive behaviours and with the students' input experiment with different strategies around managing the trigger patterns preceding them. Support the student in reflecting on what is helping in reducing the behaviours *or* what might be contributing to an increase in them
Appears restless, irritable, tired or fidgety	• Depending on the system that needs regulation, there are different activities that could be added into the day to support students in either calming or becoming more activated. Regular times for large motor movements like yoga postures, wall sits, wall push-ups and jumping jacks can support both the proprioception and vestibular systems

---

Quick tip: Being intentional with fidget toys

There are so many different kinds of fidget toys that vary in texture, light, weight, size, sound, colour and what they do. It's not enough to let kids have free reign of the fidget toys though. Not all fidget toys will appeal to all students and not all students will actually need a fidget toy at the same time either. What's important is taking the time to model their use (so it's good to have more than one of each) and work with your class to create a classroom agreement on how they're used and taken care of. It's also necessary to ensure that your students understand what they are helpful for and what they look and feel like when they aren't being used properly, and how that can impact their learning and the learning of others too.

Scarcity in designing flexible learning spaces

I once worked in one of the most beautiful schools in the world. I'd never been in a learning environment that wasn't praising teachers for covering the walls with everything that was humanly possible before. In the schools I'd been to it was expected that you have interactive displays and showcase students' work and anchor charts that would keep no wall space left uncovered. But this school was designed with huge windows to create the illusion of the natural world being an extension of the classroom. Because of that, we were asked to leave the walls bare and let the greenery and natural light come through, while finding alternative ways to provide resources for students to access when they needed them.

Their school philosophy stated the importance of nature as being a teacher in the child's learning journey. This meant that we as teachers needed to be very intentional about what to display, how to display it and how it supported our students' learning journey. My experience in this school played a significant role in how I changed the way I designed and utilised my learning spaces after that. It made me reflect on how the physical classroom environment could act as an additional teacher, potential co-regulator and a reflection of the culture of the space. Seeing the learning environment this way helped me understand just how essential it could be to all of our well-being. I needed to be very intentional about building in this space and what I hoped it would to do for everyone in it.

When we don't have access to what we believe we need to make a good learning environment it can leave us feeling frustrated and disheartened. We often struggle with the scarcity that is embedded within the education system, because it too is a part of **white supremacy culture**. This mindset conditions us to believe that there isn't enough for everyone, and it does a good job of it too. We see how schools are underfunded, and educators are left paying for their own classroom materials, are over-worked and severely underpaid. But then we also see the elaborate classroom displays, various chair styles and storage solutions on Instagram and Pinterest, and feel pressured to create something similar. This leads us to competing with each other for what we need, and what we notice is our lack of resources, rather than sharing resources and taking action together to dismantle the **structural inequities** at play in all of it. Instead, we learn we must hoard our resources and solve our problems independently because there isn't enough support or resources to go around.

Intersectional insight: Scarcity and implicit bias

When there is an economic crisis, Black, Brown and Indigenous people (but particularly Black communities) are the hardest hit. One study showed that when faced with economic scarcity and recessions, it isn't just institutional and social structures that create widening racial disparities (Krosch and Amodio, 2014), a person's perception of race also shifts depending on their social goals and motivations too. White people perceive Black **biracial** people as being darker than they are and Black people are also seen as being darker and more stereotypically Black too. This implicit bias promotes resource competition and discriminatory resource allocation by suggesting groups are fighting against each other. It increases distrust and antipathy, devaluing the other person's worth and justifying the withholding of resources because of it. This study made me wonder how the perception of learners' race would shift when it comes to being considered deserving of resources. Or how these beliefs would impact the resourcefulness that's often necessary for educators to access materials.

A scarcity mentality keeps us stuck believing that we don't have enough to make the changes we need with our learning spaces and we can't do enough to make change. But this only limits us from seeing other solutions that might be possible, creating a sense of inertia that can keep us doing the same things and expecting different results. We just don't believe there could be another way and stay stuck in beliefs that creating flexible learning spaces means spending lots of money. But this is completely untrue. Instead, we need to start becoming intentional about how we decorate learning spaces with brain science and our learners' needs in mind. That doesn't take the accumulation of more materials to make a start. For example, as Dillon (2021) notes on the *Cult of Pedagogy Podcast*, "addition by subtraction is the ultimate hack to addressing learning spaces", as it allows students to see a new iteration of the space. Oftentimes I've found that less leaves space for more solutions to become visible too.

Reflect now

What beliefs do you have over which students might be considered to be more "capable" of being in flexible learning spaces over others? How might this impact the way that you design your learning environment, the materials you provide or the behaviour you expect of your students within the space? How does a scarcity mindset show up in how you design your classroom environments and the materials that you keep?

Classroom design with ADHD in mind

Being intentional about why I'm doing anything in my classroom means making choices serve my learners, and classroom design is no exception. I think the physical layout of the learning environment needs to include some key ingredients to best support ADHD students, especially when they are younger. Since these kids are often developmentally delayed in certain executive functioning skills, remembering to structure the environment by including some external support for developing executive functioning skills is important. This might look like including more movement in between and during activities, using pictures to organise materials or to display steps to classroom rituals, processes and procedures.

I like to keep my classroom design very simple; flexible but still predictable and consistent at the same time. Too much on the walls or in the space itself can be a distraction causing dysregulation for some students, but knowing that externalising the executive functioning skills is helpful for many students as well. Trying to find your just-right balance for you and your students' needs will depend on a lot of factors. "Trial and error" is completely ok and a natural process too. Some quick starts that I've found that make a big impact include the following:

- Ask your students often what is supporting them in the classroom and what isn't. Have they noticed anything that's changed lately? This gives you some idea of what they've found most useful and what they're actually noticing or using.
- Remove materials or furniture that don't serve students' learning. We don't need a lot of fancy additions to make learning spaces flexible and we don't need to keep things from the previous teacher or from ten years ago either.
- Think about how you can use the areas that get less use within the whole school environment, like the hallway or cafeteria. Become familiar with who controls bookings for other common areas in your school.
- Consider how you can reduce your teacher footprint in the classroom (including the wall space) and give students agency to take up more space.
- Consider where else learning can take place (around the school, collaborations with other classrooms, in the local community) or who from your wider community could visit (parents, local businesses) and perhaps create a common list of resources from the school-wide community.
- Experiment with different table set-ups depending on the types of learning activities you're doing. Offer more choice for where students want to work.

I also want to make sure that any changes I make to the layout and walls of my classroom involve my students' input (and involvement) when possible. Offering a variety of seating layouts for students to choose from can support learner autonomy, but I can't just assume that they know how to effectively utilise these spaces initially either. That's why I discuss with them how to use the materials or flexible seating properly. We reflect on what it would look and sound like to be learning effectively in different areas of the classroom. We also discuss what might have to happen if we can't work as well, how it impacts their learning or that of others, and the consequences of these choices. This is a collaborative effort, so when I can give students more agency over the design of the learning space, their sense of ownership over it also increases. Creating more ownership of a learning environment helps foster a stronger sense of belonging too.

Since I knew that Diego became easily overwhelmed with the learning environment, being clear about how we used the different learning areas and remaining consistent about implementing those expectations was important. That consistency helped students like Diego know what to expect from me and the classroom, making it a space they could learn to let their guard down in too. Integrating more sensory support was easier to do than I realised. There were a lot of simple ways that I could reduce the noise (not just with sound but visual and lighting too) while also creating space in the schedule (and physical area) for more movement time. The goal was to create a learning environment that supported us as a group, but still allowed for space to have our individual needs met. But this was a slow, daily practice of consistently working towards making sustainable changes. This was especially true when considering they were younger learners, but was an even longer process for children with ADHD like Diego.

Supporting Diego

Diego threw down the scissors and ran over to the corner where we kept the new box of fidget toys I'd gotten for the class. He started rummaging through the box. Even though I was seeing a reduction in meltdowns within a few weeks of integrating more sensory processing options, we hadn't made much progress with Diego engaging in more learning activities that weren't as appealing for him. Today, we'd tried to tempt him by including some of his favourite topics but he was refusing to engage in the activity.

I tried to be a lot more flexible when Diego was like this. If he couldn't find it in himself to use the scissors that day, I knew that there was a reason for it, even if I couldn't pinpoint what it was. Although it was important for him to use scissors in order to build the muscle to do so, he clearly wasn't there yet. I had to work around that. Within our new fidget toy collection I had included some that were squeezable that I hoped would encourage building those muscles effectively too. We could continue to introduce them by placing them in his vision, but leave him to try them at his own pace.

"Are we going to do any of the project today?" I asked him softly. I knew he wouldn't reply. Instead, I watched him intently as he used a fidget spinner that lit up as it turned. It was clearly becoming one of his favourites.

"Diego …" He didn't turn around to look at me, which wasn't surprising since getting his attention often meant being in his vision. I went over to his level so he could see me from the corner of his eye.

"Let's bring your fidget to the table. Come sit back down." I guided him back with the fidget in hand.

Diego was great with colouring and painting. He loved to draw but still didn't understand how to use scissors and would choose to watch me use them instead.

"Let me cut these ones to get started and maybe you can cut these two here …" He looked up at the papers I'd initially started to cut, hoping that it might be easier for him and he'd want to continue, but he still wouldn't budge towards the scissors. Instead, he remained focused on the fidget toy.

"We can do it together?" I suggested, pointing at both of us.

He looked over at the scissors and awkwardly picked them up to pass them to me. I cut the first few as he watched me, fidget still in hand. When he was still hesitant to hold them, I watched to see what he would engage in. Diego decided that he could glue on what was cut and draw or rip out what he needed next. I sat by him, as he continued to do what was given to him. As other learners came up to me when they needed, Diego sat next to me continuing on what we started and this was more than enough.

> ## Key takeaways:
>
> - A dysregulated nervous system is one that feels unsafe. The brain's primary aim is to maximise safety, by feeling good and connecting with others, so if any of these aren't happening, the body will be dysregulated (Hammond, 2014).
> - Sensory needs are characterised by being over-stimulated by the stimuli in the environment (hypersensitive) or under-stimulated (hyposensitive). When the body can't regulate the stimulus effectively over time it becomes sensory overload.
> - Sensory processing challenges can often manifest similarly to ADHD presentations. All students can have sensory processing challenges at times; it's just some students with ADHD and other neurodivergence experience them more frequently or intensely.
> - **White supremacy culture** creates a scarcity mindset. This makes creating flexible learning spaces challenging when we get messages about what makes a "good" learning space, but we don't have easy access to resources.
> - The way we use the physical learning environment supports us in meeting sensory needs as well as plays the role of another teacher or learning guide. It's important that we are intentional about creating a flexible learning space that promotes safety and belonging for the student.
> - We can be culturally responsive teachers in many ways, including learning about how different cultures regulate discomfort and integrating these activities into our classrooms.

Resources to explore

Sensory needs

Interoception Curriculum: www.kelly-mahler.com/
The Neurodivergent Teacher: www.the-neurodivergent-teacher.com/
The OT Toolbox: www.theottoolbox.com/

Classroom design

The Space: A Guide for Educators by Bob Dillon and Rebecca Mead

Autism

A Day With No Words by Tiffany Hammond
The Reason I Jump by Naoki Higashido
I Will Die on the Hill: Autistic Adults, Autism Parents and the Children Who Deserve a Better World by Megan Ashburn and Jules Edwards
We're Not Broken by Eric Garcia

8

"Is he – they even old enough to choose pronouns?":

Alex's story

This chapter asks us to reflect on:

- the significant overlap between ADHD, OCD, Tourette syndrome and other tic disorders;
- supporting co-occurring anxiety and depression;
- how we build gender-affirming classrooms to support trans, non-binary and gender-expansive children;
- how the gender binary distorts our interpretation of ADHD presentations.

Alex was a fairly quiet student anyway, but lately seemed quieter than usual. They started to frequently miss school, whether that was arriving late, having to leave early or just not turning up altogether. I know that their teacher, the school administration and Alex's parents were doing everything they could think of to make attending school feel possible for them, but nothing seemed to help. As Alex's anxiety increased, their school attendance further decreased and soon their academic outcomes began to suffer – which by all accounts only made them feel worse. Even though an initial cause for their anxiety and school absences was their increasing difficulties with their tics, everyone would soon learn that this was just a small part of what they were going through.

Meet Alex:

- 11 years old, white, European ancestry
- identifies as non-binary
- fluent in the language of instruction
- insightful, kind, artistic
- loves: maths, art, music
- detests: reading
- future aspirations: graphic designer
- best known for: vocal and motor tics, not attending school
- learning challenges: ADHD, Tourette syndrome or other tic disorder
- additional information: possible obsessive-compulsive disorder (OCD) and generalised anxiety

---

From what I learned through other teachers in our team planning meetings, Alex's tics seemed less intrusive when they were younger. But as the years passed they became much more complex, making it increasingly more difficult to engage in many expected learning tasks. Their tics could result in them ripping up or scribbling on their papers. They might start making noises that made other students laugh at them and their teachers frustrated as a result. Addressing the undesirable behaviour often made the tics worse, making it appear as if Alex was doing them on purpose. This resulted in them getting into trouble with teachers and their peers. Although tics are repeated sounds and movements that are involuntary, the problem is that they can look and sound as if the student is acting impulsively, fidgeting or being aggressive and defiant – all actions, which initially sounds a lot like ADHD.

Tics, Tourette syndrome and ADHD

What makes Tourette syndrome (TS) different from other tic conditions is its onset (starting in childhood), the length of time with tics (at least a year) and the kinds of tics (both motor and vocal tics that can be either simple or complex). TS and ADHD co-occur frequently, with over half of all children with TS also having ADHD. For children where ADHD is noticed first, one in five will also experience persistent tics or have TS too. With such high co-occurrence rates it's surprising that ticcing or TS are not talked about as often as other neurodivergence. When it is talked about, the general assumption and misconception is that everyone with TS or tics swears or shouts out socially inappropriate language. But the fact is that only about 15–20 per cent of ticcers actually have coprolalia (which is tics involving swearing or using other inappropriate language).

Tics often start at around 6–7 years old. Their severity and frequency are impacted by environmental factors like stress, relaxation, excitement and sensory needs. The premonitory urge that comes before a tic is a physical sensation much like the urge before a sneeze or a burning sensation. When the tic is performed, the premonitory urge reduces. When forced to suppress tics,[1] the urge increases. For some people, it may take one tic to reduce the urge, but for others, it may be repeated until the urge disappears or feels *just right*. In the classroom some tics might appear as if they are done on purpose, being interpreted as attempts to get attention or disrupt the class. But this is not the case.

Ticcing can have a huge impact on our students' abilities to access the curriculum, and when compounded with ADHD it only increases their learning barriers. They can become distracted by tics, making it difficult or even impossible to engage in learning tasks at the same time. Motor tics can cause physical pain and discomfort. The constant need to monitor themselves forces them to focus on suppressing their tics, which requires a lot of additional energy too. Students who have tic conditions or TS often face a lot of bullying, compounding their stress and anxiety, which only intensifies tics. In fact, even speaking about their tics can cause some to tic more. Depending on how severe the tics are, this can result in students needing "to repeat grades, deal with more school problems or not care about doing well in school" (Claussen et al., 2018).

Intersectional insight: Ticcing within marginalised communities

A 2009 study done in the US found that "Tourette syndrome occurred in 3 out of every 1,000 school-aged children, and is more than twice as common in white kids as in Black or Latine kids" (NBC, Associated Press, July 2009). The discrepancies had very little to do with genetics. After looking at factors such as parental education or income they suspected they had more to do "with a difference in access to medical care or in attitudes about whether repetitive blinking or other tics require medical care" (NBC, Associated Press, 2009). Different cultures have variations in tic presentations, suggesting that cultural and social expectations have a bigger role in tic presentation than initially thought (Eapen and Robertson, 2008). Tics could also be interpreted in many ways, which I can only assume results in the need to suppress some tics for safety reasons as well, especially for Black, Brown and Indigenous Peoples.

---

1   Tourettes Action (2023) describes suppressing tics much like trying to suppress the urge to blink. They explain how "for a short period of time it is possible to keep your eyes wide open and avoid blinking – and with practice, you will get better at doing it for longer – but eventually, you will have to blink as the urge is too strong to control. Suppressing tics works in the same way."

Alex's teachers had to become knowledgeable about tics and how they might impact learning expectations. The expertise of everyone involved in Alex's care and education was essential in working alongside Alex to create a learning plan that would help them access their education more effectively and feel accepted while doing so. Alex's input was essential because they knew best what they would feel most comfortable with doing. For ticcers with tics that are considered *socially unacceptable* or *disruptive*, working with them to find solutions that don't involve exclusion from the learning environment or shaming them is imperative too. Patience and acceptance by those around them are proven to be most beneficial and effective in supporting children with TS or tic conditions. As they get older and their nervous systems mature, many tics are reduced or eliminated altogether (Giordano, 2013; Tourettes Action, accessed 16 June 2023). But in the meantime, there are also ways we can generally provide better access to learning that are extremely helpful for ADHD students too, including the following:

- Helping peers gain more knowledge and awareness of tics and Tourette syndrome through teaching and discussing it in class
- Giving more freedom to move about or leave the class for breaks to support the need to tic
- Exploring with the student how to meet sensory needs in the classroom
- Reducing the number of learning tasks or steps given at one time in order to reduce anxiety
- Sitting students near the front of the class to reduce distractions, but not so much so where they are a focal point of the class either
- Sitting student near the teacher to have easier access to assistance when necessary
- Using technology, scribing, audiobook or other strategies where necessary if tics are becoming distracting or destructive to engage in the task
- Getting students' input regularly for ideas on supporting them with tics that are more invasive or socially inappropriate
- Frequently direct teaching and modelling different executive functioning skills and providing opportunities to practise them often and when they're not dysregulated (Giordano, 2013)

Everyone working with Alex became familiar with what was referred to as a *tourettic nervous system*, characterised by a nervous system that can be easily triggered (activated) and difficult to settle when it was. This meant that Alex's nervous system was easily activated to initiate and energise actions and feelings, but the inhibition mechanisms that controlled these functions weren't as efficient yet (Mansueto, 2008). That made producing the expected behaviours for learning in classrooms (like sitting quietly or not fidgeting and moving about the class) quite difficult to accomplish. Alex's inability to perform learning activities as expected, was making them more anxious about being in the learning environment.

It wasn't until Alex was at a near-crisis point that they were finally able to access support. This created a situation where (like for many other possible ADHD children) they had to get to a point of extreme distress in order to be recognised for support in the first place. Before this point, many of Alex's behaviours had been interpreted as acting out and therefore seen as needing to be reprimanded instead. But the irony is that earlier interventions to reduce noticeable barriers to their learning could have kept things from becoming so unmanageable for everyone now. But for Alex, their learning environment not only had to account for any neurodivergence they might have, but it also had to ensure that it was gender-affirming too. If not, this could easily become another barrier to their learning (if it hadn't become one already).

ADHD and the gender binary

The education system perpetuates the harm of the **gender binary** every day. There are "different expectations for student behaviour, student achievement, and athletic prowess; sex-specific activity prompts and requirements that students line up, sit, or engage in other activities in boy-girl-boy-girl fashion; sex-specific dress codes" (skelton, 2022) where **cisnormativity** is expected. The textbooks or stories that we choose to teach from also include stereotypes that continue to "characterise girls as being more helpless and dependent than boys or perpetuate gender stereotypes, tokenism and omission of people outside the gender binary" (Nduagbo, July 2020). The education system encourages girl students in subjects that are seen as more feminine (writing and art), while subjects that are seen as masculine (maths, science) are encouraged for boys. Many educators will often make comments on the neatness and artistic quality of girls' school work but not the content, while doing the exact opposite for boys. This culture of **cisnormativity** is imbedded in education practices and policies. It disregards the vastness of students' experiences and the wholeness of their humanity. Instead, it forces them to fit within the labels of the **gender binary** and punishes, ridicules, bullies or rejects those who don't.

For transgender, non-binary and gender-expansive children, who have higher rates of ADHD compared to their cisgender peers (see Emma and Henry's stories for more on gender), school becomes a very unsafe environment. They experience

transphobia, gender policing and harassment from both students and teachers based on their **gender identity** and/or **gender expression**. "Trans students who experience this type of treatment and learning environment are less likely to be able to concentrate in class, have lower educational aspirations and poorer educational attainment" (Horton, 2020). These students are in environments designed to exclude them. Even attempts at representation (which are meant to create a stronger sense of belonging) for trans children often feed into the narrative of being victims or always at risk, rather than joy and resilience. This only works to suggest that trans children are the problem and have no possible future because they won't live as their assigned gender at birth – all while the *real* harm of the **gender binary** remains hidden. Rejection and being unwelcomed fuel a sense of unsafety in our nervous systems and ADHD brains, in particular, are quick to pick up and react to it.

Even if schools become aware of individual, intentional acts of **transphobia** or **anti-transness** taking place, they also need to recognise "the compounding effects of subtler acts of **cisnormativity**, including systemic practices that are not intended to cause harm to trans pupils too" (Riggs and Bartholomaeus, 2018). These subtle, unintended practices also send the message that trans, non-binary and gender-expansive children are not welcome and do not belong, leaving them feeling unsafe in school. "Language plays an important role in how school staff understand and engage with trans children and efforts to avoid pathologisation and ensure **trans-positivity** are critical" (Horton, 2020). For ADHD trans children, non-binary and gender-expansive children to learn in spaces where they feel safe enough, they also need to be affirmed and validated. They need to see representations that inspire and celebrate them like their cisgender peers do every day. Although it might not always be easy to manage the impulsiveness or emotional dysregulation of ADHD students, as educators we can always start to unlearn the ways that we think about gender and how we're dismantling the culture of **cisnormativity** in our classrooms. Belonging is an antidote to rejection.

Intersectional insights: Gender-affirming spaces

According to GenderSpectrum.Org, a gender-inclusive school asks themselves, "How they're accounting for the unique gender of every student?" They recommend a framework of intentional development for a school community approaching gender inclusivity based on four entry points:

Alex's carers met with their teachers to inform them that after some effort they had recently gotten Alex an ADHD diagnosis. The effort had come in having to convince clinicians that ADHD was a concern because the focus often fell to questions about Alex's **gender identity** and whether this might be influencing their school problems instead. This isn't an unusual situation for many trans, non-binary and gender-expansive people to experience. They're often forced to educate clinicians on their experiences, prove they're capable of understanding their needs, or insist that not every request for assistance be connected to their **gender identity**. Access to support should never have to be this complicated or demand justification.

> **Internal:** teachers reflect on their own understandings, beliefs and experiences around gender and how they impact their work with students. Building this foundation of gender literacy in teachers is imperative before schools can implement the other entry points successfully.
>
> **Interpersonal:** teachers and school staff are intentional about implementing gender inclusivity. They actively provide a counter-narrative to the assumptions made about gender through the language they use, by validating students' genders, teaching empathy and respect for others' identities and acknowledging gender diversity.
>
> **Instructional:** teaching and learning are intentionally used as a way to build more understanding and awareness about gender. Gender topics and representation are directly taught to students and integrated into the curriculum.
>
> **Institutional:** policies, plans and structures are created within the wider school community so that gender diversity is recognised throughout.

Over 75 per cent of trans, non-binary and gender-expansive children also have ADHD, more so than any other neurodivergence (Mandriota, 2022). In addition to this, they also tend to have significantly more disruptive ADHD presentations which result in more "behavioural problems" (Springer Science+Business Media, March 2014). Learning within a **cisnormative** culture that repeatedly insists they don't exist or actively takes measures to limit or deny access to gender-affirming care are active threats to trans children. Perhaps the heightened dysregulation (ADHD presentations interpreted as "bad behaviour") is a natural reaction to being in environments they know aren't designed to prioritise their safety.

ADHD Support: planning, prioritising and organising and managing anxiety and depression

Since Alex experienced a lot of anxiety around doing well in school but also struggled to be in school because of their neurodivergence, everyone decided support would focus on planning, prioritising and organising. They wanted to help reduce the mental load of decision-making that could quickly overwhelm them. Alex also needed to develop some executive functioning skills that would help them in future as the demands of school would increase.

Table 8.1   ADHD support: planning, prioritising, and organising and managing anxiety and depression

Planning and prioritising Being able to outline the steps towards achieving a goal or completing a task. Also making decisions on what is important and needs our attention right away and what doesn't

Organising Creating systems that help us keep track of our materials, our ideas and information

Possible ADHD presentations	Possible accommodations
Leaving tasks until the last minute (and not getting them completed), even if they know they are the most important part	• Sometimes the reasons for the activity and/or how to complete it may need to be (emotionally) convincing enough for them to do it your way. Convincing means: it's easier, quicker, more helpful and most logical … • Intentionally mention what is the most important part and (briefly!) why. Literally announcing, "This is important …" before giving the rest of the instruction.
Doesn't plan ahead for tasks that are due or plan out the structure to complete a task or project	• Too much choice can become overwhelming. Keep choices limited to two or three things and be open to suggestions for tweaks on the process, material and expressions of learning where possible • Encourage planning for two or three things that they need for a project or task. Ensure that they share what materials are needed or what steps are necessary to be completed (sharing out loud can help organise ideas and thoughts) – this thinking can be modelled too • Create visual timetables so they know what is happening in the day • Break projects down even further using cards or cues of "first, next, then, finally" so that students can see how they're moving through the task
Projects lack depth and makes work errors that the student wouldn't normally make	• This could be both challenges with prioritising and organising thoughts/ideas. Bigger projects (including writing compositions) need more scaffolding, direct teaching and additional time for planning and organising thoughts and information. For some students, it will help to give the parts of the project one at a time • Use checklists, planning and mind-mapping organisation tools and have consistent check-in times. (Executive functioning skills can't be done as effectively in an ADHD student's head, so it helps to model out loud the thinking for different strategies to get their ideas out and sort through them) • Be clear with examples of each stage of the work with things like pre-teaching difficult concepts, creating sentence starters, and helping set daily goals

Struggles with making decisions	• Give time limits for decisions or allow a specific thinking time before answering. Suggest students pause, perhaps close their eyes and connect with what feels right to them so as not to be so influenced by outside factors • Help students keep things simple by limiting the number of decisions they need to make • Introduce different strategies for making decisions, especially with completing tasks or deciding what is important. This could look like discussions and modelling thinking around cause and effect, meeting deadlines, what makes a task important vs urgent or scales of what is important and why (For example: What is most important to complete in this activity based on the success criteria? What could be prioritised and what could be left if I run out of time to complete it?)
Loses and forgets materials/homework	• Support in finding an ADHD learner's best ways to keep track of their things by giving suggestions and modelling various systems. (There may be additional underlying reasons beyond their control that are causing these problems. If so, I pull back the expectations and develop the strategies over time with scaffolding support) • Practical support can include homework folders, end-of-day checklists, planners and visual checklists for the process of packing bags. (I generally have students experience natural consequences to learn why things might be important to remember) • Reflect with students who continue to lose some materials consistently to collaborate on various systems together that might work for them. Be flexible with your expectations and consistent with your support as they try your ideas • Checklists for equipment can become easier to ignore over time and don't guarantee that things won't be lost. Visual checklists for home including pictures of the child doing the activities can be helpful, especially since they're involved in the process • Give enough time to put things away after use, but also allow for natural consequences to happen can support their ability to see the importance of certain organisation systems • Encourage them to create an area for all their school things at home so that they can easily be found before they leave for school
Forgets to put materials back after use, leaves drawers open, loses belongings often	• Stick to routines around keeping the space organised and ensuring all materials have visible and easily accessible places they belong • Allow time to put things away in their proper places after activities

(Continued)

Table 8.1   *(Continued)*

Struggles to decide what to do in various time frames	• Help students determine what tasks are shorter to do and can be done when finished early (shorter tasks like, pack up pencil case, finish a maths question) and which might take longer to do (clean out backpack), so that they begin to see that they don't need long stretches of time to do things and have a list of possible things to accomplish when they have a few spare moments (it helps to have a list of small tasks they can do if they finish their work early that the class has already contributed to)

Emotional regulation: Managing anxiety and depression

Anxiety and depression often co-occur with ADHD. In fact "18% of children diagnosed with ADHD at age 4 to 6 had major depression by the time they were 18. This is about 10 times the rate at which those without ADHD will develop depression" (Morgan, 2022). Some ADHD presentations also overlap with depression, such as trouble concentrating or acting agitated. This can make it difficult to diagnose. Alongside sadness and hopelessness depression in children can look like low mood, lack of interest or ability to engage in most activities, trouble getting along with friends, feelings of failure, changes in appetite, physical complaints (like headaches or stomach aches), trouble sleeping and low energy; (Morgan, 2022). Suicidal thoughts are also higher in students with ADHD.

Many ADHDers who are anxious learn to internalise their anxiety, so perfectionism, over-explaining, ruminating or being harsh with themselves is common too. Anxiety can also take on lots of physical forms like upset stomachs, headaches, lack of sleep, not eating properly, or aches and pains that suddenly appear as if out of nowhere. It can look also like avoidance or procrastination, becoming irritable, overly excited, aggressive or overwhelmed. A lot of students who tic also have sensory needs. The added sensory demands often increase anxiety, which in turn increases ADHD presentations, and tics as well.

Possible ADHD presentations	Possible accommodations
Becomes overly excited, irritable or frustrated	• Help the student understand what anxiety feels like in their body so that they can begin to recognise physical signs earlier • Develop a list of strategies and support items, places and activities with the student so that they have options to try when they are sensing more anxiety or feelings of depression • Develop a list of triggers that bring up anxiety, and practice (and model) strategies to reduce it frequently and during calm times • Ensure classroom routines and agenda are clear for the student and any changes are told in advance
Becomes restless and/or fidgety, irritable or overly excited in crowded or loud spaces	• Allow the student to leave a few minutes earlier to go to their next activity to avoid crowded hallways • Give advanced warning of changes or field trips (perhaps they may want to visit first to prepare them), or find alternative spaces to do activities where possible options to engage in field trip or change of schedule (attend part of it, leave earlier)

Difficulty transitioning from one environment to another (for example, the gym, playground or dining hall)	• Work with students to identify sensory needs and consider what accommodations might be necessary for short-term relief and what changes might be necessary for the long term • Give smaller amounts of work in one sitting and avoid focusing solely on what they aren't doing yet or can't do • Give plenty of warning before transitioning to the next activities or space – they may benefit from going before others leave or being accompanied by a close friend
Low self-esteem	• Daily use of simple positive affirmations that students can learn to create and use for themselves and learn how to use during challenging times • Allow time for gratitude practices throughout the day • Develop a growth mindset through modelling self-talk, providing actionable feedback and giving time to practise reflection through noticing what they've learned over a unit (for example, adding to their initial pre-assessment again at the end of a unit) • Allow times for students to explore further developing their talents or interests in something like a regular genius hour • Arrange structured break-time activities to support students in making new friends or include students in ways to help others in the school community
Frequently displays physical manifestations of anxiety (headaches, stomach issues)	• Discuss with students (and their family/carers) the possible triggers to the symptoms (to ensure that they are due to anxiety, depression and not other possible causes) • Create a quiet space in the classroom (or a place they know they can go to in the school) for students to retreat to when they need to • Be flexible about their need to leave the class and arrange with them a signal that lets you know they need a break (it could be an exit card they take from your desk or a hand signal). It might be helpful to have a trusted adult they can drop in and see when they feel they need it
Asks lots of repetitive questions (low tolerance for uncertainty)	• Stay patient, the student is trying to ask for a specific answer that will help them feel more secure about the task. They don't know what the answer will be, just that it will feel right • Reduce reassurance. It's OK to empathise with their feelings, but offering lots of additional reassurance (especially if they may also be dealing with OCD) can often make them feel worse later on. They also need to feel like they can experience some discomfort and survive it. It might help to have them start some of the work next to you or a trusted friend or adult first and they can come back and check in after a set amount of time. Reflect with the student on how they did the work and what helped them to offer insight for next time

(Continued)

Table 8.1   (*Continued*)

May struggle with attendance/may be tired often (due to ticcing, lack of sleep due to tics or worries due to OCD, anxiety or other neurodivergence)	• Work with parents and carers to reduce the demands of school work needed at home • Find times to check in with students online or with video calls so that they still feel some connection with you and the class. Include opportunities for the student to feel included even when they can't be there, like recording sharing work, calling into special events or working with friends online. Include the student in planning how they might want to be connected with others while at home • Reassess the outcomes that the student needs to accomplish. Look across the curriculum for ways that they might show many skills within a smaller amount of projects or have already achieved them • Offer alternatives for starting the day if that is a problem they are experiencing. This could include a flexible schedule, arriving earlier than other students and having a job to do for the class, or being able to wait in a well-being space before school starts. They may feel less anxious coming into class with a friend rather than alone
May inconsistently experience difficulties in accessing curriculum	• Be flexible in the support offered without assuming that since support wasn't needed previously it never could be • Discuss formative assessment with students so they can reflect on the data and recognise what went well and what help would be beneficial towards their learning goals • Review support plans often to add accommodations or modifications when needed to address a need
Feels disconnected from others or struggles to make friends	• Organise activities and clubs over longer breaks that students can get involved with to provide structure and an opportunity to meet others • Offer the chance to do break-time jobs that can get a student more involved in the wider community • If your school is doing a social skills group or club, suggest they join to meet others and share their experiences with others who might feel similar

When we decide what an ADHD learner's behaviour should be because of their assigned gender at birth, rather than what we notice is blocking their ability to engage in they're learning, we limit support options to align with gender behaviour expectations. Our education system requires children to follow white, Eurocentric **gender binary** norms. "When children fail to conform to expected gendered behaviours, the implicit teaching becomes explicit … We punished those that failed to conform" (skelton, 2022). The needs of trans children were never considered within the Eurocentric education system. Their existence is continually erased by the mere mention of a **gender binary** in the first place. It's not at all surprising that their behaviour is quickly interpreted as acting out instead of need-ing support or having ADHD. They aren't conforming to what's expected based on their assigned gender at birth and that could be interpreted as defiance, which leads to punishment or exclusion instead. There's no safety in a space that was never meant to include you in the first place. But within the education system of **white supremacy culture**, there's no safety for anyone that doesn't conform, even for the learners who look as if they should be the safest of everyone isn't left completely unimpacted.

Whiteness and ADHD

Much of what I read on ADHD speaks of how the criteria for diagnosis was based on the presentations of hyperactive cisgender, heterosexual (predominately), affluent, white boys and how they were most diagnosed. Within the **dominant culture**, this isn't that shocking. **Whiteness**' definition of masculinity creates the conditions where (white) males are expected to attain (and are more often given additional support to achieve) specific measures of success. If there's a reason they aren't achieving as expected, it behoves **whiteness** to find one. But it's when they can't perform their gender roles as expected and problems arise with issues like addiction, violence and aggression, or unmet mental health needs, the label of toxic masculinity becomes the main reason for their failings. It suggests that the problematic actions or behaviours expressed stem solely from the male as an individual rather than the influence of any systemic issues. We don't look at how the patriarchal, **white supremacy culture** harms those it's been designed to centre too. It's where the toxicity really lies.

Since inattentive ADHD was predominately believed to be in (white) girls, any white boy who behaved in similar ways could easily be left undiagnosed. Since they weren't hyperactive, they were considered "lazy", "demotivated" or "care-less" instead, while still expected to perform at optimum levels of productivity and acquire success. When they couldn't, being within a culture where problems are often placed on the individual (see Simon's story for more on blame culture), a diagnosis like ADHD would seem like a privilege. It becomes a solution to avoid the shame and blame that others like them (read: white) can do, but they cannot. When people see themselves as the problem (especially one who receives con-stant messages that they "are meant to be the best, the most powerful, etc., so why can't you be?"), the options for solutions are very limited beyond destroying others or destroying oneself.

White women remained undiagnosed, often until having children of their own diagnosed with ADHD, or until they were not effectively doing what was expected of them as wives and mothers. It's not escaped me that *inattentive* ADHD is connected with being diagnosed predominately in (white) women. Problems arose when they were seen as being *inattentive* to their assigned gender roles. But being too emotional or expressive would find women pre-dominately diagnosed with mood disorders before being considered for hyper-active ADHD too. Initially, white women weren't expected to do anything beyond school except attend to their households. They were expected to keep the home clean and organised, effortlessly juggle the demands of multiple family members' schedules, and be the emotional regulation and executive functioning brain for their family. Essentially, they were expected to be the frontal lobe for their husbands. Any inability to access executive functioning skills or to self-regulate wasn't considered an issue, at least not until it impacted the expectations of their white husbands, anyway.

ADHD diagnosis hid how the demands to conform within the Eurocentric ideals creates immense pressure on white children to live up to expectations of perfection too (but for different reasons than non-white children). It allowed for those white children who didn't quite fit their gender roles to be easier to mould into the expectations of the **dominant culture**. But being different in this society is not acceptable for anyone (unless it can be exploited by **whiteness**), and anyone can risk rejection and/or dealing with social, mental or emotional challenges because of it. The same is true for white children too. Only when you're not used to hearing "no", being corrected, not being accepted as you are, or any hint of not belonging it might be interpreted as oppression – it's not. But reacting with blame, defensiveness and denial perpetuate the problems within the systems that keep the supremacy illusion alive for **whiteness**. It insists that it's the white people that aren't perfect that are the problem, *not* their culture and they too could access all their privileges if they were just ... better.

ADHD as a gift or superpower

Although this society often considers obtaining an ADHD diagnosis a privilege, it still can be interpreted negatively by others. People with ADHD are often shamed for being too loud, too lazy, too emotional, too careless or just plain too much. Even white ADHDers aren't immune to this issue. In an attempt to combat this narrative, there's been a bombardment of lists on ADHD strengths or reasons why having ADHD is a *gift* a *superpower*. Although this is considered as a way to build self-esteem in ADHD children (or adults), it doesn't acknowledge the real challenges faced or the need for systemic change so everyone has the support necessary to thrive. The consistent inconsistency of ADHD makes accessing their *superpowers* unpredictable or unreliable. When certain traits are expected to be a *superpower* yet they don't show up (or just aren't naturally a strength for that person), it's hard to explain why and could lead to more shame or guilt. Their differences can't just be strengths and weaknesses that make them better suited for some tasks more than others – just like anyone else.

The *gift* or *superpower* narrative also further dehumanises people with ADHD for their natural brain differences too. They aren't just dehumanised by the patriarchal, **white supremacy culture** expectations of perfectionism, now they must also perform *better than that*. Being *superhuman* in areas of work or productivity that are valued by the **dominant culture** helped develop the belief that ADHDers (remember, without a mention of race, the default has always been white) are worthy enough to still belong to the group. These attempts at changing the narrative have never been about inclusivity or accessibility for *everyone*, but more about how (white) ADHDers desire to access privilege that white people *without* ADHD are accessing. They can't see that it's the expectations from their own **dominant culture** that make them feel like they must prove how they are *beyond perfect* to hopefully be considered good enough. Or that real solutions come from acceptance of the truth, not in making up more illusions to live within to further disguise it.

Non-whiteness and inattentive ADHD

A diagnosis of ADHD could explain why hyperactive, middle-class, heterosexual, white boys had unexpected behaviours that differed from those of non-white children who behaved in similar ways. Unlike non-white children, they no longer were seen to have behaviour that could be described as character flaws. But internalising hyperactive presentations can provide protection for non-white ADHD children in classrooms as if nothing (more) is *wrong with them* (*wrong* meaning: different). In many ways, this can make them safer in school environments where their behaviour is closely policed because of **internalised bias**. But oftentimes, depending on a child's race and perceived gender, common inattentive ADHD presentations such as daydreaming, not responding when called on, forgetfulness or missing information are not interpreted with a response of more leeway or attention (unlike some white children who present the same), but as anything from not understanding the language, purposely acting disinterested and careless, to selfishness, shyness or even defiance.

When considering **internalised bias** of race and gender alongside inattentive ADHD presentations it's why East and Southeast Asian students remain undiagnosed because they are assumed to naturally be quiet. They aren't expected to become societal leaders, so their inattentiveness isn't seen as involving possible challenges with sustaining attention and self-regulation. Instead, they're interpreted as part of their character. It's also why Black, Brown and Indigenous students are often blamed for their inattentiveness, being considered to have character flaws like rudeness. Black children are seen as being older than they actually are, which makes it easier to justify their harsher treatment. They are punished more often for subjective infractions like "disrespect" as if, since they are considered older, they deserve "adult consequences", rather than the *real* adults having to confront their actions and biases that might have led to the "disrespect" in the first place.

Any behaviour that impacts the educators' ability to teach can be interpreted as the non-white students' character, rather than a sign of needing support. It's why many learners and their families might feel uncomfortable with disclosing any ADHD diagnosis too. These students aren't given the leeway to have their inattentive ADHD presentations seen as tiredness or just having an off day. They aren't automatically offered compassion because they have ADHD. Their ADHD diagnosis isn't considered a *superpower*. Their behaviours aren't often considered through the lens of their cultural background or lived experiences either. Instead, their ADHD presentations (or even having an ADHD diagnosis) are labelled as something that's *wrong* with them. A problem because of *who they are*.

> ### Reflect now
>
> What preconceptions have you had about ADHD in your students and how accurate were they? What initially influenced your beliefs about ADHD and what beliefs are you questioning now?

Internalising ADHD presentations doesn't necessarily make it easier to manage or guarantee that ADHDers are treated better. Often, students still end up being treated negatively, but it might show up in comments about their work habits or attitude instead. They can internalise these comments and use them as negative self-talk to develop coping mechanisms to hide what they learn is "wrong" about themselves. The hope is in doing this, they can better fit the expectations of the learning environment. But when these coping strategies become ineffective with meeting the rising demands around them, their success can come crumbling down. They soon discover that they never actually addressed the underlying needs the coping mechanisms hid in the first place, and by then, they're in a lot more distress (see Emma and Henry's stories for more on inattentive ADHD).

Quick tip: ADHD and co-occurring anxiety

ADHDers can have some anxiety because they're worried about things that they struggle with due to ADHD, often feeling that nothing they can do will change it. When worries manifest around executive functioning skills like wanting to complete things but not being able to, being disorganised or always arriving late for their appointments, meeting ADHD needs can help reduce some anxiety. Co-occurring anxiety with worries and fears about other issues could be present while the ADHD is being treated. If that's the case then it could mean checking to seeing whether there's additional support needed for the anxiety.

Alex's carers hoped that the ADHD diagnosis would change everything, but Alex still seemed to be going through a lot and it was only getting worse. Before Alex's resistance to attending school, their parents described them as very interested in learning and desperately wanting to be there, but just couldn't make it past all their fears. It was clear to them that Alex had difficulties with focus and attention. They noted how they were restless and fidgety, constantly bouncing around the home, checking windows and doors to see if they were actually locked. They would get lost in thought, not always finishing tasks and often forgetting where they put their things. They noticed when Alex was under stress (like with issues that were school related), they'd get even more restless.

But now, as their focus centred on all their missed classes, their anxiety increased. Alex had become a shell of themselves, overwhelmed with obsessive thoughts, fears and doubts that resulted in them performing many actions over and over again. These "tics" were stealing chunks of Alex's days, keeping them from living their life as they once knew it to be. As the "tics" intensified, their sleep became more disrupted and they experienced more fears than ever before.

Even though since Alex had gotten older and some of their tics had decreased, while others had disappeared entirely (which is common for many children as the nervous system matures), their behaviour now was something completely different. Although Alex's ADHD presentations also seemed worse, they still began to wonder if it wasn't just ADHD.

The co-occurrence of ADHD, OCD and TS

What Alex's parents soon realised was that not only could ADHD co-occur with Tourette syndrome (TS), other tic conditions and anxiety, but that it could co-occur with obsessive-compulsive disorder (OCD) too. OCD is characterised by a person having such an overwhelming amount of "obsessive fears, doubts and urges that they may perform rituals or compulsions to neutralize or undo these thoughts or feelings to try to feel better" (ADAA, accessed June 2023). OCD often has themes (fears that it regularly attaches intrusive thoughts or urges to) and some of these themes can be socially inappropriate, making them even more terrifying to experience or talk to others about.

Even though the thoughts, urges or fears (obsessions) are incredibly distressing if other people hear about them, people with OCD don't act on them or even have a history of doing so. Just because a student has a fear of harming their friends doesn't mean they actually want to do this or would even *attempt* to. But the thoughts and urges seem so real, as if they *could* be true and that makes them feel even scarier. This makes the person with OCD do even *more* compulsions in hopes of making themselves feel better and reducing their fear and anxiety. But the relief is only temporary and the obsessions return even more relentlessly. When OCD is not managed, obsessions and compulsions become time-consuming, causing more distress and significantly impacting the student's life.

OCD is a neurodivergence that can change throughout a person's life. In around 40 per cent of people, OCD remains chronic. It co-occurs most with Tourette syndrome (TS) and ADHD. The overlap for children that might have both ADHD and OCD is around 21 per cent (Abramovitch and Mittelman, 2013). Around 60 per cent of children with TS have been reported to have OCD presentations, 50 per cent of children with OCD are reported to have had tics, and 15 per cent of those had TS (Mansueto, 2008). OCD can appear without warning or a person could have a diagnosis of it, but not have any noticeable presentations of it. Worries can attach themselves to new fears and new compulsions can appear or disappear. The severity of OCD can also change over time too. What makes OCD even more difficult to ascertain is that some compulsions could be confused with complex tics or ADHD or interpreted as misbehaviour. A key difference between tics and compulsions is the anxiety behind them. Before a compulsion, there's a lot of anxiety. With tic premonition urges, there usually isn't. With ADHD, impulsive actions are often done with little thought as to why or the consequences until much later.

ADHD and co-occurring generalised anxiety can create enough disruptions in a person's life on their own. But when considering the involvement of other neurodivergence, it becomes a completely different story. There are just so many ways that co-occurring neurodivergence can manifest and complicate a student's access to learning. But working with parents and carers, other teachers, specialists and, where possible, the student themselves is our best chance in providing support that best suits their needs. We don't have to have find all the answers to reducing learning barriers on our own. The more insights we get about our students, through working with others, the more solutions become visible.

Can ADHD and OCD truly co-occur?

Before meeting Alex, their teachers never would have believed that OCD was more than handwashing or liking materials to be organised. They never understood just how debilitating OCD really was and how, if left untreated, destructive it could be. They never realised what they were noticing in their classes were signs of Alex's rising distress. Instead, what they thought they were looking at was just ADHD, which wasn't that surprising because unmanaged OCD can look a *lot* like ADHD too. It even affects executive functioning skills as well, only stemming from different underlying causes.

What makes ADHD and OCD co-occurring together challenging to manage is how they can impact how a person reacts to their environment. ADHD is often considered an "externalising disorder, meaning it affects how they outwardly relate to their environment (which might be seen with impulsive actions like blurting out answers or fidgeting). OCD, on the other hand, is characterised as an "internalising disorder", meaning that the anxiety felt from the environment is turned inwards" (Abramovitch and Mittelman, 2013). It might seem odd that OCD and ADHD would co-occur because those with OCD are seen to be a lot more risk averse and those with ADHD more impulsive, but in my experience I've seen how they can and often do.

When OCD and ADHD co-occur it makes it more challenging to access executive functioning skills. But having OCD while treating ADHD with stimulant medication could also result in making OCD worse. For some people it might be that some stimulant medications may intensify the focus on intrusive thoughts, which in turn increases the compulsions, rather than improve the ability to focus on the task at hand. "Thus, the more obsessive, intrusive thoughts that an individual experiences, the fewer resources would be available for other tasks (such as listening to a teacher in class), especially complex ones" (Abramovitch and Mittelman, 2013). But by finding support for OCD, the idea is that executive functioning skills could become more accessible and therefore be improved. This suggests that for some people, what seems like ADHD could actually be unmanaged OCD instead.

Without proper treatment for it (which might include exposure and response prevention therapy and/or possibly medication), OCD can end up creating significant disruptions to students' lives. Learners with OCD need to build capacity to face and accept the uncertainty and doubt from the obsessive thoughts and urges without immediately engaging in the compulsions. This is an extremely challenging and very fearful undertaking and best done with a professional. The impact OCD can have on students' academic work can be devastating. Left untreated it can result in abrupt and dramatic drops in academic achievement so significant that it can be difficult or impossible to catch up.

Support for OCD with ADHD in mind

If a student has both ADHD and OCD, supporting them in reducing the impact of the OCD will address some ADHD-like presentations too. Temporary classroom accommodations best suit a student with OCD because of the way that presentations can fluctuate and change over time. There are many ways we can reduce barriers to their learning by reducing their engagement in compulsions. This could look like allowing for extra time or creating a time limit, or being flexible with formats used to express learning, seating or deadlines. Supporting them with any social challenges may be important as well if they are becoming impatient or avoidant with peers who are unintentionally triggering fears. We might provide alternatives for what they're avoiding, create signals to track time to warn of the start or end of tasks, and checklists to help guide task completion in order to reduce their uncertainty.

When a student with OCD is struggling with such deep fears and anxiety, it is tempting to reassure them by engaging in answering their repeated questions, allowing them unlimited time to complete compulsions or taking time to talk with them about their fears. Unfortunately, when it comes to OCD, these responses aren't helpful because they unintentionally give in to the learner's compulsions. No amount of reassurance will take away their fears, not to mention that asking for reassurance is a compulsion too. Instead, it's important that we empathise and take time to regularly check in with the student, so they know that we care. The goal for people with OCD is to build capacity to accept more uncertainty and doubt so they can reduce engaging in their compulsions and go back to engaging in the preferred activities of any ordinary day.

Supporting Alex

As teachers, parents and those involved with Alex's learning met to devise a way forward, the group found themselves getting stuck on what wasn't happening for Alex. They could list all the ways Alex was failing or tasks they weren't doing, but it was at this point that it was suggested that they look at what Alex could do. By ascertaining what Alex had successfully achieved so far they could start asking themselves better questions to guide their plans of remediation, modifications and accommodations. When they could turn their attention to reflecting on "What can Alex do?", it led them to start asking themselves better questions like the following:

- What procedures or planning did we implement that might have contributed to their latest accomplishments?
- What cognitive abilities or prior knowledge might they have that enabled them to be successful that we could build new knowledge on?
- What topics of interest or lessons had Alex been most successful in completing?
- What strategies or coping skills did we notice them using in order to acquire knowledge?

- How could we enhance or build on their current learning strategies in ways that might better serve their goals?
- What was happening in the environments they worked best in?

Planning through connecting with Alex's strengths first allowed them to build on them while transferring those skills to other areas of their learning. Alex's teachers needed to meet them at their current capacity for learning. There were times when remediation would be necessary, but it couldn't be the whole plan. A deficit view of Alex might also lead to setting lower expectations and that wasn't what they needed either. They needed to feel like they could be successful and that happens when there is appropriate challenge.

Learning activities were planned very intentionally to make sure they weren't void of meaning. Anything Alex engaged in would take small steps towards rebuilding their capacity for being back in the classroom. Everyone needed to let go of how they thought things should be for Alex and accept where they were now. Small successes would be a lot easier to achieve when starting from where they were showing their strengths. A lot more possibilities for supporting our students become visible when we start with noticing what students can do and assessing what resources and expertise we have at our disposal to complement and enhance them. They'd find the same to be true while designing a learning support plan for Alex too.

Key takeaways:

- Our expectations of ADHD behaviour can exclude many students that don't fit gender stereotypes, especially when considering the expected behaviour is defined through Eurocentric ideas for white, cisgender children.
- Gender-affirming environments help create safer learning spaces for trans, non-binary and gender-expansive children. It starts with educators interrogating what they've learned to believe about gender.
- Supporting planning, prioritising and organising can help reduce the overwhelm of decision-making while scaffolding skills development in our ADHD learners.
- Tic conditions and Tourette syndrome commonly co-occur with ADHD and can have a detrimental impact on a learner's self-esteem and academic work. Creating an accepting and patient space best supports these students.
- OCD can co-occur with ADHD even when they both seem to affect learners in different ways. Unmanaged OCD can to lead to delays in executive functioning skills and can look a lot like ADHD too.

Resources to explore

Gender-affirming

Whipping Girl: A Transsexual Woman on Sexism and the Scapegoating of Femininity by Julia Serano

Beyond the Gender Binary by Alok Vaid-Menon

The Trevor Project: www.thetrevorproject.org/

Tourette syndrome

Tourette's Action: www.tourettes-action.org.uk/

Tourette Association of America: https://tourette.org

Obsessive-Compulsion Disorder (including PANS/PANDAS)

PANS PANDAS UK: www.panspandasuk.org/

International OCD Foundation: https://iocdf.org/

OCD Action: https://ocdaction.org.uk/

School Avoidance

Can't Not Won't: A Story About a Child Who Couldn't Go to School by Eliza Fricker

Conclusion

I was officially diagnosed with ADHD when I was 40 years old.

This discovery led me to begin writing on Instagram about being diagnosed later in life. I hoped I could connect with others like me to better understand what I'd been unknowingly dealing with my whole life. But the nuances of living with ADHD for people in more marginalised groups were rarely discussed in mainstream ADHD advocacy. **Intersectionality** was not actively used in these spaces and white people dominated the narrative. I'd soon come to learn that everything I'd read about ADHD centred the experiences of **whiteness.** That made me want to continue sharing my experiences because there were so few of us Black ADHD content creators out there. Slowly but surely I began to connect with others and grew a small but engaged following.

However, following the murder of George Floyd by police in May 2020, my account went viral. Like many other Black content creators, I was suddenly thrust into visibility, considered a valued *resource* of information in my area of expertise because I was Black. My content was shared widely so that white ADHD coaches, advocates and specialists could be seen as "good white people" who amplified the work of Black ADHDers. I was asked to be on countless podcasts and contribute to many collaborations. I was offered speaking gigs, asked to lead training and other paid opportunities.

I turned down each and every one.

Even after everything that happened, I *still* wasn't seen as human, just another possible *resource* to be exploited for their gain. I innately knew the offers of working together were never intended to be a reciprocal relationship. In their urgency to *connect* with me, they revealed how *disconnected* from their own humanity they truly were. It's difficult to build a connection with others when we suppress and accept so little about ourselves. I think our students experience something similar when the underlying messages of our learning relationships in schools demand and/or imply that we must hide or leave so much of ourselves at the door too. No one ever feels truly safe within them.

But it was also during the summer of 2020 that many people I knew personally ended up finding my Instagram account too, including some of my ex-students who were diagnosed with ADHD. They shared how they finally understood why they enjoyed our classes together. This brought me a sense of joy (and relief!) because I had a lot of fun learning with them even though I didn't see myself as a particularly exceptional teacher. You wouldn't have found any of my work on Pinterest. I made plenty of mistakes, took on way too much extra work and definitely wasn't always the beacon of self-regulation with them either. But as much as I was an imperfect, messy human at times, the care, compassion and openness I had for them was very real too.

I didn't know much (especially as a newish teacher), but one thing I innately felt and strongly believed was that the quality of relationships I developed with my students was *everything*. I needed them to know without a doubt that I *saw* them in their messy humanness and I would *still* be there regardless. I needed to be OK with them seeing my humanness sometimes too. If we could do that then maybe we had a better chance of eventually accepting each other as we were and from that point working together to thrive.

I didn't have the words for it back then, but now I realise it was all about *connection*.

As a Black, transracial adoptee growing up with untreated ADHD, my obvious differences from everyone around me kept me disconnected from myself as I tried to change who I was to find a way to fit in. But with being constantly dehumanised and receiving messages from society that I was less than everyone around me, all I ever *really* wanted was to *be enough*. In my young mind that meant connecting with my teachers because maybe then they could teach me that I finally was. I don't think I ever forgot the influence my teachers had to either build me up or destroy me with a single decision or word. If I wanted to be the teacher that built more children up than tore down I had to connect with them too.

Teaching and learning are not activities that should be done in complete isolation. We truly need each other within our classrooms, our school communities and beyond. There's a vulnerability in teaching and learning because it requires connection and that means showing more of who we really are under the labels that we're made to wear. But in **white supremacy culture** being different means our natural imperfections could risk us being excluded from the group. Much like our ADHD students, we're fearful of rejection too. We try to meet expectations about who we think we should be as teachers and who we learn they should be as students by learning to disconnect from our inner knowing and each other.

Instead, we need to lean into our communities and build more capacity to work towards reconnection, embracing who we *are* as educators and accepting who they really *are* as learners too. The more we trust in our own inner wisdom and cultivate self-compassion for our own humanity, the more we see the humanity in and find compassion for our ADHD students too. We go beyond the imposed limits of labels to finally see the possibilities for teaching and learning that arise when we all can start with being who we are. In this way, we become conduits for building connections.

It's through connection that we all learn best.

Glossary

ableism/internalised ableism: the discrimination of and social prejudice against disabled people based on the belief that they are "less than" those who are "typically able". It's rooted in the belief that disabled people require "fixing" and defines people by their disability. Ableism also includes harmful stereotypes, misconceptions and generalisations of disabled people. These beliefs can also be turned towards oneself (internalised ableism) where the person believes they should be able to do the same typical things independently as those who are able when they can't and would benefit from support.

appropriation: when a **dominant culture** (in this book it refers to **white supremacy**) assumes it's their right to take cultural elements (symbols, art, language, customs, etc.) for one's own use, commodification or profit, often without understanding, acknowledgement or respect for its value in the original culture.

body doubling: being in the presence of another person while completing difficult or necessary tasks. This strategy works as co-regulation support for the nervous system to create more ease in order to engage in the activity.

cisgender: someone whose **gender identity** is the same as the sex they were assigned at birth.

cisnormativity: is the presumption that most people do, or should, conform to the norms about the gender they've been assigned at birth in their society. It assumes that everyone by default chooses to accept the gender that their parents or societal authorities have assigned them. It also assumes that all cultures by default have a **gender binary** similar to or based on Eurocentric cultural norms.

code-switching: involves changing one's style of speech, appearance, behaviour and expression in ways that will optimise the comfort of others in exchange for fair treatment, quality service and employment opportunities (McCluney et al., 2019). Black children are taught to selectively code-switch from African American Vernacular English (AAVE) to "standard" English depending on comfort of the group they're engaging with.

collectivist culture: prioritising the needs of the group over the individual. They are characterised by interdependence and social connectedness. It sees power as being with the people rather than a few individuals, which can make it easier to create a system that has shared goals.

colonialism: when a group of people, nation or social construct dominates or controls another nation, people or area. Through political and economic control the dominant country settles in another more vulnerable country for exploiting its people and natural resources. It then typically tries to force its own cultural values and language on the Indigenous Peoples it colonises.

colourism: discrimination based on skin colour that leads to the systematic oppression of dark-skinned people. It's rooted in **white supremacy** and **colonialism**, and upholds the belief that the lighter skinned you are (read: appearing closer to white), the better/more valued you are. This then makes you more entitled to preferential treatment. It is also often witnessed within marginalised communities with how dark- and light-skinned members treat each other.

culture: according to Resmaa Menakem, author of *My Grandmother's Hands*, "Culture is how our bodies retain and reenact history—through the foods we eat (or refuse to eat); the stories we tell; the things that hold meaning for us; the images that move us; what we are able (and unable) to sense or feel or process; the way we see the world; and a thousand other aspects of life. Culture lives in our bodies" (2018, pp. 245–246).

cultural humility: a lifelong process of self-reflection and self-critique starting with the person unpacking and examining their own beliefs and cultural identities in order to learn about how that influences the ways they view another's cultures and beliefs. The term was first coined by Melanie Tervalon and Jann Murray-García.

declarative language: this is different from imperative language as it doesn't require a response from the other person. Instead, we share information that invites the person to engage with what's been said on their own terms. This can include making statements about things like sharing your own feelings or experiences, commenting or describing your thoughts or ideas on a topic or situation, praising a specific action or ability and thinking aloud, or problem-solving statements.

dominant culture: dominant culture refers to the cultural values, beliefs and practices that are prevalent in society. These are often associated with mainstream or dominant groups. It's characterised by how it can shape and influence societal norms and expectations and make other cultures follow them. In countries like the US, Canada, the United Kingdom and Australia, the dominant culture is often used to refer to a culture that's white, able-bodied, **cisgender**-male dominated and heterosexual. It also tends to centre those that are more affluent. Throughout this book, dominant culture refers to the culture of **white supremacy**.

emergent bilingual/multilingual: students who are continuing to develop their **home language** while also learning an additional language.

emotional flooding: when a temporary emotion can overwhelm a person, taking up all of the space of one's head, having them react in ways that are often not equal to the event. Emotional flooding makes it difficult for the person to connect to their thinking brain and decide how they would like to respond, leaving them reacting instead.

gender binary: a system that classifies sex and gender into a pair of opposites, often imposed by culture, religion or other societal pressures. Within the gender binary system, all of the human population must fit into one of two genders: man or woman (the model does not include gender identities that exist outside the binary system). The gender binary system is also harmful towards **cisgender** people because of how it reinforces gender roles and stereotypes.

gender-expansive: someone whose **gender identity** and/or **gender expression** expands beyond, actively resists and/or does not conform to the current cultural or social expectations of gender, particularly in relation to male or female. Examples of gender identities that are gender-expansive include non-binary, gendervague, autigender or demigender.

gender expression: how a person chooses to outwardly express their gender, within the context of societal expectations of gender. This is not the same as transgender.

gender identity: a person's innate sense of their own gender, which may or may not align with the gender assigned at birth. At birth people are assigned male or female genders, but there are many more gender identities, including nonbinary, agender, genderfluid or genderqueer.

home language: the first language we learn to speak and is generally the language of our parents and community.

individualistic culture: prioritises human independence and freedom. It sees people as autonomous who can act as they want as long as they also respect the freedom of others. It's characterised by self-reliance and a focus on personal goals.

internalised bias/unconscious bias: the ways people's behaviour is influenced because of repeated exposure to different messages and past experiences that they have not reflected on. These can be attitudes, beliefs and judgements that – since the person is not aware of them – can become very powerful determinants of their behaviour. It's why a person can insist they are not racist, but then behave in ways that are not congruent with what they think they believe.

intersectionality (intersectional): a tool used to consider people's experience of inequality or disadvantage in society depending on their multiple social identities: race, ethnicity, class, sexuality, religion, national origin, age and disability status. When people with different social identities are treated differently within structural systems, such as education, criminal justice, healthcare, employment or housing, they have vastly different realities, lived experiences and opportunities to live whole, meaningful and healthy lives.

microaggressions: the verbal, non-verbal and environmental snubs, slights or insults that communicate hostile, derogatory or harmful messages to target persons simply because they belong to a marginalised group. Microaggressions can be intentional or not and still inflict harm.

neuroception: a neurobiological process that results in the subconscious's ability to perceive situations, people and interactions as safe, dangerous or life-threatening. It was coined by Dr Stephen Porges in 2004.

perspective-taking: because of lagging self-talk, ADHDers can struggle to understand others' thoughts and feelings, or how they come across when engaging with others. They find it challenging to think about others' thoughts and understand how their actions could be perceived by others without direct teaching, modelling and real-life practice to develop this skill.

"Pull yourself up by your bootstraps!" mentality: the belief that one can improve their success or prosperity in life through hard work and self-determination, rather than getting assistance from someone else. This belief doesn't account for the systematic oppression that creates multiple barriers to success that many marginalised communities faced in their history and/or continue to do so today.

racial literacy: Joseph-Salisbury (2020) defines racial literacy as "the capacity of teachers to understand the ways in which race and racism work in society, and to have the skills, knowledge and confidence to implement that understanding in teaching practice".

school-to-prison pipeline: when education and public safety policies push students into the criminal legal system. The use in schools of zero-tolerance disciplinary policies and involvement of the police in minor misbehaviour often lead to arrests and juvenile detention referrals. This can result in criminal charges and incarceration. Schools can also indirectly push students into the pipeline through suspension, expulsion, discouragement and even high-stakes testing requirements. The pipeline also disproportionately impacts the most marginalised students: Black, Brown and Indigenous students, disabled students and LGBTQIA2S+ students.

sensory bin: a box of hands-on tools for children to explore their world through their senses. Sensory play may calm, focus and engage a child. They can be used to learn cooperative play, assist with language development, improve fine motor skills or even support cognitive tasks.

sensory diet: a set of activities that make up a sensory strategy to meet an individual's needs. These are specific activities, scheduled into a child's day, which are used to help them regulate activity levels, attention and adaptive responses. They are unique to every individual based on their sensory profile (which sensory systems are they experiencing discomfort or dysregulation and therefore need regular support).

structural inequalities: a system that creates conditions where one group of people has an unequal status in relation to another group. This is systematically rooted in the normal operations of social institutions such as education, employment, laws and regulations and healthcare.

transphobia/anti-transness: an irrational fear, aversion, prejudice or discrimination towards someone because they are transgender, including denying their gender identity or refusing to accept it. Transphobia/anti-transness may be targeted at people who are or who are perceived to be trans, and can include acts like trying to remove trans people's rights, or denying access to gender-affirming care and abuse.

white supremacy culture: white supremacy is the pseudo-scientific concept of race in order to create an elite class of people based on **whiteness**. It is a hierarchy of racialised value created to disconnect and divide white people from Black, Brown, Indigenous and other melanated peoples. It also divides races from each other, including white people from each other. It disconnects us all from ourselves, each other and the natural world too.

whiteness: refers to the specific dimensions of racism that serve to elevate white people over everyone else. This definition counters the dominant representation of racism in mainstream education as isolated in discrete behaviours that some individuals may or may not demonstrate, and goes beyond naming specific privileges (McIntosh, 1989).

white-presenting: refers to people who have a cultural and/or racial identity that is not white, but who experience what has been referred to as "white skin privilege" because of how they look. This allowed Black enslaved people who appeared white to hide their Black identities for their survival. It's also why "white-presenting" has also been referred to as "white-passing" in the past.

whitewashing: the history taught in the Eurocentric education system leaves out important events and the point of view of historically excluded communities. It creates an entirely different picture of past events that leaves out marginalised groups while hiding the truth of some historical situations to centre **whiteness**. It makes history more palatable for white educators to teach.

References

About the Book, Preface and Introduction

Admin, L. (2012, June 18). *ADHD and adoption*. Lanc UK. www.lanc.org.uk/adhd-and-adoption/

Dawson, P., and Guare, R. (2009). *Smart but scattered: The revolutionary "executive skills" approach to helping kids reach their potential*. The Guilford Press.

Larson, K., Russ, S. A., Kahn, R. S., and Halfon, N. (2011). Patterns of comorbidity, functioning, and service use for US children with ADHD, 2007. *Pediatrics*, *127*(3), 462–470. https://chadd.org/about-adhd/co-occuring-conditions/ (accessed 13 June 2023).

Lhamon, C. E., Timmons-Goodson, P., Adegbile, D. P., Herio, G. L., Kirsanow, P. N., Kladney, D., Narasaki, K., and Yaki, M. (2019, July). *Beyond suspensions: Examining school discipline policies and connections to the school-to-prison pipeline for students of color with disabilities*. Washington, DC: The United States Commission on Civil Rights.

Matthews, M., Nigg, J. T., and Fair, D. A. (2014, July 2). *Attention deficit hyperactivity disorder*. Current topics in behavioral neurosciences. www.ncbi.nlm.nih.gov/pmc/articles/PMC4079001/

Peñarrubia, M., Navarro-Soria, I., Palacios, J., and Fenollar-Cortés, J. (2021, May 17). ADHD symptomatology, executive function and cognitive performance differences between family foster care and control group in ADHD-diagnosed children. *Children* (Basel), *8*(5), 405. doi: 10.3390/children8050405. PMID: 34067856; PMCID: PMC8156241.

Reinblatt S. P. (2015). Are eating disorders related to Attention Deficit/Hyperactivity Disorder? *Current treatment options in Psychiatry*, *2*(4), 402–412. https://doi.org/10.1007/s40501-015-0060-7

Saline, S. (2023, February 21). ADHD and anger in the family: Manage outbursts with stop-think-act. Dr. Sharon Saline. https://drsharonsaline.com/2021/06/02/adhd-and-anger-in-the-family-manage-outbursts-with-stop-think-act/

1 "He's so defiant!": Darnell's story

American Academy of Child and Adolescent Psychology. (2019, June). *Oppositional defiant disorder: FAQs*. AACAP.org. www.aacap.org/aacap/Families_and_Youth/Resource_Centers/Oppositional_Defiant_Disorder_Resource_Center/FAQ.aspx

Barry, T.D., Lyman, R.D., and Klinger, L.G. (2002). Academic underachievement and attention-deficit/hyperactivity disorder: The negative impact of symptom severity on school performance. *Journal of School Psychology*, *40*(3), 259–283.

Campbell, A. (2020). Educational experiences of multiracial students: A literature review. *Journal of Educational Research and Innovation*, *8*(1), 1.

Conroy, R. (2021, October 12). *The role of implicit bias: Dyslexia diagnosis and race*. The Windward School. www.thewindwardschool.org/the-windward-institute/the-beacon/article/~board/beacon-archives/post/the-role-of-implicit-bias-dyslexia-diagnosis-and-race

Fields, L. (2021, October 25). *Risks of untreated ADHD*. WebMD. www.webmd.com/add-adhd/childhood-adhd/risks-of-untreated-adhd

Frazier, T. W., Demaree, H. A., and Youngstrom, E. A. (2004). Meta-analysis of intellectual and neuropsychological test performance in attention-deficit/hyperactivity disorder. *Neuropsychology, 18*(3), 543.

Hsu, E., Davies, C. A., and Hansen, D. J. (2004, February 27). Understanding mental health needs of Southeast Asian refugees: Historical, cultural, and contextual challenges. *Science Direct*. www.sciencedirect.com/science/article/abs/pii/S0272735803001491

Mayes, S. D., and Calhoun, S. L. (2006). Frequency of reading, math, and writing disabilities in children with clinical disorders. *Learning and Individual Differences, 16*(2), 145–157.

McConville, K. (2019, September 23). *Language barriers in the classroom: From mother tongue to national language*. Concern Worldwide US. www.concernusa.org/story/language-barriers-in-classroom/

McGrath, L. M., and Stoodley, C. J. (2019, November 21). Are there shared neural correlates between dyslexia and ADHD? A meta-analysis of Voxel-based morphometry studies. *Journal of Neurodevelopmental Disorders*. BioMed Central. https://doi.org/10.1186/s11689-019-9287-8

Molitor, S. J., Langberg, J. M., and Evans, S. W. (2016, January 21). The written expression abilities of adolescents with attention-deficit/hyperactivity disorder. *Research in Developmental Disabilities*. www.ncbi.nlm.nih.gov/pmc/articles/PMC5134244/

Office of the Surgeon General (US); Center for Mental Health Services (US); National Institute of Mental Health (US). (2001, August). Mental health care for Asian Americans and Pacific Islanders. Chapter 5 in *Mental health: culture, race, and ethnicity: A supplement to mental health: A report of the Surgeon General*. Rockville, MD: Substance Abuse and Mental Health Services Administration (US). Available from: www.ncbi.nlm.nih.gov/books/NBK44245/

Okonofua, J. A., and Eberhardt, J. L. (2015). Two strikes. *Psychological Science, 26*(5), 617–624. https://doi.org/10.1177/0956797615570365

Olivardia, R. (2022, October 29). The dyslexia and ADHD connection. *ADDitude*. www.additudemag.com/adhd-dyslexia-connection/#:~:text=Is%20There%20a%20Link%20Between,and%20it%20is%20vastly%20misunderstood

Riccio, C. A., Homack, S., Jarratt, K.P., and Wolfe, M.E. (2006). Differences in academic and executive function domains among children with ADHD predominantly inattentive and combined types. *Archives of Clinical Neuropsychology, 21*(7), 657–667.

Rosales, J., and Walker, T. (2021, March 20). *The racist beginnings of standardized testing*. NEA.org. www.nea.org/advocating-for-change/new-from-nea/racist-beginnings-standardized-testing#:~:text=Since%20their%20inception%20almost%20a,from%20early%20childhood%20through%20college

2 "They're just shy": Emma and Henry's story

Baum, S., Preuss, L., Novak, C., and Dunn, M. (2011). *The mythology of learning: Understanding common myths about 2E learners: A series of articles from Bridges Academy*. Glen Ellyn Media.

Kaiser Permanente. (2018, April 18). *ADHD and Depressive Disorders More Frequently Diagnosed in Transgender Youth*. (n.d.). Neuroscience from Technology Networks. https://www.technologynetworks.com/neuroscience/news/adhd-and-depressive-disorders-more-frequently-diagnosed-in-transgender-youth-299702

Mazzone, L., Postorino, V., Reale, L., Guarnera, M., Mannino, V., Armando, M., Fatta, L., De Peppo, L., and Vicari, S. (2013, July 11). Self-esteem evaluation in children and adolescents suffering from ADHD. Clinical Practice and Epidemiology in Mental Health. www.ncbi.nlm.nih.gov/pmc/articles/PMC3715757/

Serano, J. (2018). *Whipping girl: A transsexual woman on sexism and the scapegoating of femininity*. Seal Press.

Wexelblatt, R. (2023, April 25). The social executive function skills that elude kids with ADHD. *ADDitude*. www.additudemag.com/social-skills-for-kids-friendships-adhd/

3 "She cries over everything!": Ameera's story

Awad, G. H., Hashem, H., and Nguyen, H. (2021). Identity and ethnic/racial self-labeling among Americans of Arab or Middle Eastern and North African descent. *Identity*, *21*(2), 115–130.

Hammond, Z. (2014). *Culturally responsive teaching and the brain: Promoting authentic engagement and rigour among culturally and linguistically diverse students*. Corwin, a SAGE Company.

Horton, C. (2020, July 27). Thriving or surviving? Raising our ambition for trans children in primary and secondary schools. *Frontiers*. www.frontiersin.org/articles/10.3389/fsoc.2020.00067/full

Menakem, R. (2017). *My grandmother's hands: Healing racial trauma in our minds and Bodies*. Penguin Books.

Miodus, S., Allwood, M. A., and Amoh, N. (2021). Childhood ADHD symptoms in relation to trauma exposure and PTSD symptoms among college students: Attending to and accommodating trauma. *Journal of Emotional and Behavioral Disorders*, *29*(3), 187–196. https://doi.org/10.1177/1063426620982624

Porteous-Sebouhian, B. (2021, July 29). ADHD and trauma. *Mental Health Today*. www.mentalhealthtoday.co.uk/blog/awareness/how-trauma-informed-care-from-childhood-could-help-identify-and-treat-adhd

Siegfried, C. B., Blackshear, K., National Child Traumatic Stress Network, with assistance from the National Resource Center on ADHD: A Program of Children and Adults with AttentionDeficit/Hyperactivity Disorder (CHADD). (2016). *Is it ADHD or child traumatic stress? A guide for Clinicians*. Los Angeles, CA and Durham, NC: National Center for Child Traumatic Stress.

The Bell Foundation. (2021). *Effective Teaching of EAL Learners*. https://www.bell-foundation.org.uk/eal-programme/guidance/effective-teaching-of-eal-learners/

Venet, A. S. (2021). *Equity-centered trauma-informed education*. W.W. Norton and Company.

4 "He never does anything you tell him to!": Dhruv's story

Awad, G. H., Hashem, H., and Nguyen, H. (2021). Identity and ethnic/racial self-labeling among Americans of Arab or Middle Eastern and North African descent. *Identity*, *21*(2), 115–130.

Baglivio, M. T., Wolff, K. T., Piquero, A. R., Greenwald, M. A., and Epps, N. (2017, July). Racial/ethnic disproportionality in psychiatric diagnoses and treatment in a sample of serious juvenile offenders. *Journal of Youth and Adolescence*, *46*(7), 1424–1451. doi: 10.1007/s10964-016-0573-4. Epub 2016 Sep 24. PMID: 27665279.

Bangera, N. (2018, May 15). *Why autonomy in education should be schools' primary goal*. The Swaddle. https://theswaddle.com/what-is-autonomy-in-education/

Baron-Cohen, S., Cale, E. M., Cyders, M. A., Daffern, M., Erskine, H. E., Frith, U., Goldberg, L. R., Gow, A. J., Green, J., Jang, J., Jones, S. E., Lenzenweger, M. F., Reilly, C., Aguilar-Cárceles, M. M., Association, A. P., Ashworth, S., Biederman, J., Blonigen, D. M., Burke, J. D., … Gov. (2020, July 15). Individual differences, ADHD, adult pathological demand avoidance, and delinquency. *Research in Developmental Disabilities*. www.sciencedircct.com/science/article/abs/pii/S0891422220301633

Baxley, T. P. (2008). Issues in education: "What are you?" Biracial children in the classroom. *Childhood Education*, *84*(4), 230–233. https://doi.org/10.1080/00094056.2008.10523014

Campbell, A. (2020). Educational experiences of multiracial students: A literature review. *Journal of Educational Research and Innovation*, *8*(1), 1.

Djoub, Z. (2022, February 21). *Learner autonomy: Understanding the process*. EduLearn2Change. https://edulearn2change.com/article-learner-autonomy-understanding-the-process/

Egan, V., Bull, E., and Trundle, G. (2020). Individual differences, ADHD, adult pathological demand avoidance, and delinquency. *Research in Developmental Disabilities*, *105*, 103733. https://doi.org/10.1016/j.ridd.2020.103733

Ehrlich, C. (2022, October 15). *At Peace Parents podcast*. www.buzzsprout.com/2084398

Hammond, Z. (2014). *Culturally responsive teaching and the brain: Promoting authentic engagement and rigour among culturally and linguistically diverse students*. Corwin, a SAGE Company.

Rozek, C. S., and Gaither, S. E. (2020). Not quite White or Black: Biracial students' perceptions of threat and belonging across school contexts. *The Journal of Early Adolescence*, *41*(9), 1308–1337. https://doi.org/10.1177/0272431620950476

Ugwuegbula, L. (2020, July 2). *The role of education in perpetuating racism and white supremacy: Rethinking the Eurocentric curriculum*. Samuel Centre for Social Connectedness. www.socialconnectedness.org/the-role-of-education-in-perpetuating-racism-and-white-supremacy-rethinking-the-eurocentric-curriculum/

5 "He can't do anything by himself!": Simon's story

Addy, L. (2004). Speed up!: A kinaesthetic programme to develop fluent handwriting. LDA.

Barkley, R. (2018). *Barkley Sluggish Cognitive Tempo Scale—Children and Adolescents (BSCTS-CA)*. The Guilford Press.

Fassbender, C., Krafft, C. E., and Schweitzer, J. B. (2015, May 21). *Differentiating SCT and inattentive symptoms in ADHD using FMRI measures of cognitive control*. NeuroImage. Clinical. www.ncbi.nlm.nih.gov/pmc/articles/PMC4474281/

Fliers, E. A., Franke, B., and Buitelaar, J. K. (2011). Motorische problemen bij kinderen met ADHD. Onderbelicht in de klinische praktijk [Motor problems in children with ADHD receive too little attention in clinical practice]. *Nederlands Tijdschrift voor Geneeskunde*, *155*(50), A3559. Dutch. PMID: 22186361

Gregory, A. (2018, February 16). *Addressing blame culture in your school is vital … for pupils and teachers*. Teachwire. www.teachwire.net/news/addressing-blame-culture-in-your-school-is-vital … for-pupils-and-teachers

Haberman, M. (2010). The pedagogy of poverty versus good teaching. *Phi Delta Kappan*, *92*(2), 81–87. https://doi.org/10.1177/003172171009200223

Hammond, Z. (2014). *Culturally responsive teaching and the brain: Promoting authentic engagement and rigour among culturally and linguistically diverse students*. Corwin, a SAGE Company.

Hinton, J. (2020, October 22). *From dependent to independent learners: Bridging the opportunity gap*. www.jeffreyahinton.com/post/from-dependent-to-independent-learners-bridging-the-opportunity-gap

Houston, L., and Paquet-Bélanger, N. (2017, September 22). *Working memory difficulties: Strategies for the classroom*. LD@school. www.ldatschool.ca/working-memory-difficulties/

Hove, M., Zeffiro, T., Li, Z., and Valera, E. (2015, May 21). *Postural sway and regional cerebellar volume in adults with attention-deficit/hyperactivity disorder*. National Center for Biotechnology Information. https://pubmed.ncbi.nlm.nih.gov/26106567/

Kidd, J., Kaufman, J., Baker, P., and Allen, D. (2020, June 13). *Learned helplessness in our students and learning how we help!* Foundations of Education and Instructional Assessment. https://courses.lumenlearning.com/atd-hostos-education/chapter/foundations-of-education-and-instructional-assessmentsociological-influenceshelplessness/

Re, A. M., and Cornoldi, C. (2010). ADHD expressive writing difficulties of ADHD children: When good declarative knowledge is not sufficient. *European Journal of Psychology of Education, 25*(3), 315–323.

Tindle, R., and Longstaff, M. G. (2015, December 31). Writing, reading, and listening differentially overload working memory performance across the serial position curve. *Advances in Cognitive Psychology*. www.ncbi.nlm.nih.gov/pmc/articles/PMC4710969/

Tivers, E. and Barkley, R. (2017, April 14). *Russell Barkley on the meaning of ADHD*. ADHD reWired. www.adhdrewired.com/russell-barkley-meaning-of-adhd/

Womack, J. (2013, July 1). Learned helplessness – how to make students responsible? Education 589 Eagle Projects.

6 "She's the ideal student!": Ji Yeon's story

Bradbury, A. (2013). *From model minorities to disposable models: The de-legitimisation of educational success through discourses of authenticity*. UCL Discovery.

Cortina, K. S., Arel, S., and Smith-Darden, J. P. (2017, October 5). School belonging in different cultures: The effects of individualism and power distance. *Frontiers*. www.frontiersin.org/articles/10.3389/feduc.2017.00056/full#:~:text=In%20summary%2C%20collectivist%20cultures%20emphasize,reliance%2C%20independence%20and%20personal%20goals

Gay, G. (2002). Preparing for culturally responsive teaching. *Journal of Teacher Education, 53*(2), 106–116. https://doi.org/10.1177/0022487102053002003

Hammond, Z. (2014). *Culturally responsive teaching and the brain: Promoting authentic engagement and rigour among culturally and linguistically diverse students*. Corwin, a SAGE Company.

Horton, C. (2020, July 27). Thriving or surviving? Raising our ambition for trans children in primary and secondary schools. *Frontiers*. www.frontiersin.org/articles/10.3389/fsoc.2020.00067/full

Kennedy, D. (2020, September 11). The ADHD symptoms that complicate and exacerbate a math learning disability. *ADDitude*. www.additudemag.com/math-learning-disabilities-dyscalculia-adhd/

Purpura, D. J., Day, E., Napoli, A. R., and Hart, S. A. (2017). Identifying domain-general and domain-specific predictors of low mathematics performance: A classification and regression tree analysis. *Journal of Numerical Cognition, 3*(2), 365–399.

Sharma, M. C. (2022). *Some remediation principles for dyscalculia and acquired dyscalculia*. British Dyslexia Association. www.bdadyslexia.org.uk/dyscalculia

Talusan, L. A. (2022, January 12). *Why I am tired of talking about the model minority myth*. Teaching While White. www.teachingwhilewhite.org/blog/why-i-am-tired-of-talking-about-the-model-minority-myth

Vargus, M. (2008). *Culturally responsive teaching*. Research Gate. www.researchgate.net/publication/326657963_Culturally_Responsive_Teaching

Wong, B. (2015). A blessing with a curse: Model minority ethnic students and the construction of educational success. *Oxford Review of Education, 41*(6), 730–746. https://doi.org/10.1080/03054985.2015.1117970

7 "He just won't sit still!": Diego's story

Child Mind Institute. (2021, August 25). *How sensory processing issues affect kids in school*. https://childmind.org/article/how-sensory-processing-issues-affect-kids-in-school/

Dillon, K. (n.d.). *Sensory anxiety: Not your ordinary anxiety*. Sensory Processing – STAR Institute. https://sensoryhealth.org/node/1129

Gonzalez, J., and Dillon, B. (2021, March 12). *Episode 91: Twelve ways to upgrade your classroom design*. Cult of Pedagogy. www.cultofpedagogy.com/pod/episode-91/

Krosch, A. R., and Amodio, D. M. (2014, June 24). *Economic scarcity alters the perception of race*. Proceedings of the National Academy of Sciences of the United States of America. www.ncbi.nlm.nih.gov/pmc/articles/PMC4078865/

Menakem, R. (2017). *My grandmother's hands: Healing racial trauma in our minds and Bodies*. Penguin Books.

Nason, B. (2014). *The autism discussion page: On anxiety, behaviour, school and parenting strategies*. Jessica Kingsley.

Schmengler, H., Cohen, D., Tordjman, S., and Melchior, M. (2021). Autism spectrum and other neurodevelopmental disorders in children of immigrants: A brief review of current evidence and implications for clinical practice. *Frontiers in Psychiatry, 12*, 566368. https://doi.org/10.3389/fpsyt.2021.566368

8 "Is he/they even old enough to choose pronouns?": Alex's story

Abramovitch, A., and Mittelman, A. (2013, Winter). *OCD and ADHD dual diagnosis misdiagnosis and the cognitive "cost" of obsessions*. International OCD Foundation. https://iocdf.org/expert-opinions/expert-opinion-ocd-and-adhd-dual-diagnosis-misdiagnosis-and-the-cognitive-cost-of-obsessions/

Anxiety & Depression Association of America (ADAA). (2023). *The not-so-obvious symptoms of OCD in school*. https://adaa.org/understanding-anxiety/obsessive-compulsive-disorder/ocd-at-school/hidden-symptoms

Associated Press. (2009, June 4). *Tourette's most common in White Kids, boys*. NBCNews.com. www.nbcnews.com/health/health-news/tourettes-most-common-white-kids-boys-flna1c9464090

Claussen, A. H., Bitsko, R. H., Holbrook, J. R., Bloomfield, J., and Giordano, K. (2018, May). *Impact of Tourette syndrome on school measures in a nationally representative sample*. Journal of Developmental and Behavioral Pediatrics. www.ncbi.nlm.nih.gov/pmc/articles/PMC5930055/

Eapen, V., and Robertson, M. M. (2008). *Clinical correlates of Tourette's disorder across cultures: A comparative study between the United Arab Emirates and the United Kingdom.* Primary care companion to *Journal of Clinical Psychiatry.* www.ncbi.nlm.nih.gov/pmc/articles/PMC2292447/

Giordano, K. (2013). *Classroom strategies and techniques for students with Tourette syndrome.* Tourette Syndrome Association Education Committee.

Greene, R. W. (2021). *The explosive child: A new approach for understanding and parenting easily frustrated, chronically inflexible children* (6th ed.). HarperCollins.

Horton, C. (2020, July 27). Thriving or surviving? Raising our ambition for trans children in primary and secondary schools. *Frontiers.* www.frontiersin.org/articles/10.3389/fsoc.2020.00067/full

Mandriota, M. (2022, May 3). *ADHD and gender identity: How they're linked and tips for parents.* Psych Central. https://psychcentral.com/adhd/people-with-adhd-more-likely-to-question-gender-identity#adhd-and-gender-identity

Mansueto, C. S. (2008, Winter). *OCD and Tourette syndrome: Re-examining the relationship.* International OCD Foundation. https://iocdf.org/expert-opinions/ocd-and-tourette-syndrome/

Morgan, K. K. (2022, May 23). *Are kids with ADHD more likely to be depressed?* WebMD. www.webmd.com/add-adhd/childhood-adhd/adhd-children-depression-the-link#:~:text=It's%20also%20common%20for%20kids,without%20ADHD%20will%20develop%20depression.

Nduagbo, K. C. (2020, July 23). *How gender disparities affect classroom learning.* ASCD. www.ascd.org/el/articles/how-gender-disparities-affect-classroom-learning

Riggs, D. W., and Bartholomaeus, C. (2018, February 1). *CISGENDERISM and certitude: Parents of transgender children negotiating educational contexts.* Duke University Press. https://read.dukeupress.edu/tsq/article-abstract/5/1/67/133887/Cisgenderism-and-CertitudeParents-of-Transgender?redirectedFrom=fulltext

skelton, j wallace. (2022). Schools often fail to expect trans and nonbinary elementary children: What gender independent, nonbinary, and trans children desire. *Teachers College Record.* https://doi.org/10.1177/01614681221126243

Springer Science+Business Media. (2014, March 12). Wishing to be another gender: Links to ADHD, autism spectrum disorders. *ScienceDaily.* Retrieved June 17, 2023 from www.sciencedaily.com/releases/2014/03/140312103102.htm

Tourettes Action. (2023). *What is Tourette syndrome?* What is TS? www.tourettes-action.org.uk/67-what-is-ts.htm

Glossary

Joseph-Salisbury, R. (2020). Runnymede Perspectives: Race and racism in English secondary schools. Runnymede: Intelligence for a Multi-Ethnic Britain. https://assets.website-files.com/61488f992b58e687f1108c7c/61bcc0cc2a023368396c03d4_Runnymede%20Secondary%20Schools%20report%20FINAL.pdf

McCluney, C., Robotham, K., Lee, S., Smith, R., and Durkee, M. (2019, November 15). *The Costs of Code-Switching.* Harvard Business Review. https://hbr.org/2019/11/the-costs-of-codeswitching

McIntosh, P. (1989). White privilege: Unpacking the invisible knapsack. Peace and Freedom. https://psychology.umbc.edu/wp-content/uploads/sites/57/2016/10/White-Privilege_McIntosh-1989.pdf

Index

Note: Page numbers followed by *t* indicate material in tables.